THE GREAT BOOK OF
TANKS

THE GREAT BOOK OF

TANKS

The world's most important tanks from
World War I to the present day

DAVID MILLER

SALAMANDER

A Salamander Book

8 Blenheim Court
Brewery Road
London N7 9NY
England

© Salamander Books Ltd 2002

A member of **Chrysalis** Books plc

9 8 7 6 5 4 3 2 1

ISBN 1 84065 475 9

CREDITS
Cover Design by John Heritage
Index Compiled by Chris Bernstein
Production: Don Campaniello
Editorial Director: Marie Clayton
Editor: Colin Gower
Colour Reproduction: Anorax Imaging Ltd
Printed in Taiwan

CONTENTS

INTRODUCTION

❖

THIS BOOK DESCRIBES all the important tank designs to have entered service since the first operational tank - a British Mark I, rolled off the production line on 16 January 1916. The first tank action was at Flers-Courcelette on 15 September that year and since then the tank's unique combination of firepower, mobility and protection has exerted a dominating influence on the battlefield, while the number and quality of its tanks has been, and remains, the yardstick by which every army is measured. When the British shipped the first of these revolutionary vehicles to France in great secrecy in mid-1916 their nature and purpose was disguised by describing them as "water tanks" - "tanks" for short - the name by which they have been known ever since. Such early tanks were intended to overcome the stalemate in trench warfare, but they brought with them new problems; it took some time to work out their best tactical use, while novel methods of command and control, of cooperation with infantry and artillery, and of logistic support had to be devised.

The basic factor from which no tank designer can escape is that any new design must be a compromise between greater firepower (ever more destructive guns), protection (increasingly effective armor) and mobility (greater battlefield agility). This has resulted in a development cycle in which weight increases to the point where tanks become either too big or too heavy (or both) forcing designers to revert to smaller, lighter designs, thus starting the cycle over again. During World War II, for example, a typical 1939 tank, the British Cruiser Mk IV, weighed 15 tons, but by 1945 the German Tiger II weighed 70 while the prototype Maus weighed no less

than 130 tons. Determined efforts throughout the 1950s and 1960s kept the weight down to about 40 tons, but by the end of the 20th century the US Army's M1A1 Abrams weighed 56 tons and the British Challenger 2 a massive 62 tons, but there is no doubt that the next generation will be much smaller and lighter.

During World War I the basic mission of the tank was to enable the infantry to fight its way across "No Man's Land" and through the first line of enemy trenches; if the tanks could then help in the subsequent exploitation that was a bonus. But between 1919 and 1939 the major European armies put much effort into improving both tank design and tactics, and it was realized that the tank was a major battlefield weapon in its own right. The British carried out maneuvers with experimental "tank brigades" and the Russians quietly developed some revolutionary tank designs, but it was the Germans who evolved the highly mobile and effective operations known as "Blitzkrieg," which enabled them to overrun Western and most of Eastern Europe between 1939 and 1942. American, British and Russian tanks increased in quality throughout the war, but it was eventually their sheer numbers that told, so that by 1945 Germany's armored forces, good as they were, had

Above Inset: *The first fully effective tanks were the instantly recognisable British rhomboid-type, such as this Mark IV (Female). These tanks were slow, very noisy and unreliable, but they signified a complete revolution in the way in which future ground wars would be fought.*

Right: *Some 80 years separate these ultra-modern US Army M1 Abrams tanks, here seen on a Cold War exercise in Germany, from the curious, unreliable rhomboid machine inset at the top of the page.*

been thoroughly defeated.

Throughout the Cold War (1949-1992) the primary theater for any land battles would have been western Europe, and with this in mind the Soviet Union produced tanks of good design in vast numbers, while NATO tried to offset this by a smaller number of tanks, but of even higher quality. Tank development continued apace and the main battle tank (MBT), as it was now called, became a very sophisticated and complicated weapons system. Indeed, during the second half of the 20th century, the importance of the tank had never been greater and it played a vital role in combat in Korea, the various Arab-Israeli wars, the Iran-Iraq wars, and, most recently, in Operation Desert Storm in the Gulf and in Russia's war against Chechnya.

Above left: *The first successful prototype of an armored track-laying vehicle was this "land-ship" known less formally as "Little Willie." The most significant difficulty in the early trials was with the original tracks, made of cast links, but when these were replaced by metal plates (as seen here) the machine was considered a great success.*

Left: *German tank development in World War I was not a success, but they learnt the lessons and in the inter-war years developed a series of tanks which were used in the famous blitzkrieg as was this PzKpfw III Ausf J in the attack on Moscow in 1942.*

Below: *The first great tank battle was at Cambrai (20 November 1917), where this British Mark II (Male) has become stuck in a German trench. The naval 6-pounder QF (quick-firing) gun is mounted in a "sponson." The hatch behind the 6-pounder covers a port for a 8mm Hotchkiss machine-gun.*

The last two decades of the 20th Century saw some remarkable advances which included: new types of armor; more powerful guns, growing through 105mm to 125mm; autoloaders, which enabled the crew to be reduced; and far more powerful engines. In addition, integrated fire control systems (IFCS) enabled the crew to use their weapon with greater accuracy and effectiveness, while new detectors were used both to spot the enemy and to know when the enemy was trying to find them.

The future of the tank has been brought into question from time to time as new weapons have challenged its supremacy on the battlefield, and in the early years of the 21st century questions are again being asked about the effectiveness of such large and heavy machines in the low-intensity, rapid reaction and littoral wars, which

Left: *Universally acknowledged as one of the greatest of tank commanders in any army, the German General Heinz Guderian fought throughout World War II from the initial smashing victories of 1939-42 to the final disastrous defeats in 1945.*

Below: *A British brigadier uses his walking stick to point to an objective on a sand-table model during a briefing for a group of very thoughtful-looking officers during the Battle of Tobruk in November 1941. The officer behind the brigadier's walking-stick and wearing a black beret is dressed in the desert uniform of the Royal Tank Regiment.*

Above: *During the US deployment to strife-torn Beirut, Lebanon in August 1958, a US Army M48 tank maneuvers in the sand. The driver's head can just be seen below the bustle of the reversed turret. Note also the four large drums mounted at the rear of the tank, which carry extra fuel to extend the range. They also constituted a major fire hazard and would be ditched at the very first sign of opposition.*

Right: *Turrets for British Chieftain tanks on the production line at the government-owned Royal Ordnance Factory at Leeds in the mid-1970s. The gun on the nearest turret has yet to have its thermal cladding applied, showing just the bare barrel. This also shows how the design of the nose of the turret meant that no separate mantlet was required, a feature of most modern British tanks.*

seem to have become the pattern. Tank designers have, however, been through this before and there can be little doubt that the main battle tank will remain the primary weapon on the battlefield for many years to come.

TANK DESIGN

The tank designer must balance several competing factors in arriving at a design which will meet the requirement of the operational staffs. At its simplest this is a trade-off between protection, firepower and mobility, so that the design may not meet all its criteria exactly, but at least does approach each one; alternatively, limits in one may be deliberately accepted in order to optimize the other two. In the

late 1940s, for example, the very well-armed and well-protected Soviet JS-2 and T-10 heavy tanks posed a serious threat to NATO, which believed that the only way to defeat them was with a 120mm gun. But, at that time, such a gun was large and heavy, and could only be carried by an equally large and heavy tank. As a result, the three tanks developed to counter this threat - British Conqueror, US M103 and French AMX-50 - were slow and lacked agility, but this was accepted by the respective armies in order to maximize firepower.

Fortunately, technological advances come to the designer's rescue, and modern production methods and materials enable 120mm guns to be constructed with thinner and much lighter barrels, while engines are more powerful and lighter. Today's British Challenger 2, for example, has a combat weight of 61 tons, slightly less than that of the Conqueror of the 1950s (65 tons), but its engine has a power output of 1,200bhp compared with the latter's 810bhp; as a result it is very much more agile. Another example was the French AMX-30 of the 1960s, which was considerably lighter than the contemporary British Chieftain and US M60, since the French Army was prepared to accept thin armor to gain battlefield mobility, something which, in any case,

was in keeping with the national penchant for dash and elan.

THE THREAT

No single weapons system on the battlefield has to face such a plethora of threats as the MBT, which may be attacked from above by aircraft, indirect fire

Above: *Loader secures ammunition in an M60 during training in Germany in 1978.*

Right: *Weapons on the roof of this M1 Abrams comprise a 0.5in heavy machine-gun (left) and a 62mm light machine-gun (right).*

Below: *The M551 Sheridan was armed with a unique 152mm gun/missile launcher, which eventually proved to be unsuccessful.*

weapons and top-attack direct-fire weapons; from the front, rear and sides by direct-fire weapons, particularly from other tanks, or antitank guided missiles launched from helicopters or ground launchers; and, finally, from beneath by mines. Furthermore, the nature of the threat extends from attack on the hull by high-velocity, high-density, 'punch-through' projectiles such as tungsten-

carbide and depleted uranium APFSDS, through chemical attack using HESH and HEAT, to 'mobility kill" attacks aimed at the engine and running gear. In addition, the crew can be attacked through the use of nuclear and chemical weapons, and the mobility of the tank may be reduced by obstacles, either natural (e.g. rivers) or man-made (e.g. anti-tank ditches and minefields).

THE TANK GUN

The tank's main gun is intended to impose its supremacy across the battlefield. The past 40 years have seen an unending competition with each advance in protection being countered by improvements to the gun and its ammunition, and vice-versa. At the end of World War II the largest caliber 'normal' tank gun was the Tiger II's 88mm weapon,

but most tanks had guns of between 76mm and 85mm caliber, although the US M23 had a 90mm gun. After the war, the Soviet Army has led the way to higher calibers, being the first to 100mm on T-54, to 115mm on T-62 and then to 125mm on T-64. In the West a brief early excursion in the USA and UK to 120mm was reversed by the outstanding British 105mm, which became, in effect, the standard tank gun outside the Warsaw Pact, the only major nation not to adopt it being France. The British themselves, however, then moved to 120mm with the rifled L11, to be followed later by the Germans with the Rheinmetall smoothbore and by France with the GIAT

120mm smoothbore. A further increase in caliber, say to 152mm, is by no means impossible, but it seems unlikely at the moment, not least because the trend is towards much lighter tanks designed for use in low-intensity operations.

A longer barrel leads to greater accuracy, but a point is eventually reached where the effects of barrel vibration, tank motion, "droop" and thermal effects (for example, rain on a hot barrel) begin to outweigh these advantages. (Barrel "droop" is the result of mechanical effects where the weight of the barrel causes extremely slight bending, but with modern high velocity, flat-trajectory rounds, the slightest

deviation results in a miss). These problems can be countered: modern production techniques result in stiffer barrels, muzzle reference systems measure droop, and thermal sleeves ensure an even temperature along the tube.

AMMUNITION

Ammunition's ability to penetrate armor can be improved either by increasing muzzle velocity or by increasing the diameter of the round. The sub-caliber round, which utilizes kinetic energy to 'punch' its way through armor, is made of very dense material (such as tungsten carbide) and is held in the barrel by a

Left: *On training in the Egyptian desert during Exercise Bright Star 1987, US Army 105mm APDS (Armor-Piercing Discarding Sabot) rounds are laid out prior to loading the tanks. The white driving-band secures the multi-segment sabot in place until the round leaves the muzzle; the band then disintegrates, the sabot falls away and the solid shot continues at high velocity to the target.*

Explosive Plastic (HEP) (known as High-Explosive Squash-Head (HESH) in the UK) in which the greater portion of the round is an explosive contained in a thin steel case. On hitting target the case fractures and the explosive filling spreads in a cake, whereupon it is detonated and the resulting explosion generates stress waves, which throw lethal metal scabs from the inside. This round does not actually penetrate the tank at all and its effects are not degraded by spin.

In the 1960s the USA developed the XM163 152mm gun/launcher system, which could fire either a guided missile or a conventional round of ammunition. The system achieved limited operational status in the M60A2 MBT and the Sheridan light tank, but was not a success. The Russians, however, took up the idea and have developed a successful 125mm gun/launcher which equips its latest tanks.

SECONDARY ARMAMENT

A tank requires a secondary armament to supplement its main gun, traditionally to deal with nearby infantry, although there is an increasing requirement for such weapons also to be used in the anti-aircraft and anti-helicopter roles. There is usually one coaxial machine-gun and a second mounted on the roof of the turret.

AUTOLOADERS

Autoloaders are being installed in an increasing number of tanks. The Swedes introduced one in the 1960s in their S-tank, which is both simple and reliable, with a firing rate of some 25 rounds per minute. However, the gun is in a fixed mounting, which makes for mechanical simplicity but imposes severe tactical limitations. Where the gun is mounted in a revolving turret, however, the complexities of transferring rounds from a fixed stowage to a rotating turret are somewhat daunting and have deterred many armies, and the Russian Army was known to have had severe problems with the automatic loader in the T-64.

An autoloader is required to select a projectile and a charge from their

sabot, which falls away as the round leaves the muzzle (hence the name, Armor-Piercing Discarding Sabot, APDS). To achieve maximum terminal effect the penetrator must have a slim nose and the overall diameter of the round must be kept to a minimum to reduce velocity losses along the trajectory, which results in a long, thin projectile, but with spin stabilization the length-to-diameter ratio cannot exceed 5:1 or else control is lost. This has led to the development of the "long rod penetrator" with a length:diameter ratio of 12.._, which uses fins to maintain stability (Armor-Piercing Fin Stabilized Discarding Sabot [APFSDS]).

France, Germany and Russia use smoothbore guns, but the British and Americans have developed 105mm and 120mm APFSDS rounds with slipping driving bands to enable them to be used in rifled barrels.

The High Explosive Anti-Tank (HEAT) projectile (also known as Hollow-Charge), has a conical cavity in the nose of the explosive filling, with a copper liner. When exploded at an appropriate stand-off distance a thin, high velocity jet of molten metal pierces the armor, and a diverging spray of high-velocity metal particles kills or wounds the crew.

The third major type of round is High

respective stowage areas, line them up with the open breech and then ram them home, but this simple statement conceals some very complicated requirements. The majority of armies require their MBTs to fire, at the very least, two kinds of ammunition, while, if separate charges are used (as is almost inevitable with ammunition of 120mm caliber or greater), then the appropriate charge must be selected as well. Next, the projectile and charge must be moved from their stowage to the gun, which will introduce problems of alignment and, in some designs, of turning as well. The turning depends upon the stowage selected.

Where the rounds are stowed vertically (as in the T-64) they must be lifted clear and then rotated before they can be offered up to the gun. In the T-72, however, the rounds are stowed horizontally in a carousel, which holds 40 boxes below the turret basket. The selection of rounds having been made, the carousel rotates and the box is lifted until it is level with the breech, whereupon a swinging arm comes forward and rams the projectile. The box is then lowered to enable the charge to be rammed. This method does away with the requirement for turning the round, but the gun must return to precisely the same position each time (in both azimuth and elevation) on each occasion for the round and charge to be rammed. This inevitably slows down the rate of fire.

The autoloader is inevitably heavy and complicated, and must take up a fairly large amount of space. It will also reduce the total number of rounds that can be carried. It may, furthermore, go wrong, in which case there must be a manual reversionary mode or the tank will have to withdraw to a place where the faults can be identified and repaired. However, the great advantages lie in doing away with the human loader, with all the savings in space, manpower and training costs that this implies.

AMPHIBIOUS CAPABILITY

Many armies require their tanks to have an amphibious capability, so that they can continue advancing without having to wait for cumbersome, slow-moving bridging equipment to be brought up to river crossings. In order to float, a vehicle needs to have sufficient buoyancy, and some light vehicles (such as the Soviet PT-76 tracked reconnaissance vehicle) and a number of APCs can float without any

further aid or preparation. MBTs, however, need flotation equipment, and collapsible canvas screens have been used on some tanks, but they require some time to erect, are very conspicuous and are vulnerable to hostile fire.

Most tanks are capable of submerged fording, many of them up to the tops of their turrets, enabling rivers up to about 7ft (2.2m) deep to be crossed, provided careful reconnaissance has confirmed that the bottom will bear the load. Some Western tanks, such as Leopard 1 and AMX-30, also have extension tubes which can be fitted to the commander's cupola, which enable fording to a depth of about 13ft (4m) to be accomplished. These are wide enough for the crew to use as an escape route, if necessary, but the capability is rarely practiced and would probably not be used on any scale in time of war. The Soviet Army used a similar snorkel tube, enabling the tank to ford rivers up to 18ft (5.5m) deep, but was so narrow that there was no question of it being used as an escape route, which made the system very unpopular with crews.

Left & below: *The Sherman DD (duplex drive) was fully amphibious, using a extending screen. Shown below, the screen is fully erected and the two propellers are visible seen below the rear of the tank. On the left, the tank has returned to land and the screen is in the process of collapsing, prior to the fully combat-capable tank driving away.*

PROTECTION

For many years tanks have been constructed of steel armored plate, usually nickelchrome-molybdenum steel in the form of rolled plate or castings. Armor effectiveness is enhanced by good design, for example by sloping surfaces and avoiding shot-traps, or simply by using thicker plates, which means, of course, a heavier tank. Protection can also be increased by concentrating the armor in the areas of greatest threat, particularly the front. Other protective measures include placing the engine in the front of the tank (as in the Israeli Merkava), using side-skirts to detonate HEAT rounds before they hit the suspension, and spaced armor.

A major advance in the early 1970s was the British Chobham armor (named after the research establishment where it was designed), which consists of a sandwich of several different materials which can defeat both kinetic and chemical energy rounds. Even with Chobham armor, sloping enhances its effectiveness, although the turret of the German Leopard 2 has vertical sides, suggesting a total belief in the efficacy of the protection being provided.

An even more recent advance is "active armor," consisting of a series of explosive plates covering vulnerable parts of the tank. These plates are built in different sizes and shapes to facilitate fitting them to the tank in a manner similar to the heat dissipating tiles used on the Space Shuttle. They are basically explosive charges which detonate when hit, exploding outwards and dissipating the jet of a HEAT round, blowing off the explosive scab of a HEP round and, possibly, deflecting the penetrator of an APDS round.

Far Left: US Marine Corps M48 wades ashore onto a Vietnamese beach, September 7, 1965, during Operation Piranha. The boxes on the rear of the turret contain the crew's rations.

Above: The Shir 2, renamed Challenger, has the same powerpack, armament and fire control system as the Shir 1 but with a hull and turret of Chobham armor. This gives a high degree of protection against both kinetic and chemical attack over the frontal arc.

Below: No matter how well-armored a tank seems when it appears, there is always a need to uparmor it in service. This German World War II PzKpfw IV Ausf H has extra plates on the sides of the hull and around the turret, and the track sections on the front of the hull are also intended to increase protection.

NBC Protection

Tanks could be required to fight on a nuclear battlefield. The thick armor provides a degree of nuclear protection, but recent Russian tanks also have an interior lining of a synthetic material, containing lead, which provides enhanced protection against nuclear fallout, neutron radiation and electromagnetic pulse (EMP). Most modern tanks also incorporate an NBC protection system, which functions by maintaining a slight overpressure within the crew compartment, provided by air which has passed through various filters. This enables the crew to continue to operate without respirators in a contaminated environment.

Size

The overall width of the tank is limited by the dimensions of rail and road transporters, bridges, ships, etc, but perhaps the chief constraint is the maximum permitted railway load width of 10ft 4in (3.125m). Some tanks exceed this but can still be transported by rail, either by removing such items as track-guards (where this is possible) or by using carefully selected routes. Length is similarly limited by a variety of factors. For high speed movement across uneven surfaces, the greater the length of track on the ground the better, while the greater the area of track on the ground the less the ground pressure and thus the better the ability of the tank to move across soft terrain. However, the combination of tracks which are laterally rigid and the concomitant use of skid steering imposes limits on the configuration of the tank, because in order to be maneuverable the ratio of the length of track in contact with the ground to the distance between the track centerlines must lie between 1.1:1 and 1.8:1. Examples among modern tanks are: 1.12:1 for the Soviet T-72, 1.53:1 for the Israeli Merkava and 1.36:1 for the US M1.

The height of the tank again depends upon a number of factors. Adequate ground clearance is necessary to prevent "bellying down" and is normally of the order of 18in (45.72cm). The primary factor in the distance between the floor and roof of the hull is the height of the seated driver, which is about 3.25ft (0.99m), while the distance between hull floor and the turret roof is dictated by a combination of the height of a standing loader (say 5.5ft, 1.68m) and the depression required of the main gun.

Above: *This M4 Sherman being lifted onto a Z-craft for its short journey to the shore, shows the sloping front, which was designed to deflect incoming armor-piercing rounds, thus preventing them penetrating.*

Opposite: *Israeli M48 tank is covered in blocks of Blazer explosive reactive armor (ERA), which is designed to explode as soon as it is hit by an incoming APDS or APFSDS round, thus deflecting it harmlessly away.*

CREW

During World War II most tanks had five-man crews, consisting of commander, loader, gunner, driver and bow machine-gunner, but when the need for the latter disappeared the crew was reduced to four. This number was long considered to be the irreducible minimum on the grounds that four men are required to perform the many tasks apart from just fighting the tank, including guards, radio watch, tank maintenance, replenishment and cooking. The first modern MBT to reduce the crew to three was the Swedish Strv-103 (S-tank),

German Armored Unit Uniforms and insignia

1 Officer's field cap
2 NCO Panzer jacket
3 Panzer marksmanship lanyard
4 Panzer trousers
5 General officer's collar tab
6 Lieutenant general's shoulder tab
7 Throat microphone
8 Vehicle intercom headphones
9 Officer's cap

10 Major's shoulder strap
11 Pair of lIeutenant's shoulder straps
12 NCOs shoulder straps
13 Helmet with cover
14 Self-propelled gun crew NCO jacket
15 Army waist bell and holster for P.38
16 M1943 helmet
17 Trousers for 14
18 General officers vehicle pennant
19 Waffen-SS Panzer field service cap
20 Waffen-SS Pea Pattern camouflage
   Panzer uniform

21 Pistol bell and Radom P.35p holster
22 Web gaiters for 23
23 Short combat boots
24 Four SS shoulder straps, see caption
25 SS divisional cuff titles, see caption
26 Luftwaffe officer's service cap
27 1st Lt. Panzer jacket and trousers
28 Luftwaffe enlisted man's waist belt
29 Luftwaffe web gaiters

Memorial Museum, Bayeux

but like so many features of this design this was considered by Western experts to be a one-off experiment, and tanks like Leopard 1 and 2, Chieftain, Challenger, M60 and M1 continued to be designed for a crew of four. There was, therefore, considerable surprise when the Soviet T-64 appeared with an autoloader and three-man crew, as have all subsequent Soviet/ Russian tanks.

In a four-man crew the driver sits at the front, usually centrally although where the engine is located at the front (as in the Israeli Merkava) he has to be moved to one side. The remaining three men are in the turret, the loader standing on one side and the commander and gunner seated on the other.

British Army Uniforms and Equipment

1 Royal Armoured Corps pattern steel helmet
2 Beret with the insignia of the Royal Tank Regt.
3 Armored crew denim overalls
4 Binoculars and P.37 compass pouch
5 First aid kit for armored fighting vehicles
6 Royal Tank Regt. designating pennant
7 P.37 web gaiters dyed black for armored personnel

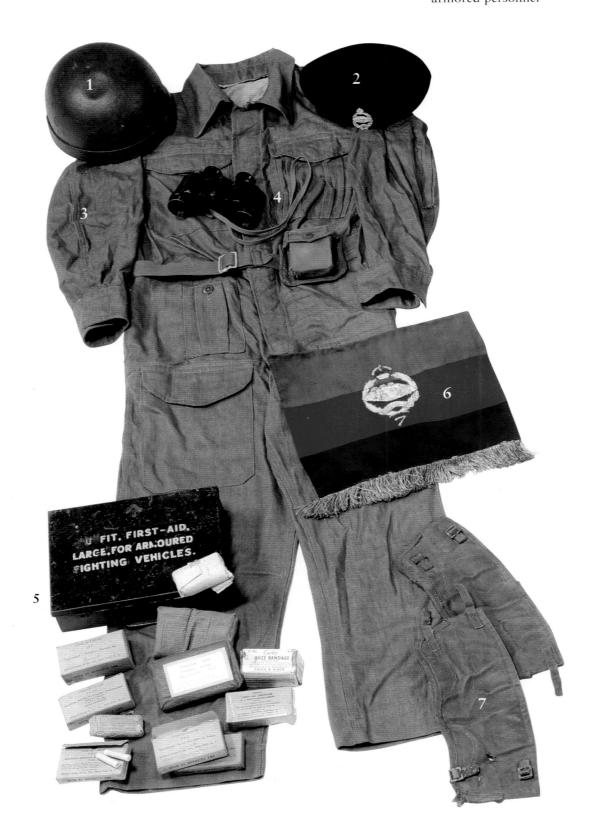

Above: *Chieftain tank of the British Army's Royal Hussars. The driver sits upright when driving with his head out of the hatch (as here) but is in a semi-reclining position when the hatch is closed (note thickness of the hatch). The projector on top of the barrel was used on exercises to indicate whether "hits" had been scored on "enemy" tanks.*

Previous page, Top: *US Army M60A1 main battle tank crosses a German-laid AVLB (armored-vehicle laid bridge) on a Cold War exercise in Germany. Such mobile bridges are essential to cross even quite narrow rivers, such as that shown here. In the background four umpires with white helmet bands discuss the progress of the exercise.*

Previous Page, Bottom: *A British Churchill tanks undergoes a maintenance period during the campaign in Italy. The trooper on the right is using a very large spanner to adjust the tension on a track. The driver sat between the "horns" of the Churchill, giving him a very limited view; compare with the Chieftain driver on this page (above).*

FIRE CONTROL SYSTEMS

For many years range calculation was achieved by eye, but as battle ranges grew this became unsatisfactory and the optical rangefinder was introduced; typically, such devices have a magnification of between x8 and x10 and feature split-image coincidence, as on many modern 35mm cameras. The British Army did not like optical rangefinders and from the 1950s to the 1980s used a 0.5in (12.7mm) ranging machine-gun (RMG), which fired tracer ammunition, ballistically matched to the main gun's ammunition. This was very popular with the British, as it was cheap, simple to use, reliable, and also took full account of wind and trunnion tilt.

However, its range was limited to 2,000yd (1,800m), whereas modern main guns are capable of firing out to some 3,500yd (3,200m); it also tended to slow down the rate of engagement; and its use could give away the fact that an anti-tank round was about to be fired. Both optical devices and RMGs have been replaced by laser rangefinders, which are virtually instantaneous in operation and extremely accurate. They are, however, detectable, so that the most advanced MBTs are now being fitted with sensors to tell their crews that they are being "lased."

ANTI-TANK WARFARE

When originally faced with tanks in World War I the Germans scoffed at what they called these "ridiculous weapons," but were quickly forced to find a means of combating them. Ordinary field-guns in the direct-fire mode were used initially, but the Allies responded by doubling tank armor from 0.5in (12mm) to 1.0in (24mm), which, coupled with increased speed and revised tactics reduced losses from 54 percent (Battle of the Somme, 1916) to 24 percent (Amiens, 1918). The Germans also developed a 37mm anti-tank gun with a solid shot capable of penetrating some 1.6in (40mm) of armor - the world's first true anti-tank weapon.

Above: *Bren Gun Carrier of the Indian Army drives past a burning German PzKpfw III, This picture gives an excellent impression of the flat, featureless desert arena over which so much of the North African campaign was fought. It also makes it clear that early World War II tanks were not particularly large, especially when compared with today's M1s, Challengers and Leopard 2s.*

Anti-tank weapons have always had two simple goals: to pierce the enemy's armor and, having achieved that, to incapacitate the crew or the tank, or both. For many years these objectives were reached by making bigger shells, fired from ever heavier conventional guns. By the middle of World War II, however, these guns had become so large that they were difficult to site tactically. Guns also started to use the same types of projectile as the tanks (ie, APDS, HEAT and HEP/HESH). Designers also turned to recoilless guns and then, in the post-war period, to a completely new weapon, the guided missile, and a completely new delivery platform, the helicopter.

No single weapon, delivery system or warhead has proved to be the complete answer and the effectiveness of each has, of course, depended as much upon its tactical handling by the soldier-operators as upon its technical excellence The purpose of the defensive anti-tank battle is to render an aggressor's tank force ineffective through a combination of deception, delay and destruction and to achieve this the anti-tank defenses must possess depth and flexibility, with all the elements being welded together into a cohesive entity.

ATTACKING ARMOR

For the aggressor the tank force is the mobile fighting arm which is designed to smash its way through the enemy's defenses and then drive into the relatively weaker rear areas to capture the objectives which will ensure strategic victory. This was how the German panzers were used against Poland in 1939 and France in 1940, and it is how the Warsaw Pact intended to use its forces against NATO during the Cold War. To prevent this, defensive forces must optimize their anti-tank capability, and this happened to such an extent in NATO that the armies in Western Europe became virtually one great anti-tank system, with all other roles subordinated to this task.

Left: *Sheridan light tank of the 10th Cavalry launches its MGM-51C Shilelagh missile. The same 152mm barrel could also be used to fire conventional anti-tank rounds.*

Below: *US Army M60A3 tanks of the 3rd Armored Division deploy from the United States Air Force's Sembach Air Base in West Germany on 26 April 1982.*

ANTI-TANK GUNS

During World War II the majority of anti-tank weapons were guns, firing a variety of armor-piercing rounds from a closed tube in the traditional way. Progress was rapid. The British, for example, started the war with the 2pdr gun capable of penetrating 2in (50mm) of armor plate at 1,000yd (914m) and ended with the 17pdr (76.2mm caliber) with an APDS round which could penetrate 8in (203mm) of armor at 1,000yd (914m). On the other side, the famed German 88mm/Flak 41 fired two types of anti-tank munition: an armor-piercing (ie, solid shot) round weighing 22lb (10kg) and sub-caliber (ie APDS) round weighing 16.5lb (7.5kg); at a range of 2,200yd (2,000m) these could penetrate 5in (127mm) and 6in (152mm) armor plate, respectively. By 1945 these heavy anti-tank guns had become too large and cumbersome for infantry use and in most armies there was a rapid move away from them towards the much lighter and more easily concealed recoilless guns, rocket launchers and guided missiles. Nevertheless, wheeled anti-tank guns did remain in service with a number of armies for many years, especially those in the Warsaw Pact.

Left: *One way to increase anti-tank capability is with tank-destroyers, which mount a heavy gun on a chassis that is much lighter and less well protected than a conventional tank. One example was the US Army's M10 tank destroyer, seen here on Leyte in January 1945.*

Above: *The most famous anti-tank gun of World War II was the German 88mm/Flak 41 - always known simply as "the 88" - which was designed and built as an anti-aircraft gun. The example seen here is in use in the North African desert in April 1941 and clearly shows that although very effective, the 88 was also very large and offered no protection whatsoever to its numerous crew.*

SP ANTI-TANK GUNS

Tracked Self-Propelled Anti-Tank guns (SPAT), also known as "tank destroyers," have enjoyed periodic popularity during and since World War II, the idea being to give the weapons greater mobility and to enable them to get into and out of action more rapidly than a wheeled gun. Some of these SPATs have rotating turrets, which gives them the appearance of a tank, although the hull and turret are constructed of light plate rather than the heavy armor of an MBT.

Other types of SPAT have the main gun mounted in the upper glacis plate with very limited lateral movement. The Soviet Army retained the SU-100 SPAT in service for many years following the end of World War II, while the ASU-85, which can be dropped by parachute, remains in service with airborne units of the Russian Army. The West German Army followed World War II practice when it produced the Jagdpanzer 4-5 in the 1960s, armed with a 90mm gun in the glacis plate; some 750 served with the Bundesheer and 80 with the Belgian Army, but it left service in the 1970s. Unlike these SPATs, the Austrian Jagdpanzer Kurassier has a fully traversing turret (actually, the oscillating turret and 105mm gun from the French AMX-13 light tank) which is mounted on a modified APC chassis. Finally, many authorities would argue that the Swedish S-tank is merely a sophisticated SPAT, rather than a true battle tank, especially as it cannot fire on the move. The Swedish Army also has a large number of Infanterikanonvagn 91 (Ikv-91) tank destroyers in service and in the 1990s had a revolutionary articulated tank destroyer under development, but this has since been cancelled.

The SPAT is somewhat cheaper than the MBT, but tactically it is neither as effective nor as ubiquitous, and its value is questionable. Very few armies maintain any further interest in the weapon, especially as light tanks with soft recoil, large-caliber guns seem to provide a better solution.

RECOILLESS WEAPONS

Recoilless guns use Newton's Law that "action and reaction are equal and opposite," the projectile being fired from a tube is open at both ends so as it moves forwards it is counterbalanced by the rearward expulsion of a large volume of high-velocity gas. The absence of recoil means that small weapons can be fired from a man's shoulder (for example, the World War II 3.5in rocket launcher and the modern 84mm Carl Gustaf), while the heavier weapons such as the British 120mm Wombat and the Soviet 107mm B-11 were fired from simple wheeled mounts. While these recoilless guns are light, uncomplicated and easily transported, they suffer from two major drawbacks: the sound of firing is both loud and easy to distinguish, and the back-blast is accompanied by both flash and a pall of smoke. It is thus difficult to fire the weapons without giving their position away and this, together with their low muzzle velocity, imposes tactical limitations. The former problem has, however, been solved in an ingenious way by the German Armbrust, a 67mm recoilless gun in which the explosion is contained by two pistons, eliminating the flash and smoke normally associated with such a weapon. The heavier versions of the recoilless gun are gradually losing favor, but the lighter, shoulder-fired recoilless guns are still very much in vogue, since they represent the best means of giving the infantry an effective close-range tank-killing capability.

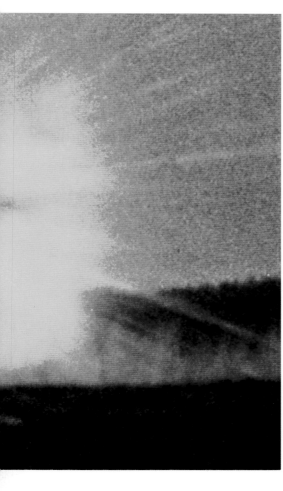

Above left: *A devastating impact as an anti-tank weapon hits a target tank on a range. In real life such a hit would kill all crew members and render the tank completely unusable, making repair impossible.*

Below left: *A Copperhead, cannon-launched. Lazer-guided projectile impacts on a tank. This round is fired from a 155mm artillery tube and is designed for a first-round hit .*

Below top: *The Soviet RPG-7 anti-tank rocket system is the most widely used weapon in the world and is especially popular with guerilla forces.*

Below bottom: *The Dragon is the standard medium-range ATGW of the US Army and Marine Corps.*

SELF-PROPELLED RECOILLESS GUNS

Recoilless guns have been mounted on vehicles: the British, for example, mounted the 120mm BAT on the FV 432 APC, while the Americans have mounted their 106mm M40A1, both on the M113 APC and on various wheeled field cars. A specialized armored vehicle used by the US Marines in the 1950s and 1960s was the M50 Ontos, comprising six 106mm recoilless rifles (RCLs) mounted on a light tracked vehicle. The only other country to show any interest in this concept has been Japan, which developed the Type 60, a tracked vehicle mounting two 106mm RCLs on an extendible arm. The problem of back-blast and obfuscation remained, however, and neither vehicle could fire on the move.

Left: *The infantry need close-in anti-tank weapons systems to give them a final line of defense against attacking tanks. One of the most effective means of providing this is using shoulder-launched rocket systems, such as this British LAW-80 (Light Anti-armor Weapon), fielded in the 1980s. The tube incorporates a semi-automatic spotting rifle and the rocket will penetrate over 650mm of armor. It is discarded after use.*

Below: *A Copperhead missile immediately prior to impacting on its target - a derelict M47 tank. Unseen by the human eye is the laser spot resting on the side of the turret and upon which the projectile's seeker is homing, using the fins to make fine adjustments to the flight path and ensuring a kill every time.*

Above: *One of the most successful infantry-manned anti-tank systems of recent years is the US Army's TOW (Tube-launched, Optically-guided, Wire-controlled). The missile has a caliber of 120mm, enabling it to carry a large diameter (and thus highly effective) hollow-charge warhead. It has been sold to many foreign armies and will remain in service for many years to come.*

Above Right: *McDonnell MH-6 "Little Bird" launches a TOW missile from a fuselage-mounted, twin launch tube. None of the many anti-tank systems is totally effective on its own, but a combination of launchers (air, ground mobile, ground static) and methods of attack is required to provide a barrier which only a very few main battle tanks will be capable of penetrating.*

ANTI-TANK GUIDED WEAPONS

Apart from MBT's main guns, the most important anti-tank weapons are guided weapons (ATGW), which have developed rapidly over the past 30 years. The Egyptian army made very successful use of ATGWs in the 1973 Yom Kippur war leading some commentators to conclude that tanks were no longer valuable weapons of war, but a more sober assessment showed that although the ATGWs scored early successes due to tactical surprise, they were easily countered. The majority of tank kills had been, as in the past, caused by the guns of other tanks.

ATGWs are launched from either tubes or from zero-length launchers, which can be mounted on helicopters, on vehicles or on the ground.

Until recently, all ATGWs had shaped charge (HEAT) warheads, which gave them a considerable tank-killing capability, combined with a light missile of minimal dimensions, which is sufficiently cheap to be purchased in large numbers, even by the smaller armies. Further, the effect of the warhead is not dependent upon the range of the weapon nor its velocity of impact. ATGWs do, however, have several disadvantages, particularly their relatively low speed, leading to long flight times at

ranges over 1,000yd (914m) and their considerable minimum range, typically 200-300yd (183-274m). For many years, the two "givens" in anti-tank warfare were that APDS rounds of sufficient density and velocity could only be fired from guns, and that missiles could only be armed with HEAT warheads. The US Army has, however, developed the Line-Of-Sight Anti-tank Weapon (LOSAT), which reverses those concepts by using a high-density penetrator delivered by a hyper-velocity rocket-powered missile, rather than a gun-fired projectile. The 9.3ft (2.8m) long, 6.4in (162mm) diameter missile has four stabilizer fins and a large

proportion of its volume is taken up by the single-stage rocket motor which accelerates the missile to 3,400mph (5,470km/h) in less than 4 seconds. This is very much faster than any previous battlefield missile and the warhead is claimed to penetrate any known armor, even at high oblique angles of impact. The launcher will be mounted on an HMMWV wheeled vehicle.

Virtually all battlefield guided missiles are line-of-sight systems, but the US Army's Enhanced Fiber-Optic Guided Missile (EFOGM) uses a fiber-optic cable which transmits TV pictures from the missile to the firer. As a result, the missile can attack targets out of the firer's view (behind a hill

or a building, for example), the firer can seek targets of opportunity during the missile's flight, and is even capable of attacking aircraft. The missile is based on that of the TOW, but with the addition of a high-resolution, infrared video camera in the nose, and a fibreoptic cable dispenser in the tail. This cable relays TV images down to the gunner's station, and control data up to the missile. The Fire Unit is a modified version of the HMMWV, with a crew of two and an eight-missile launcher.

Right: *Water obstacles (ie, rivers, streams and lakes) provide serious barriers to tanks' progress and overcoming them was a major preoccupation for Warsaw Pact armies during the Cold War. One method, which was very unpopular with tank crews, was to use a long, narrow snorkel tube, which is mounted on this Czech Army T-54 in front of the open loader's hatch. Because this is a peacetime training exercise, however, a longer and larger diameter tube has been mounted behind, on the commander's hatch, to enable the crew to escape if the crossing runs into difficulties.*

Below: *Various types of "tank barriers" have been tried. The devices seen here, known as "dragon's teeth," were produced in vast numbers in Germany in 1944-45 in a vain effort to prevent the Allied advance. This is the scene looking across the France-German border at the aptly-named village of Steinfeld (which means "stone field"). Such barriers were difficult to get through but the tanks simply went round them.*

OBSTACLES

Natural and man-made obstacles continue to be an essential part of any anti~tank plan. Natural obstacles include rivers, canals, dense woods, lakes and buildings, although most require enhancements to optimize their anti-tank capability. The danger of complacency arising from the apparent impregnability of obstacles was illustrated in the 1973 Yom Kippur war, when the Israelis' western boundary lay on the Suez Canal, which the Israelis reinforced with a sand wall some 50-70ft (15-21m) high and of considerable width. The combination of the canal, the sand wall and the defenses of this "Bar-Lev Line" impressed the Israelis more than it did their enemy, and a junior lieutenant in the Egyptian Engineer Corps produced the answer: use the water of the canal and high pressure hoses to wash away the sand wall. The achievement of both strategic and tactical surprise, coupled with the Israelis' complacency, meant that the obstacle was not covered by fire at the critical time and the Egyptian infantry

Above Top: *Engineers of the British Eighth Army examine German anti-tank mines which have been lifted to clear the way forward in the Desert campaign. Such mines will either penetrate the belly of the tank and kill the crew, or, more usually, they will destroy or break one of the tracks, thus immobilizing the tank - known as an "m-kill" (m = mobility).*

Above: *The aim of the anti-tank battle has been achieved, as US Marines pass a Soviet-supplied, North Korean T-34 tank - a scene from the Korean War in September 1950, as UN forces swept northwards.*

assault, together with the sappers' use of a 'low-tech' device in an imaginative way, soon cleared the way for armored divisions to sweep through into the Sinai Desert. This episode illustrates the strengths and weaknesses of a "barrier mentality," especially in the anti-tank battle. The right sort of barrier ought to be effective, but cannot be totally effective,unless watched and protected as any other defensive position.

MINES

Minefields can either stop or seriously delay an enemy, or can channel the enemy into ground of the defenders' choosing, but, as with any obstacle, minefields must be covered by fire. Most anti-tank mines have a pressure-sensitive firing device, although some also have rods which react to lateral forces, while others respond to magnetic or seismic disturbance. The force of the explosion will normally break a track and damage at least some of the roadwheels and suspension (resulting in a "mobility" kill), although the belly-plate may also be pierced. Some mines are constructed on the hollow-charge principle and can penetrate belly-plates up to 2.8in (70mm) thick, doing considerable damage inside the tank. The biggest practical problem with mines is that they cannot, in general, be laid in peacetime and need to be positioned very quickly once hostilities commence using mechanical layers, together with minelaying helicopters, artillery shells and rockets.

Mark I Tank

❖❖❖

THE FIRST PROTOTYPE track-laying armored vehicle, known as "Little Willie," was built at the William Foster works in England and ran its first tests in September 1915. Even as this "land-ship" was being built, a second design was being prepared to meet a new requirement for a vehicle which would cross an 8ft (2.44m) trench and surmount a 4ft 6in (1.37m) parapet. This requirement could only be met by a high prow, resulting in the rhomboidal shape that remained a characteristic of British tanks until the end of the war. The prototype, usually known as "Mother," but also sometimes called the "Wilson Machine" or "Big Willie," ran for the first time on 16 January 1916, and lived up to every expectation, completing a specimen "battlefield obstacle course" with ease. This led to a firm order for 100 (later increased to 150) Mark1 "tanks," while, in parallel with this manufacturing work, a new unit designated, for security reasons, Heavy Section, Machine Gun Corps, was formed to man them.

The hull was a rectangular box structure made of armor plate with a large, rhomboidal track frame attached to each side. These frames had the high prows and large radius curves along their bottom edges that contributed to the machine's incredible performance over obstacles, while the return track was carried up inclines at the rear and then forward along skidways on each side of the hull roof.

Below: British Mark I (Male) on 25 Sept 1916. The wheels at the back were to assist steering but were found to be superfluous and removed. Note shute in rear of sponson for used cartridge cases.

SPECIFICATIONS

Country of origin: United Kingdom.
Crew: 8.
Armament: (Male) two 6pounder QF guns; four 8mm Hotchkiss machine-guns. (Female) four .303in (7.7mm) Vickers machine-guns; one 8mm Hotchkiss machine-gun.
Armor: 6mm-12mm (0.23-0.47in).
Dimensions: Length 32ft 6in (0.75m); male width 13ft 9in (4.12m); female width 14ft 4in (4.3m); height 8ft 0½in (2.41m).

Weight: Combat 62,720lb (28,450kg) for male; 60,480lb (27,434kg) for female.
Engine: Daimler six-cylinder inline water-cooled petrol engine developing 105hp at 1,000rpm.
Performance: Speed 3.7mph (5.95km/h); range 23½ miles (37.8km); vertical obstacle 4ft 6in (1.35m); trench 11ft 6in (3.45m); gradient 24 per cent.

top and covered with wire mesh to ensure that they fell harmlessly to the ground.

While the new vehicle was still being designed, doubts were expressed about its ability to hold off massed infantry, so it was decided to complete half of those on order with an all-machinegun armament. To differentiate between the two versions, those with the 6-pounders were dubbed "males" and those with all machineguns became "females."

The Mark I had a crew of eight. The commander and driver sat side-by-side in the cupola, high in front of the vehicle, but their forward vision was very limited by the track "horns." Inside were two "gearsmen" crouched on either side of the gearbox, while the two-man gun crews knelt or squatted on tiny seats in the gun sponsons. In the middle sat the roaring six-cylinder engine, which had no silencing arrangement of any sort, and around the

Below: *The conditions on the Western Front were absolutely desperate, as proved by this Mark I ((Male) which has been brought to a halt by the wet mud and is now incapable of going either forwards or backwards.*

Left top: *A disarmed British Mark I in the U.S. after the war. The steel rails above the roof were used to support an unditching beam or fascines.*

Left bottom: *An almost pristine Mark I (Female). Note the camouflage and the corporal with his special tank crew helmet.*

crew compartment ran the unsprung tracks. As a result, the noise and heat were appalling, normal conversation was impossible, and simple instructions were passed by banging on the engine casing, together with hand signals!

Much against the wishes of those who were campaigning for the first mass tank attack to be a surprise action on good ground, the Mark I tanks were thrown into action at Flers-Courcelette on 15 September 1916. The ill-fated Somme offensive had totally bogged down, the going was dreadful and many of the crews were inexperienced. Very few of the 49 tanks that started out reached their objectives, but those that did swept all the opposition before them. Army staffs took note and orders for further tanks quickly followed.

Below: *After the Battle of Ypres a deserted and disarmed Mark I (Female) sinks slowly into the morass. This picture gives a good view of the driving compartment, which was occupied by the driver and commander, but the slits gave very limited vision.*

Schneider Assault Tank

❖

IN MAY 1915 the French Schneider company purchased two Holt crawler tractors and as a result of trials the French Army placed an order for 15 powered by a 45hp engine, for use as artillery tractors. Meanwhile, Colonel Estienne had been pressing for a tracked vehicle capable of crossing trenches and barbed wire, and in December 1916 he and a Schneider engineer designed a new vehicle based on the Holt chassis. The hull was of armor plate 0.45in (11.5mm) thick, with a boat-shaped front, which incorporated a barbed-wire cutter. The engine was at the front, offset to the left, with the driver to its right. Armament consisted of a 75mm Schneider gun mounted in the front of the hull on the right, with two Hotchkiss Model 1914 machine-guns, one in each side of the hull. Ammunition comprised 90 rounds of 75mm and 4,000 rounds for the machine-guns. Later production models had an additional layer of armor 0.31 in (8mm) thick to give protection against the German armor-piercing "K" bullet which had a tungsten-carbide core.

SCHNEIDER ASSAULT TANK ~ 49

Schneiders were first used in action at Chemin des Dames (16 April 1917); of the 132 deployed, 57 were destroyed, with many more damaged beyond repair, mostly due to the gasoline tanks catching fire and blowing up. Some 400 Schneider tanks were built, the last being delivered in August 1918. Some were disarmed and used as supply carriers later in the war.

Below: *A French Schneider demonstrates its hill-climbing ability. Note the girder, intended to prevent ramming the far side of a trench, and the rivetted construction, adapted from methods used in ship-building.*

SPECIFICATIONS

Country of origin: France.
Crew: 6
Armament: One 75mm howitzer; one 8mm machine-gun in each side of the hull.
Armor: 0.45in (11.5mm) maximum.
Dimensions: Length 20ft 9in (6.32m); width 6ft 9in (2.05m); height 7ft 7in (2.3m).
Weight: Combat 32,187lb (14,600kg).
Engine: Schneider four-cylinder water-cooled petrol engine developing 55hp.

Performance: Road speed 4.6mph (7.5km/h); range 30 miles (48km); vertical obstacle 2ft 9in (0.787m); trench 5ft 9in (1.752m); gradient 57 per cent.

St Chamond Assault Tank

❖❖❖

THE PROTOTYPE ST CHAMOND tank was completed in February 1916 by Compagniees Forges et Anciennes de la Marine et Homecourt at its St Chamond works (hence the name) and after trials 400 were ordered. The St Chamond was based on a lengthened Holt tractor chassis, with a riveted, armored, boat-shaped hull. An unusual feature was that the design used electric drive, with a Panhard petrol engine driving a generator which powered two electric motors, one for each track. Early production vehicles were armed with a 75mm St Chamond gun but later versions mounted the standard 75mm Model 1897 gun. There were also four 8mm Hotchkiss machine-guns: one each in the front, sides and rear of the hull. Some 106 rounds of 75mm and 7,600 rounds of machine-gun ammunition were carried.

The St Chamond was first used in action in May 1917, when 15 out of the 16 deployed became stuck in the first line of German trenches. This was caused by the long overhang, which resulted in the nose

digging into the ground and compared badly with the British Mk 1 tank, whose lozenge shape enabled it to cross trenches 11 ft 6in wide (3,505m) and climb a vertical obstacle of 4ft 6in (1.372m). Some 400 St Chamonds were built, the last being completed in March 1918 after it had been decided to concentrate on building larger numbers of the smaller Renault FT-17s.

Below: *The St Chamond's gun was fixed in the glacis plate, and the tank's long forward overhang severely limited its ability to cross the wide German forward trenches. Only 400 were built.*

SPECIFICATIONS

Country of origin: France.
Crew: 8.
Armament: One 75mm gun; four 8mm machine-guns.
Armor: 0.67in (17mm) maximum.
Dimensions: Length 28ft 6in (8.687m); width 8ft 9in (2.667m); height 7ft 9in (2.362m).
Weight: Combat 48.50lb (22,000kg).
Engine: Panhard four-cylinder petrol engine developing 90hp.

Performance: Road speed 5mph (8km/h); range 37 miles (59.5km); vertical obstacle 1ft 3in (0.381m); trench 9ft (2.438m); gradient 57 per cent.

Mark IV Tank

❖

THE MARK IV WAS THE WORKHORSE of the newly-formed Tank Corps in World War I. Derived from the Mark I, it incorporated improvements introduced in the Marks II and III, although all three of those early models were built only in comparatively small numbers. The Mark IV continued the rhomboidal shape and was outwardly little different from its predecessors, but there were many detailed changes. The crew compartment was better ventilated and escape hatches were located in the roof as well as the sides; the fan drew cooling air for the engine from inside the tank and blew it out through the radiator, which was at the back between the rear horns; and a silencer was at last fitted to reduce some of the deafening noise inside. The engine was improved, with aluminum pistons enabling revolutions to be increased and more power to be developed, although the tank was still underpowered. Twin carburetors improved the induction flow and the vacuum fuel system ensured that petrol reached the engine at all times,

overcoming earlier problems with the gravity arrangement, which sometimes starved the engine of fuel when plunging into deep trenches or on steep slopes.

The armor was the improved type fitted to the Marks II and III, and kept out the German tungsten-cored anti-tank bullets, while closer attention to riveting of the joints reduced the bullet "splash" which

Below: *A Mark IV tank pushes through trees brought down by shell-fire. The officer carries the blackthorn walking stick; behind him are fascines - bundles of sticks to be dropped into trenches to ease crossing them.*

SPECIFICATIONS

Country of origin: United Kingdom.
Crew: 8.
Armament: Two 6pounder guns and four .303in Lewis machine-guns (male); six .303in Lewis machine-guns (Female).
Armor: 12mm (0.47in) maximum; 6mm (0.25in minimum.
Dimensions: Length 26ft 5in (8.05m); width 13ft 9in (4.19m); height 8ft 2in (2.48m).
Weight: Combat 62,720lb (28,450kg) for the male; 60,480lb (27,434kg) for the female.

Engine: Daimler six-cylinder water-cooled inline petrol engine developing 100hp or 125hp.
Performance: Speed 3.7mph (5.92km/h); range 35 miles (56km); vertical obstacle 4ft 6in (1.371m); trench 10ft (3.048m).

had been a hazard on the Mark I. Splash was still a danger, however, and crews were issued with leather face masks and goggles, though few could tolerate wearing them. The track rollers were strengthened and so were the drive-chains from the gear-shafts. A plain idler wheel was fitted on the front, and wider tracks were tried. The second gear-shaft, which took a great deal of strain in action, had been found to twist, so in the Mark IV it

was made from nickel steel. The sponsons were hinged to allow them to be swung in for rail travel. An unditching beam was fitted as standard and carried on top of the hull at the rear.

The 6-pounder guns were shorter (23 calibers compared to 40), which greatly reduced the danger of the muzzle digging into the ground when the tank was crossing wide trenches, and also made it easier for the crew to handle the gun when

Below: *A British Mark IV waiting to join the attack during the Battle of Polygon Wood (26 September 1917). The camouflage net became standard practice in World War II.*

Left top: *A captured Mark IV leads a German attack (note cross on the tank). The circular container on the back of the man in the center foreground contained flame-thrower fuel.*

Left bottom: *Troops of the Canadian Mounted Rifles follow a Mark V (Female) into the attack at Bonny, France (12 June 1918).*

stowing the sponsons. Due to a shortage of Hotchkiss machine-guns, Lewis guns were substituted, which proved to be a mistake because the large cooling-jacket meant that a larger hole had to be made in the armor, which allowed splinters and bullet splash to enter. In addition, the jacket itself was vulnerable to the intense small arms fire which a tank attracted. Later Mark IVs reverted to the Hotchkiss,

much to the relief of the crews. The eight-man crew was distributed in the same way as in the Mark I (q.v.).

Despite its shortcomings, the Mark IV was a formidable fighting vehicle, especially the "male," and when the first German tanks appeared in April 1918 some "females" were given a "male" sponson on the right-hand side so that they could protect themselves, the

Below: What tanks were meant to do; a British Mark V (an improved Mark IV) advances into the village of Meaulte, which has just been captured in the great advance on 22 August 1918.

Right top: An abandoned Mark IV after the battle of Cambrai; quite how it got itself into this unusual predicament is not clear.

Right bottom: Another of the tasks for which tanks were originally designed - crushing the wire entanglements on the Western Front.

resulting marriage being called a "hermaphrodite." Altogether 420 male and 595 female Mark IVs were produced, and the type was used from the Battle of Flers in September 1917, through Cambrai to the end of the war. The Germans were also quick to press captured Mark IVs into service, as they were far superior to anything they could design. Although there were five later marks of rhomboidal tank, by 1919 these large, slow moving, vulnerable vehicles were obsolete and were replaced by lighter, faster models.

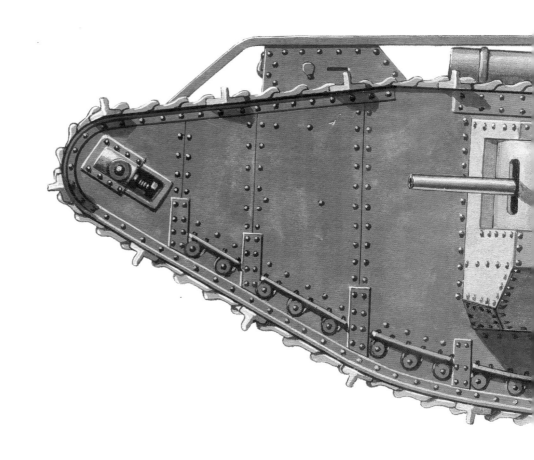

Right: *This view of a Mark IV (Male) shows the characteristic rhomboid shape, the sponson sticking out to the side, the top of the control compartment, and the large silencer and exhaust leading down to the rear of the tank. The square object at the after end of the overhead rail is the unditching beam.*

Below: *These soldiers are cheerful and purposeful because they are advancing and in open country. The tanks are Mark Vs, the occasion the Battle of the St Quentin Canal (29 September 1918). The devices atop the tanks are "Cribs", used to help the tanks cross large gaps.*

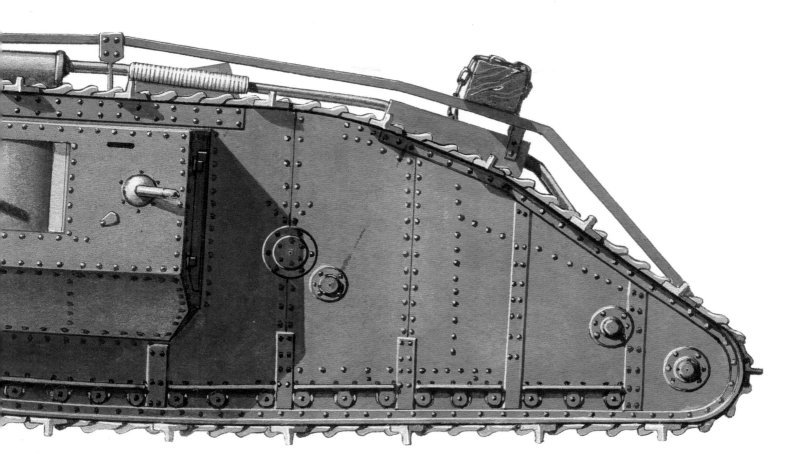

Leichte Kampfwagen (LK) II Cavalry Tank

TAKEN BY SURPRISE by the appearance of Allied tanks, the usual German reaction was to copy the British designs. Thus, when a Mark A Whippet (qv) was captured, it was immediately copied by Krupp, although some of the faults were corrected. The LK II had much the same general layout, with the engine in the front and a rear transmission, central driver, and a rear turret. Since a revolving turret was too difficult, a fixed box with a front-mounted 5.7cm gun was fitted.

The LK II was considerably lighter than the Whippet, but it had much the same protection. Its 55hp Daimler engine made it both fast and agile, and its lighter weight meant that it was able to make better use of its power. In the event, the LK II never entered service, and it seems that no more than two were actually completed by the Germans, but when the war ended the design was sold to Sweden, which, following some modifications, took it into service as the m/21.

One major change was to fit a small rotating turret mounting a 3.7cm gun atop

the fixed turret, and another was to increase the crew to four and fit a small radio to a proportion of the fleet.

In 1926 a new version of the LK II appeared in Germany, which was effectively an amalgam of the LK II and the Vickers Medium although it was far more advanced than the previous model. It had a sprung track, using coupled bogies, a lower silhouette, a full rotating turret mounting the 3.7cm gun, and reasonably sloped armour. The weight increased by 0.98 ton (1,000kg) but the speed and agility improved markedly.

SPECIFICATIONS

Country of origin: Germany.
Crew: 3.
Armament: One 5.7cm gun or two 7.92mm Maxim machine-guns.
Armor: 0.24in (6mm) minimum; 0.43in (11mm) maximum.
Dimensions: Length 16ft 7in (5.06m); width 6ft 4in (1.95m); height 8ft 2in (2.5m).
Weight: 18,739lb (8,500kg).
Engine: Daimler four-cylinder water-cooled inline petrol engine developing 55bhp.

Performance: Road speed 10mph (16km/h); range 40 miles (65km); trench 6ft 6in (2.04m); gradient 45 degrees, for short climbs only.

Above: *The German LK II was based on the British Whippet (see overleaf).*

Left: *Germany's first tank, the LK II. had a front-mounted engine and a fixed turret.*

Mark A Whippet Medium Tank

❖

ONCE THE RHOMBOIDAL MARK I tanks were in production, the designer, Tritton, turned his attention to a lighter, faster tank to undertake the traditional cavalry tasks of exploiting a breakthrough and pursuing a retreating enemy; effectively, an armored replacement for the horse. The new tank was initially named the "Tritton Chaser" but the name "Whippet" was officially adopted. The layout resembled that of an armored car, with the engine at the front and the driver at the rear, looking out over a long bonnet. One poor feature was that the petrol tank was in front of the engine, placing it in the most likely position to receive anti-tank fire, although it was armored. The prototype had a rotating two-man turret, but to get the tank into service more quickly production tanks had only a fixed, box-like structure with a machinegun in each of the four faces, which meant that the commander and gunner had to handle four machine-guns within the confines of a very small fighting compartment.

The tank had two engines, one for each

track, with the driver using a steering wheel connected to the two throttles, but the process was very difficult to manage, one common problem being that drivers regularly stalled one engine whereupon the tank spun round, shed a track and became immobilized. Also, whilst faster than a rhomboidal tank, the Whippet was nothing like as fast as a horse. The range - 40 miles (64km) - was too short for a vehicle intended to exploit a breakthrough, and crews often carried extra gasoline in cans strapped on the outside of the hull, a suicidal habit in action.

SPECIFICATIONS

Country of origin: United Kingdom.
Crew: 3.
Armament: Four .303in Hotchkiss machine-guns.
Armor: 14mm (0.55in) maximum; 5mm (0.2in) minimum.
Dimensions: Length 20ft (6.09m); width 8ft 7in (2.61m); height 9ft (2.74m).
Weight: Combat 31,360lb (14,225kg).

Engine: Two Tylor six-cylinder water-cooled inline petrol tractor engines, each developing 45hp.
Performance: Speed 8mph (12.8km/h); range 40 miles (64km).

Despite the shortcomings, the Whippet was considered a great success. In one epic action, a Whippet named "Musical Box," commanded by Lt Arnold, became detached from the main body of its tank battalion during an advance at Villers-Bretonneux on 8 August 1918. On seeing a German gun position harassing advancing British infantry Arnold attacked, killing some 30 German gunners and enabling the infantry to continue their advance. Thereafter "Musical Box" was continuously in action for nine hours, dispersing a complete enemy infantry battalion, and was only stopped when hit by artillery fire whilst attacking a divisional transport column far behind what had been the enemy front line.

As an experiment, a Tank Corps' workshop in France rebuilt a Whippet, giving it sprung bogies, which improved the ride considerably and then fitted a single 360hp Rolls-Royce Eagle aircraft engine and much modified controls. As a result cross-country performance was greatly increased and a road speed of 30mph (48km/h) was easily attained. The implications were ignored, however, and the design was abandoned in 1919, with all 200 being scrapped, apart from a few that were sold to Japan.

Left: The Whippet, as its name implies, was intended to be a fast-moving and agile tank, able to exploit a breakthrough. Because it was designed to operate in open country it did not need the great rhomboidal track system of other British tanks. Note the forward-mounted engine, mud-chutes and the non-rotating turret, which mounted one 0.303in machine-gun in each face.

Renault FT-17 Light Tank

THE FIRST PROTOTYPE FT-17 ran in February 1917 and a production order was then placed with Renault, but rapid increases in the numbers required - 3,500 by the end of 1918 - meant that other companies were brought into the program. Nevertheless, there were many delays mainly due to problems in producing the turrets.

The FT-17 was a narrow box of riveted 0.63in (16mm) steel. The driver sat in the front, and the engine and transmission was at the rear, while in the center was the commander/gunner in a small turret, the first in any tank to be capable of 360º rotation. Most FT-17s were fitted with a tail at the rear to increase their trench-crossing capabilities, but this was removed for transport. Armament varied and there were many minor variants. FT-17s were first used in action in May 1918 and early losses were heavy, but reduced as the crews gained experience. One of the advantages of the Renault was that its small size enabled it to be transported by lorry from one part of the front to another, whereas

the heavier tanks had to be brought up by rail and then proceed to the front line under their own power.

Many FT-17s were exported in the 1920s and in many cases they were the first armored vehicles of some armies. Such was the demand, that exports had to be stopped, otherwise the French Army would have ended up with no Renaults at

Below: *After the French capitulation, many French-built Renault FT-17 tanks were pressed into service with the German Wehrmacht as the PzKpfw 18R 730(f). Sole armament was a puny 8mm machine-gun.*

SPECIFICATIONS

Country of origin: France.
Crew: 2.
Armament: One Hotchkiss 8mm machine-gun (see text).
Armor: 22mm (0.87in) maximum; 6mm (0.24in) minimum.
Dimensions: Length (with tail) 16ft 5in (5m); width 5ft 9in (1.74m); height 6ft 7in (2.14m).
Weight: Combat 15,432lb (7,000kg).

Engine: Renault four-cylinder water-cooled petrol engine developing 35bhp at 1,500rpm.
Performance: Road speed 4.7mph (7.7km/h); road range 22 miles (35km); vertical obstacle 2ft (0.6m); trench crossing (with tail) 5ft 11in (1.8m); (without tail) 4ft 6in (1.35m); gradient 50 per cent.

all. In the 1930s, those FT-17s remaining in service were rearmed with new 0.75mm Hotchkiss machine-guns and then became known as the FT-31. There were still large numbers in service in 1939, including some 1,600 with the French Army. Many of the latter were captured and then pressed into service by the German Army as the PzKpfw 18R 730(f). They were used mainly for an internal security role, and for guarding airfields and other strategic targets. Some of the tanks had their turrets removed, the turrets being installed as coastal defences.

Below: *Renault FT-17 returns from an operation on the Aisne front in 1940. Note that it is fully closed down, with the commander inside the turret, rather than sitting on the back flap.*

Left top: *Dozens of FT-17s (and a single Char B1) at a Wehrmacht depot in Poland in 1941, prior to conversion for German use.*

Left bottom: *A somewhat jaded FT-17, showing the suspension and track system, with enormous front driving sprocket.*

Right: *A scene in North Africa as a column of British Indian Army Bren-gun carriers drive through a demolished road-block which has been defended by an PzKpfw 18R 730(f) (ex-French FT-17) and a sole anti-tank gun.*

Below: *US infantry and armor troops move up to the front-line on 26 September 1918. Their Renault FT-17 tanks are fitted with long-range gasoline tanks in anticipation of deep penetration into German-held territory.*

Right: *French-built Renault FT-17 tanks of the US Army's 326th Tank Battalion move towards the front line near Boureuilles, France, 26 September 1918.*

Right bottom: *French Army tanks on the streets of Frankfurt, Germany in April 1920, watched by apprehensive German civilians.*

LES TANKS DANS LES RUES DE FRANCFORT – 6 AVRIL 1920.

Left: *Two American soldiers in a Renault FT-17, making it clear just how small these tanks really were. The construction is crude, based on riveting techniques, and resistance against anti-tanks weapons poor.*

Sturmpanzerwagen A7V

ALARMED BY THE British introduction of tanks, the German General Staff sought "quick fixes," essentially to use captured British tanks or to manufacture copies. They also produced their own design and contracts were hurriedly finalized on 22 December 1916. Prototypes started trials in mid-1917, in the course of which many weaknesses were revealed, particularly with the engine cooling and tracks. These had still not been resolved by December 1917, when the impatient General Staff simply went ahead and ordered 100 tanks, to be ready in time for the Spring offensive. The tank was designated A7V, from the initial letters of the committee that first called for it: the *Allgemeine Kriegesdepartment 7 - Abteilung Verkehrwesen* (= General Staff Department Number 7 - Traffic Section).

The design was simply an armored strongpoint on tracks, consisting of a tracked chassis and suspension with a large steel box on top carrying a 5.7cm low-velocity gun and six 7.92mm machine-guns. The result was a heavy,

ungainly vehicle, unable to move on any surface other than a flat, hard road, since the very limited ground clearance (15.75in/40cm) ensured that it bellied down on any rough or muddy ground, of which there was no shortage on the Western front. The problems were exacerbated by the lack of any "lift" at the front, preventing the vehicle from pulling itself out of a trench. The only positive element in the track arrangement was that it was protected by armor.

The interior of the hull contained the two engines centrally sited below the cupola housing the driver and commander. The tracks ran on 24 sprung bogies, allowing a top speed of 8mph (13km/h) in ideal conditions, but the tank's weight was too much for engines and transmission, and reliability was appalling.

The crew, the largest carried by any tank, was led by the commander. The driver was assisted by two mechanics who maintained and repaired the engines; all three came from the engineer corps. The 5.7cm gun was manned by two artillerymen and the six machine-guns were manned by two infantrymen each. Thus, there were 18 men

from three different corps, which did not help teamwork. Their working conditions were terrible, with limited vision, tremendous noise and smell from the engines, and communication only by shouting and hand signals.

Only 20 of the 100 ordered in 1917 were completed, which were grouped into units of five vehicles each. Their first operation was on 29 March 1918 and the last on 8 October. A few were destroyed or captured in battle and all but one of the survivors were scrapped in 1919. The one

survivor is #506 "Mephisto" which was captured at Villers-Brettoneux on 24 April 1918 and is now in a museum in Queensland, Australia.

Opposite: An A7V in the summer of 1918. This version was equivalent to the British "female" tank, armed with seven 7.92mm machine-guns. This German design was, in essence, a large and very slow-moving mobile strong-point.

Below: The second version mounted a 57mm gun in the front-plate, together with five 7.9mm machine-guns, two on either side and one in the rear. Note also the commander's "bridge."

SPECIFICATIONS

Country of origin: Germany.
Crew: 18.
Armament: One 5.7cm gun; six or seven 7.92mm Maxim machine-guns.
Armor: 0.59in (15mm) minimum; 1.18in (30mm) maximum.
Dimensions: Length 24ft 1in (7.34m); width 10ft 0½in (3.07m); height 10ft 10in (3.3m).
Weight: 65.918lb (29,900kg).

Engines: Two Daimler four-cylinder water-cooled inline engines each developing 100bhp at 1.600rpm.
Performance: Road speed 5mph (8km/h); range 25 miles (40km); trench 7ft (2.13m).

Fiat 2000 Heavy Tank

A PROTOTYPE OF A tracked vehicle, with two turrets, each mounting a single machine-gun, was built in 1915 for the Italian Army, but trials were unsuccessful. In 1917, the Italians obtained a Renault light tank and a Schneider medium tank for trials, but the French refused to supply them in quantity, so a version of the FT-17 was produced under licence (see Fiat 3000), while the Italians designed their own heavy tank, the FIAT 2000; a prototype completed in late 1918 saw no action.

The FIAT 2000 was advanced for its time. The driver sat at the front of the hull with excellent vision and the engine was at the rear. Compared to other tanks of the period, the interior was roomy as most of the mechanical components were under the floor. Main armament was a 65mm gun in a turret with all-round traverse, and there were also seven 6.5mm machine-guns, three machine-guns in each side of the hull, one in the rear. There were ten road wheels, eight in pairs on sprung bogie units, and two located between each end bogie and the idler or drive sprocket.

The FIAT 2000 did not have the cross-country capability of the British Mark IV, but was superior to the French Saint Chamond and Schneider tanks, and was well armed. A further four vehicles were completed in 1920, which remained in service until at least 1934.

Below: *The Italian Fiat 2000 had a 65mm gun mounted in a turret with 360° traverse, one of the earliest to use such an arrangement. Note also the track skirts with mud chutes.*

Opposite: *The prototype Fiat 200 demonstrates its ability to climb a wall; the type saw no combat, but four vehicles served until 1934.*

SPECIFICATIONS

Country of origin: Italy.
Crew: 10.
Armament: One turret-mounted 65mm gun; seven FIAT 6.5mm machine-guns.
Armor: 20mm (0.79in) maximum; 15mm (0.59in) minimum.
Dimensions: Length 24ft 3in (7.4m); width 10ft 2in (3.1m); height 12ft 6in (3.8m).
Weight: Combat 88,185lb (40,000kg).

Engine: Fiat A12 six-cylinder petrol engine developing 240hp.
Performance: Maximum road speed 3.7mph (6km/h): range 47 miles (75km); vertical obstacle 3ft 3in (1m); trench 9ft 10in (3m).

Medium C Tank

✦

THE MEDIUM C combined the experience of the Mk IV and the Medium A (Whippet) into one machine and was intended to lead the proposed Allied breakthrough in 1919. The main improvement was that the crew was grouped together in one compartment and interconnected with voice tubes. This enabled the commander, who occupied a small rotating cupola at the back of the turret, to control the tank, which had been impossible in the Mk IV. Also, the engine was placed in a separate compartment at the rear, reducing the noise and fumes in the fighting compartment.

The suspension was uninspired, with unsprung bogies, and speed was low; the maximum was 7.9mph (12.64km/h) and that could only be achieved on a good road. The fixed turret had mountings for five machine-guns, although only four were ever fitted, the fifth being pintle-mounted on the roof for anti-aircraft fire. It was intended at one time to build a second version armed with a 6-pounder gun, but, as far as is known, only one was

ever built.

It was planned to build the Medium C in large numbers, but all production ceased in February 1918 after some 200 had been built. The design proved to be a significant advance and the stepping stone to the fully-sprung, fast models, with the Vickers Medium being the next logical step and which laid the basis for all modern tanks.

Below: *The British Medium C was intended to lead the Allied breakthrough in 1919. The crew was grouped together and the version seen here had a fixed turret mounting four 0.303in machine-guns; a second version was armed with a single 6-pounder gun and two machine-guns.*

SPECIFICATIONS

Country of origin: United Kingdom.
Crew: 4.
Armament: Four .303in Hotchkiss machine-guns.
Armor: 14mm (0.55in) maximum; 6mm (0.25in) minimum.
Dimensions: Length 25ft 10in (7.856m); width 8ft 11in (2.71m); height 9ft 8in (2.94m).
Weight: Combat 43,680lb (19,813kg).

Engine: Ricardo six-cylinder water-cooled inline petrol engine developing 150bhp at 1,200rpm.
Performance: Speed 7.9mph (12.64km/h); range 75 miles (120km); vertical obstacle 4ft 6in (1.371m); trench 10ft (3.352m); gradient unknown.

Char 2C Heavy Tank

❖

IN 1916 THE FCM (Forges et Chantiers de la Mediterranee) started the design of a "breakthrough tank." Known as the Char FCM 1A it was a huge vehicle, weighing 39 tons (40,000kg) and two prototypes were completed in late 1917 before attention switched to the Char 2C. Ten of the latter were completed in 1918, but did not enter service until 1919; had the war not ended, it was anticipated that 300 Char 2Cs would ve been built for the planned 1919 offensive.

Char 2C's main armament was a turret-mounted 75mm gun, with four 8mm machine-guns, one in the hull front, one in each side of the hull in the forward part of the tank, and the last in an independent turret at the rear of the tank. The tanks were originally powered by two Mercedes engines, but these were later replaced by more powerful Maybach engines. The Char 2C had the distinction of being the first tank to have two turrets; it also had one of the largest crews at 12 men. It was exceptionally heavy and had it been used operationally would have been more of a

liability than an asset. One Char 2C was rebuilt as the only Char 2C-bis, which had additional armor, Sautter-Harlè engines and a 155mm howitzer. Ten Char 2Cs were modified in the 1930s and were operational when war broke out in 1939, although when the Germans attacked in 1940, the Luftwaffe destroyed most on their special railway wagons before they could take any part in fighting.

Below: *The French Char 2C was a massive vehicle, weighing some 70 tonnes and with a 13-man crew, but armed with only a 75mm main gun and four 8mm machineguns.*

SPECIFICATIONS

Country of origin: France.
Crew: 12-13.
Armament: One 75mm gun; four 8mm machine-guns.
Dimensions: Length 33ft 8in (10.27m); width 9ft 8in (2.95m); height 13ft 2in (4.01m).
Weight: Combat 154,320lb (70,000kg).

Engine: See text.
Performance: Road speed 8mph (12km/h); range 100 miles (160km); vertical obstacle 4ft (1.219m); trench 13ft 6in (4.114m); gradient 50 per cent.

Fiat 3000 Light Tank

❖

WHEN FRANCE REFUSED to export Renault FT-17s, FIAT, assisted by Ansaldo and Breda, designed a vehicle similar to the FT-17 but using Italian components. The Army placed an order for 1,400, but this was reduced to 100 when World War I ended in November 1918. The first prototype was not completed until 1920 and the type entered service in 1923.

The Carro d'Assalto FIAT 3000 Model 21 (FIAT 3000) was lighter and much faster than the FT-17, with the production vehicles being armed with turret-mounted twin 6.5mm machine-guns. In 1929 a FIAT 3000 was fitted with a 37mm gun in place of the machine-guns, and most surviving examples were then rebuilt as the FIAT 3000 Model 30 (or FIAT 3000B). In addition to the new armament the suspension was improved and a more powerful engine was fitted. The 37mm gun was offset to the right in the turret. Some FIAT 3000s were also fitted with a radio for use in the command role, and trials versions included a 105mm self-

propelled howitzer and another with twin 37mm guns.

Until the arrival of the British Carden-Loyd Mark VI vehicles in 1929, the FIAT 3000 was the only tank operated in the Italian Army in any quantity, and they used it in action in Abyssinia, Libya and in Italy itself, where it was last used in the defense of Sicily in 1943.

Below: *The Fiat 3000 was designed and constructed in Italy after the French refused the Italian request to supply Renault FT-17s. This is the Fiat Model 30B (Model 1930) armed with a 37mm main gun.*

SPECIFICATIONS

Country of origin: Italy.
Crew: 2.
Armament: Twin SIA or FIAT Model 29 6.5mm machine-guns.
Armor: 6mm (0.24in) minimum, 16mm (0.63in) maximum.
Dimensions: Length (without tail) 11ft 9in (3.61m); length (with tail) 13ft 8in (4.17m); width 5ft 5in (1.64m); height 7ft (2.19m).
Weight: Combat 12,125lb (5,500kg).

Engine: FIAT four-cylinder petrol engine developing 50hp at 1.700rpm.
Performance: Road speed 15mph (24km/h); range 59 miles (95km); vertical obstacle 2ft (0.6m); trench 4ft 11in (1.5m); gradient 60 per cent.

Vickers Mark II
Medium Tank

BRITAIN'S FIRST TRULY post-World War I tank, the "Vickers Medium" incorporated many advances over war-time designs, most notable the fully revolving turret. In order to reduce costs the hull was fabricated from flat plates with few curves making it very box-like, although this gave the crew plenty of space inside. The engine was in front on the left, with the driver alongside on the right, with an excellent view. Of the four men in the turret, one fired the 3-pounder; the second loaded for him and handled the co-axial machine-gun; the third was the radio operator and fired one of the hull machine-guns; and the fourth was the commander, who handled the other hull machine-gun, if necessary. Ventilation was reasonable, and the great heat of the old rhomboidals was gone; indeed, there were even a few crew comforts such as a smokeless cooker, some cooking utensils and three day's rations. The Vickers Mediums were also the first fast tanks in British service; the official top speed was 16mph (26km/h), but drivers were able to

reach 30mph (48km/h), if they were allowed to do so!

Approximately 160 were produced and served in the Royal Tank Corps throughout the difficult interwar years. Some even survived to 1939 when they were used for training gun crews and drivers. A few were used operationally in North Africa in the early months of World War II, while others were dug into the ground in England as anti-invasion pillboxes.

SPECIFICATIONS

Country of origin: United Kingdom.
Crew: 5.
Armament: One 3-pounder gun; one .303in Vickers machine-gun mounted co-axially; two .303in Vickers machine-guns mounted in hull.
Armor: 12mm (0.47in) maximum 8mm (0.31in) minimum.
Dimensions: Length 17ft 6in (5.33m); width 9ft 1½in (2.78m); height 9ft 10½in (3.01m).
Weight: Combat 30,128lb (13,666kg).

Engine: Armstrong Siddeley eight-cylinder air-cooled inline developing 90bhp.
Performance: Speed 16mph (25.6km/h); range 120 miles (192km); vertical obstacle unknown; trench 6ft 6in (1.981m); gradient unknown.

Left: *The Vickers Mark II Medium was the first tank to enter British Army service after World War I. The first of the second generation tanks, it was a great success; it was the first British tank with a fully rotating turret, which mounted a 3-pounder gun with a coaxial Vickers 0.303in machine-gun. It also had two machine-guns in ball-mountings in the tank sides, one of which can be seen at the rear of this tank. The Vickers Mark II Medium provided the basis for all the tactical experiments carried out by the British armored units in the 1920s and 30s, and a few were still in service in the early days of World War II, but by then they were totally obsolete.*

T3 Christie Medium Tank

AMERICAN ENGINEER, J. Walter Christie, produced his first tank design in 1919, and a second in 1921, but the breakthrough came in 1928 when the first tank with "Christie suspension" appeared, which had four large road wheels and removable tracks. Running on road wheels, the T3 could achieve 70mph (113km/h); on tracks its speed was 30mph (48km/h).

The US Army ordered five as the T3 Medium Tank. The hull was constructed of 0.5in (12.7mm) thick armor and there were four rubber-tired 27in (68.6cm) diameter road wheels on each side, mounted on swinging arms with a travel of 16in (40.65cm) and tracks which could be removed/replaced by two men in 30 minutes. In road-running mode the tracks were removed, the two front wheels were used for steering, the middle pairs were raised clear of the ground and the rear pair were driven by chains from the driving sprocket. While very fast, the large angular movement resulted in heavy wear, while the suspension springs reduced the available space in the hull. Main armament was a

turret-mounted short-barreled 37mm gun.

Nine T3s were built, five for the US Army, two for the Polish Army (although not delivered and taken into US service as T3E1) and two for the Soviet Union, which were designated BT-1 s, and led to the T-34 (q.v.). The British later bought a single example.

Below left: *One of three T3s to enter service with the US Army's 67th Regiment, seen here in its fast, road-running configuration, with tracks removed and stored on the guards.*

Below: *The glacis plate was well-sloped and carefully designed to defeat attack by anti-tank weapons. Note 37mm gun above driver's head.*

SPECIFICATIONS

Country of origin: USA.
Crew: 3.
Armament: One 37mm gun; one .3in machine-gun mounted co-axial with main armament; one .3in machine-gun in each side of turret; one .3in machine-gun in hull.
Armor: 16mm (0.625) maximum; 12.7mm (.5in) minimum.
Dimensions: Length 19ft 1in (5.82m); width 8ft 1in (2.46m); height 7ft 7in (2.31m).
Weight: Combat 24,200lb (10,977kg).

Engine: Ordnance Liberty 12-cylinder water-cooled petrol engine developing 338bhp at 1,400rpm.
Performance: Road speed (wheels) 46mph (74km/h), road speed (tracks) 27mph (43km/h); vertical obstacle 3ft (0.9m); trench 8ft 3in (2.5m); gradient 42 per cent.

T-26 Light Tank

THE MIGHTY SOVIET ARMY armored forces which so convincingly defeated the German tank armies in 1943-45 had very modest beginnings in the 1920s, mainly due to the upheaval and disruption caused by the Revolution of 1917 and the subsequent conflicts with the White Russians and various Western and Japanese armies. The earliest influences on the Soviet Army armored doctrine were the French, who promoted their concept of light tanks tied to infantry formations in a purely supporting role. As a result, the first tank produced by the Soviet Army was the KS Light Infantry Tank, which was based on the Renault FT-17 and nicknamed the "Russky Renault" This entered service in 1920, but Soviet tank designers decided that they could do better, which led to the MS-1, armed with a single 37mm Hotchkiss cannon and weighing 12,125lb (5,500kg). This was in production from 1929 to 1931, but was withdrawn from front-line service in 1932 and appears to have been a poor design, because in 1930 the Soviet Army was

already looking for a replacement, ordering several indigenous tank designs to be prepared. They also took the precaution of purchasing a number of tanks to a similar specification from the British company, Vickers-Armstrong. These had the company designation Vickers-E and when competitive trials were held against the Soviet T-19 and T-20 designs, the British type easily won. As a

Below: The Soviet T-26 was produced from 1931 until 1940, during which some 12,000 were built in a variety of versions. Note the hull machinegun, a feature common in 1930s tank design.

SPECIFICATIONS

Country of origin: Russia.
Crew: 3.
Armament: Various (see text).
Armor: Between 6mm (0.24in) and 25mm (0.98in) according to model.
Dimensions: Length between 15ft 2in (4.62m) and 16ft (4.88m); width between 8ft (2.44m) and 7ft 11in (2.41m); height between 7ft 8in (2.33m) and 6ft 10in (2.08m).

Weight: Between 17.637lb (8,000kg) and 20.944lb (9,500kg) according to model.
Engine: Model T-26 four-cylinder air-cooled petrol engine developing 91hp at 2,200rpm.
Performance: Road speed between 17.5mph (28km/h) and 20mph (32km/h) according to model; range between 63 miles (100km) and 140 miles (225km) according to model; vertical obstacle 2ft 5in (0.79m); trench 5ft 10in (1.90m); gradient 40 degrees.

result of the trials a few modifications were incorporated and the type was then placed in full-scale production as the T-26 Light Tank on a production run lasting from 1931 to 1940, during which some 12,000 were manufactured, in a multiplicity of models.

The initial production model was virtually identical to the British original apart from a few alterations to the shape of the hull front and the configuration of the two independently rotating machine-gun turrets. The hull was made of armor plates of varying thicknesses (0.25in (6mm) to 1in (25mm)) which were riveted together. The driver sat at the right front and the main armament consisted of two machine-guns in a curious twin turret arrangement in which each had a certain degree of movement independent of the other. These mounted a variety of weapons, including machine-guns of differing calibers. There was also a special command version, fitted with a high-frequency radio and a "hand-rail"-type antenna of the type which enjoyed a vogue in the 1930s, and which extended across

the front of the vehicle and down both sides, but not across the rear.

Next was planned a version in which one of the two turrets was removed and the remaining turret mounted a new long-barreled 37mm cannon, but only a small number were produced, because a further decision had already been made to move onto yet another model with a completely new and larger turret mounting a single 45mm cannon. Mass production of this single-turreted model started in 1933 and later in the 1930s the survivors of the earlier twin turreted tanks were retrofitted with the same turret.

In 1938 the Red Army became involved in conflict with the Japanese in the Far East and General Blyukher, commander of the Special Far-Eastern Army, sent urgent reports to the effect that the riveted T-26 tank hulls had proved ineffective against Japanese anti-tank fire. It was therefore decided to adopt a new version with an all-welded hull and turret, which was designated T-26S. Some of the earlier riveted models were retrofitted with the welded turret of this tank.

Prior to World War II, the T-26 saw action in the two main battles with the Japanese in Manchuria, with the Communist forces in the Spanish Civil War, and in the Russo-Finnish War. The T-26 underwent many alterations and modifications, and several special-purpose vehicles were developed around its chassis, including self-propelled guns, flame-throwers, bridge-layers, smoke and chemical tanks, artillery tractors, remote-controlled tank mines, and many others. The T-26 was not a great design, but it nevertheless played an important role in the development of Soviet tanks.

Below: A Soviet Army unit shows off its T-26 to a visiting delegation. In this tank, the main gun is a long-barrelled 37mm weapon and the hull machine-gun has been removed.

Right top: T-26 armed with 27mm main gun and 7.62mm machine-gun in an unusual twin turret arrangement. The "handrail" around the upper hull is, in fact, a radio antenna.

Right bottom: T-26s move forward in an attack, closely watched by infantrymen. The T-26 was high for its size.

T-28 Medium Tank

❖

FOLLOWING THE BRITISH Independent of 1926, there was something of a vogue for multi-turreted tanks and the British produced the A6 as a possible successor to the Medium Mark II (q.v.). The A6, also known as the "16-tonner," was successful but the financial climate prevented production, although the Soviets managed to obtain the plans through a spy. In 1932 the Leningrad Kirov plant built a new prototype based on the British design, which had a main armament of a 45mm gun and weighed some 17.3 tons (17,575kg). Following trials a new design was prepared, armed with a 75mm gun, which raised the weight to 27.6 tons (28,000kg) and this was accepted for service as the T-28 on 11 August 1933. All T-28s were fitted with two-way high frequency radio equipment and had the characteristic frame antenna around the top of the main turret. They were also fitted with smoke-emitters. Later production vehicles were fitted with a stabilizer for the main gun, considerably enhancing the accuracy when fired on the

move and the first known application of a device now universally used.

The T-28 was particularly noted for its quiet, smooth motion and unusually good ability to cross trenches and other obstacles. During 1938 these tanks were modified with the original 16.5 caliber gun being replaced by one 26 calibers long.

T-28 tanks were employed against the Japanese in 1939 and also during the Russo-Finnish War, and in the latter it was discovered that the armor was inadequate, resulting in the addition of appliqué plates

SPECIFICATIONS

Country of origin: Russia.
Crew: 6.
Armament: One 76.2mm gun; three DT machine-guns.
Armor: 20mm to 80mm (0.79in to 3.15in) depending on model.
Dimensions: Length 24ft 5in (7.44m); width 9ft 3in (2.82m); height 9ft 3in (2.82m).
Weight: 61.729lb (28,000kg) to 70,547lb (32,000kg) depending on model.

Engine: One M-17L 12-cylinder water-cooled petrol engine developing 500hp at 1,450rpm.
Performance: Road speed 23mph (37km/h); range 140 miles (220km); vertical obstacle 3ft 5in (1.04m); trench 9ft 6in (2.9m); gradient 80 per cent.

which raised the weight to 31.5 tons (32,000kg). Surprisingly, this did not affect speed or agility and the tank was popular with its crews. Nevertheless, production ended in 1941.

Left: *The Soviet T-28 was based on the British A1E1 experimental tank of the mid-1920s and like the original featured a turret-mounted main gun (in this case a 76mm) and two machine-guns in "sub-turrets." This example was captured by the Finnish Army and painted in winter camouflage; it also carries the Finnish national symbol. Note the sub-turret (immediately below the main gun) which has had the machine-gun removed.*

T-35 Heavy Tank

R ED ARMY TANK DOCTRINE in the 1920s and early 1930s required "breakthrough" tanks with heavy firepower and excellent protection, and the army was also quite prepared to look abroad for inspiration. It was particularly interested in British designs, some of which were purchased, but the design of the A-1 Independent tank was obtained by espionage. This tank, which appeared in 1926 and never got beyond the experimental stage in Britain, had five turrets and the Soviet T-35 bore more than a passing resemblance, also having five turrets. The main gun was a 76.2mm, with 37mm cannon in two subsidiary turrets (front and rear of the main turret) and two 7.62mm machine-guns in the smallest turrets. The result was a vehicle with a crew of 11 men and which weighed 49 tons (50,000kg). Subsequent production vehicles dispensed with some of these turrets, and a few had 45mm guns in place of the 37mm type, while the final models had sloping welded armor.

About 60 were built and all were fitted

with radio equipment and had the characteristic frame antenna around the top of the main turret. The T-35 was outmoded by the outbreak of war in 1941, but was retained in service until the Battle of Moscow in December. It was then phased out, but many of the hulls had their tracks and suspension removed and were then installed on railroad flatcars to produce armored trains.

Below: The T-35 mounted a single 76.2mm gun in the main turret and two 37mm guns in sub-turrets, one in front, the second at the rear of the tank (the muzzle is just visible).

SPECIFICATIONS

Country of origin: Russia
Crew: 11 (when provided with all turrets; some models had some of the turrets removed).
Armament: Basic model – One 76.2mm gun; two 45mm guns; six 7.62mm DT machine-guns; one P-40 AA machine-gun. (Some later models had a few of the subsidiary weapons removed.)
Armor: 30mm (1.18in) maximum; 10mm (0.39in) minimum.

Dimensions: Length 31ft 10in (9.72m); width 10ft 6in (3.2m); height 11ft 3in (3.43m).
Weight: Combat 110,230lb (50,000kg). (Some models were lighter.)
Engine: One Model M-17T V-12 12-cylinder water-cooled petrol engine developing 500hp at 2.200rpm.
Performance: Road speed 19mph (30km/h); range 94 miles (150km); vertical obstacle 4ft (1.2m); trench 11ft 6in (3.5m); gradient 20 degrees.

Carro Veloce CV33 Tankette

◆

IN THE MID-1920s the British firm of Carden-Loyd developed a series of two-man "tankettes" which were light and usually armed with a machine-gun; armor was minimal and they relied for protection on small size and high mobility. These were popular abroad and in 1929 the Italian Army obtained a licence to manufacture Carden-Loyd Mark VI tankettes, with a number supplied from Britain, following which 25, armed with a single 6.5mm machine-gun, were built in Italy under the designation Carro Veloce Model 1929 (CV-29).

.Further development led to the definitive model, the CV-33, which had a hull with a thickness of 0.3-0.5in (7-14mm) and a two-man crew, the commander/gunner seated on the left, driver on the right. The engine was mounted transversely at the rear, connected by a drive-shaft to the forward-mounted gearbox. Suspension consisted of six small road wheels, with forward drive sprocket and rear idler, with an additional, adjustable idler behind the sixth road wheel. There were no track-return rollers.

The original production order for Series I vehicles was for 1,100 armed with a single 6.5mm machine-gun and 200 (CV-33 special) with a 37mm cannon, although only some 300 were actually built. These were followed in 1935 by the Series II, basically similar but armed with twin FIAT Model 18/35 machine-guns, and Series I vehicles were later brought up to the same standard. The weapon mounts

Below: CV-33, armed with twin 8mm machine-guns, side-by-side in a fixed turret. The tubes atop the rear of the tank are a ground mounting for an anti-aircraft machine-gun.

SPECIFICATIONS

Country of origin: Italy.
Crew: 2.
Armament: Twin 8mm FIAT Model 18/35 machine-guns.
Armor: 15mm (0.6in) maximum; 5mm (0.2in) minimum.
Dimensions: Length 10ft 5in (3.16m); width 4ft 7in (1.4m); height 4ft 2in (1.28m).
Weight: Combat 7.571lb (3,435kg).

Engine: SPA CV3 four-cylinder petrol engine developing 43bhp at 2,400rpm.
Performance: Road speed 26mph (42km/h); range 78 miles (125km); vertical obstacle 2ft 2in (0.65m); trench 4ft 9in (1.45m); gradient 100 per cent.

allowed a traverse of only 12 degrees left or right. There were a number of variants of the CV 33. The flamethrower, Carro Lancia Flamme, carried a flamethrower and either towed a two-wheel, 109 gallon (500 liter) trailer or carried a 13 gallon (60 liter) tank on the rear decking. The maximum range of the flamethrower was about 110 yards (100m) and the vehicle was used in North Africa.

There were other usual variants, including a command tank, a bridgelayer, and a tractor towing a supply trailer. Armament varied; some had an additional 8mm anti-aircraft machine-gun, while in others the machine-guns were replaced by a Solothurn 20mm anti-tank gun.

A revised version, CV-35, entered production in 1934-35. This had a redesigned hull of bolted construction, and

was armed with a single Breda 13.2mm machine-gun. The last model to enter service was the L 3/38, which had a new suspension.

About 2,500 CV-33/CV-35s were built both for the Italian Army and for export. The CV-33 was used in the Spanish Civil War, where its shortcomings soon became apparent when it encountered the Russian tanks used by the Spanish Republican

forces. The tankette still formed a major part of the Italian armored forces when World War II started, but the British in North Africa had no trouble dealing with it as its armor was so thin.

Left: Reconnaissance versions of CV-33 on the march. The horses show just how small these two-man vehicles actually were.

Top below: Flamethrower version of the CV-33, with turret-mounted flamegun and fuel trailer; this model was often used in Italy's colonial wars.

Bottom below: CV-33 on a training course, simulating a defensive wall. It has just climbed bridges laid against the wall and is about to fall forward onto the ramparts. Note twin machine-guns and the details of the suspension. Viewed on their own, pictures such as this suggest the CV-33 was large; in fact, it was a very small machine and a tight fit for its two-man crew.

T-37 Light Amphibious Tank

❖❖❖

DURING 1930 SOME EXAMPLES of the British Carden-Loyd Light Amphibious Tank were purchased from the Vickers-Armstrong company, which were used as the basis for a series of experimental vehicles. The first of these, the T-33 (also known as MT-33) was completed in 1932 and subjected to extensive tests. This failed acceptance tests as did the next version, the T-41, but the subsequent T-37 was more successful, passing its tests in August 1933. A few more modifications were implemented and the tank entered production in late 1933.

Some 1,200 T-37s were built, successive production series incorporating improvements such as a cupola for the commander and the use of die-formed armor on the hull. Platoon and company commander's tanks, designated T-37U/TU (TU = Command Tank), were provided with radio equipment and the characteristic, hand-rail aerial running round the hull. All vehicles were armed with one 7.62mm DT machine-gun in a turret.

T-37s were issued to armored reconnaissance formations as well as tank battalions of infantry and cavalry units, where they replaced the obsolescent T-27. During 1935 T-37 tanks were successfully transported by air, carried by TB-1 and TB-3 bombers, and were later deployed in this manner during the Soviet occupation of Bessarabia in 1940. Several trials were also carried out in which these tanks were launched into the water direct from their aircraft.

SPECIFICATIONS

Country of origin: Russia.
Crew: 2.
Armament: One 7.62mm Degtarov machine-gun.
Armor: 9mm (0.35in) maximum; 4mm (0.16in) minimum.
Dimensions: Length 12ft 4in (3.75m); width 6ft 7in (2m); height 5ft 11in (1.82m).

Weight: Combat 7,055lb (3,200kg).
Engine: One GAZ-AA four-cylinder water-cooled petrol engine developing 40hp at 3,000rpm.
Performance: Road speed 21.9mph (35km/h); water speed 2.5mph (4km/h); land range 116 miles (185km); vertical obstacle 1ft 7in (0.5m); trench 5ft 3in (1.6m); gradient 40 degrees.

Left: *T-37 light tanks outside a factory, awaiting fitting of tracks and mounting of the 7.5mm machinegun. Men set the scale.*

Above: *Carrying out the role for which the tank was designed an officer conducts a reconnaissance in his T-37 light tank.*

Type 89B Medium Tank

❖

In the early 1920s the Japanese purchased some European tanks and the first indigenous design was the Experimental Tank Number 1, completed in 1927. This had a five-man crew, was powered by a petrol engine and armed with a turret-mounted 57mm gun and two 7.2mm machine-guns in small, individual turrets. Experimental Tank Number 2 weighed 9.8 tons (10,000kg) and had the same armament as the Type 87, but the forward machine-gun was now within the hull and the rear machine-gun in the after end of the turret. Powered by a petrol engine, this was produced as the Type 89A medium tank.

Production switched in 1934 to the Type 89B, the major change being replacement of the petrol engine by an air-cooled diesel, giving improved safety and easier cold-starts, and a new turret. Armament consisted of a 57mm gun, a 6.5mm machine-gun mounted in the turret rear and a similar weapon in the forward hull. The commander had his own cupola in the turret. Engine and transmission were at

the rear of the hull and the suspension consisted of nine small road wheels with the idler at the front and the drive sprocket at the rear. The Type 89 saw action in China from 1932, and was also employed in the early stages of World War II, some being used in the Philippines campaign.

Left below: *T-89 Medium tanks advancing with infantry. Note how the turret is at the rear of the tank and offset to the right.*

Right below: *At the high tide of Japanese expansion, Type 89s parade through downtown Manilla in May 1942. Note 57mm gun and hull-mounted 6.5mm machine-gun.*

SPECIFICATIONS

Country of origin: Japan.
Armament: One type 90 57mm gun; one 6.5mm machine-gun in turret rear; one 6.5mm machine-gun in hull front.
Armor: 17mm (0.67in) maximum; 10mm (0.39in) minimum.
Dimensions: Length 14ft 1in (4.3m); width 7ft (2.15m); height 7ft 2in (2.2m).
Weight: Combat 25.353lb (11,500kg).

Engine: Mitsubishi six-cylinder inline diesel developing 120hp at 1,800rpm.
Performance: Road speed 17mph (27km/h); range 100 miles (160km); vertical obstacle 3ft (0.914m); trench 6ft 7in (2m); gradient 60 per cent.

Renault AMR 33 VM Light Tank

❖

DURING WORLD WAR I the French cavalry used small numbers of armored cars in the reconnaissance role, but these lacked cross-country mobility and specifications were issued in 1922-23 for a tracked vehicle to be called the Auto-Mitrailleuse de Cavalerie (AMC). Little progress was made until 1931 when requirements for three different types of vehicle for the cavalry were drawn up, including the Auto-Mitrailleuse de Reconnaissance (AMR), a light scouting vehicle with a crew of two, armed with a single 7.5mm machine-gun. Renault built a prototype AMR and after trials an order for 123 production vehicles was placed in 1933. These vehicles entered service with the French Army under the designation AMR 33 VM.

The hull was of riveted construction, with the driver at the front, the commander/gunner in the turret, which was offset to the left of the hull, and the engine on the right side. Further development resulted in the AMR 35 ZT, of which 200 were built. This weighed 6.4

tons (6,500kg) and was powered by a Renault four-cylinder water-cooled petrol engine which developed 85hp and gave the vehicle a top road speed of 34mph (55km/h). Armament consisted of either a 7.5mm machine-gun, or a 13.2mm Hotchkiss machine-gun or a 25mm Hotchkiss anti-tank gun. Quantities of both AMR 33 VM and AMR 35 ZT were captured by the Germans. Some of these were used for reconnaissance, while others had their turrets removed and replaced by a new superstructure mounting an 80mm mortar.

SPECIFICATIONS

Country of origin: France.
Crew: 2.
Armament: One 7.5mm machine-gun.
Armor: 13mm (0.51).
Dimensions: Length 11ft 6in (3.504m); width 5ft 3in (1.6m); height 5ft 8in (1.727m).
Weight: 11.023lb (5000kg).
Engine: Reinastella eight-cylinder liquid-cooled petrol engine developing 84bhp.

Performance: Maximum road speed 37mph (60km/h); vertical obstacle 2ft (0.609m); trench 5ft (1.524m); gradient 60 per cent. (Note: data relate to AMR 33 VM.)

Left: *The Renault 35 ZT was a developed version of the 33 VM, and is seen here armed with a 25mm anti-tank gun, although others had either a 7.5mm or 13.2mm machine-gun. As usual with French tanks at this time, there was only one man in the turret.*

Above: *Another picture of the AMR 35 ZT showing its unusual suspension system. This consisted of four road wheels on each side, with two on a twin bogie in the center, pivoted at the lower end of a vertical coil, and single wheels, front and rear, on bell-cranks.*

Type 92 (Type 94) Tankette

◆

LIKE SEVERAL OTHERS, in the late 1920s the Japanese purchased a number of Carden-Loyd Mark VI machine-gun carriers, followed later by two Mark VIb carriers. Following trials, a Japanese version was developed which was put into production as the Type 92 tankette (referred to by British sources as the Type 94). The riveted hull had the engine and driver at the front and the small turret at the rear of the hull. Armament consisted of a single 6.5mm machine-gun in a manually traversed turret with a suspension consisting of two bogies on each side, each of which had two small rubber-tired road wheels. Once in service, it was found that the Type 92 threw its tracks in a high speed turn. Further redesign work was carried out on the suspension and modifications made, but the problem was never really solved.

This model was powered by an air-cooled petrol engine and armament consisted of a single Type 91 6.5mm machine-gun, although later models mounted a single 7.7mm machine-gun.

The primary role of the Type 92 was reconnaissance, although it was not really suited for this role as its "armor" could be penetrated by ordinary rifle bullets. It was, therefore, increasingly used to carry supplies in the battlefield area, often towing a tracked ammunition trailer, as well. The Type 92 was replaced in service by the Type 97.

SPECIFICATIONS

Country of origin: Japan.
Crew: 2.
Armament: One 6.5mm machine-gun.
Armor: 12mm (0.47in) maximum; 4mm (0.16in) minimum.
Dimensions: Length 10ft 1in (3.08m); width 5ft 4in (1.62m); height 5ft 4in (1.62m).
Weight: Combat 7,496lb (3,400kg).

Engine: Four-cylinder air-cooled petrol engine developing 32hp at 2,500rpm.
Performance: Road speed 25mph (40km/h); range 130 miles (208km); vertical obstacle 1ft 8in (0.508m); trench 4ft 7in (1.4m); gradient 60 per cent.

Below: *Type 92 tankettes in a pre-war parade through Tokyo streets. The men in the turrets show how small these vehicles were.*

PzKpfw 1 Light Tank

❖

GERMANY BEGAN OPENLY to rearm in 1933 and the General Staff realized that development of a full range of modern tanks would take several years, but that meanwhile there was an urgent need for vehicles which could be used by the new panzer troops for training. As a result, designs were sought for a series of armored vehicles with an overall weight of less than 6.9 tons (7,000kg) and Krupp's submission was named the winner.

Designated PzKpfw IA, the new two-man tank was inadequate even by the modest standards of the mid-1930s. The lightly armored hull offered little protection for the crew, while the low powered engine gave poor performance, fittings were minimal, and very little attention was paid to crew comfort. The suspension was suspiciously similar to that of the British Carden-Lloyd light tanks of the 1920s, while the engine was at the rear but the drive-sprocket at the front, with the transmission running along the floor of the hull to a differential beside the driver's feet. Driver and commander

shared the same compartment, and the small turret was traversed by hand. Armament comprised two MG34 machine-guns mounted side-by-side, for which 1,525 rounds were carried.

The original engine, made by Krupp, was woefully inadequate and had to be replaced by a more powerful (100bhp) Maybach diesel, although the hull had to be lengthened by 17in (43cm) to

Below: *PzKpfw Is on a formation exercise in the Baumholder training area in 1941. This was Germany's first post-World War 1 tank and was never intended to be other than an interim design.*

SPECIFICATIONS

Country of origin: Germany.
Crew: 2.
Armament: Two 7.92mm MG 34 machine-guns.
Armor: 0.28in (7mm) minimum; 0.51in (13mm) maximum.
Dimensions: Length 13ft 3in (4.03m); width 6ft 9in (2.05m); height 5ft 8in (1.72m).
Weight: 11,905lb (5,400kg).

Engine: Krupp M305 four-cylinder horizontally-opposed air-cooled petrol engine developing 60hp at 2,500rpm.
Performance: Road speed 23mph (37km/h); range 125 miles (200km); vertical obstacle 1ft 2in (0.355m); trench 4ft 7in (1.4m); gradient 58 per cent.

accommodate it and an additional road-wheel added. This in turn required changes to the suspension, with an extra road wheel and the rear idler raised clear of the ground. Designated PzKpfw IB this was a substantial improvement on the IA, although it shared the same failings of poor armor and weak armament. As with other German tanks, the chassis was used as the basis of numerous other self-propelled weapons systems, such as the

15cm Infantry Gun, although in most cases the vehicle was overloaded and so the idea was quickly dropped.

Over 2,000 PzKpfw IBs were built, and the type saw action in the Spanish Civil War (1936-39), Poland (1939), the Low Countries (1940), and Africa, Greece, the Balkans and even Russia during 1941. In the earlier of these campaigns the PzKpfw Is survived largely because of the lack of any effective anti-tank armament in

service with their enemies, and even this vehicle was virtually immune to most infantry weapons. But, as soon as a light gun, even the much derided British 2-pounder, could be brought to bear the PzKpfw I was doomed. Nevertheless, these tanks played a vital role in training the panzer troops in the late 1930s, which then roared across Europe demonstrating the art of blitzkrieg to a startled and frightened world.

Left: *Panzerjäger (tank hunter) version of PzKpfw IB armed with 4.7cm Pak anti-tank gun advancing through a French village in the summer of 1940.*

Above: *Rare picture of Infanterie-begleitpanzer version in 1939. Note twin 7.65mm machine-guns and the very early version of the "interleaved suspension."*

BT-7 Fast Tank

❖

During the 1930s the rapidly expanding Soviet armored force was based on two types of tank: the T-26 light infantry tank (q.v.), and the BT-series of fast tanks. The official name was Bistrokhodny Tank (= fast tank), but it was commonly known to the tank-crews as either Betka (= beetle) or Tri-Tankista (= three tankers) since it had a three-man crew.

Most Soviet designs of the early 1930s were based on British prototypes, but the BT-series used the suspension system developed by J.W. Christie in America (see T-3 entry), one example of which had been purchased by Soviet officials in 1930. This was given rigorous tests and two prototypes of a developed version, designated BT-1, were delivered in September 1931. These had machine-gun only armament and after further trials a small number were produced as the BT-2. Initially these were still armed with machine-guns, but the armament was then upgraded, first to the BT-3 armed with a 37mm in the original machine-gun turret and then to the BT-4 with a 45mm cannon

in a turret virtually identical to that installed in the T-26 light tank. Commanders' vehicles (BT-5U) were provided with two-way high-frequency radio equipment, mounted in the turret overhang (thereby reducing the number of rounds carried) and were fitted with the characteristic 1930s frame antenna.

Below: *Soviet Army BT-7 tanks drive through Gorkiy Street in Moscow on the way to the front line on 7 November 1941, a parade intended to boost civilian morale. This design was developed from the Christie tank bought from the USA in the early 1930s.*

SPECIFICATIONS

Country of origin: Russia
Crew: 3
Armament: One 45mm M1935 gun; one co-axial 7.62mm DT machine-gun. (Some vehicles had an additional 7.62mm DT machine-gun in turret rear and a P.40 machine-gun.)
Armor: 22mm (0.87in) maximum; 10mm (0.39in) minimum.
Dimensions: Length 18ft 7in (5.66m); width 7ft 6in (2.29m); height 7ft 11in (2.42m).
Weight: 30.644lb (13,900kg).

Engine: One Model M17T 12-cyliner water-cooled petrol engine developing 500hp at 1,650hp/ton.
Performance: Road speed on wheels 46mph (73km/h); road speed on tracks 33mph (53km/h); range on wheels 450 miles (730km/h); range on tracks 270 miles (430km); vertical obstacle 1ft 10 in (0.55m); trench 6ft 7n (2m); gradient 60 per cent.

BT tanks were intended to be used in large, independent, long-range armored units, penetrating deep into the enemy's rear areas, where they would attack vital installations such as headquarters, supply bases and airfields, in a tactic known as desantnya. One of the attractions of the Christie suspension was its ability to run on either tracks or road wheels. Tracks were used when moving across country or along poor roads, whilst wheel drive was used for long strategic road drives, with the tracks stored on the track guards. The Red Army claimed that the time taken to change from one mode to the other was 10-15 minutes, but, as far as is known, this ability to run on wheels, while tested in peacetime exercises, was never actually used in military operations.

As the result of large-scale Red Army exercises during the early 1930s, it was realized that the long-range desantnya groups needed artillery fire-support during their attacks, which led to the development of support tanks using the same chassis. These were given the suffix "A" and the first model, BT-5A, which entered service in 1935, was armed with a short-barreled 76.2mm gun in a fully traversing turret. Following combat experience, the Red Army demanded that the BT be redesigned with welded armor, which also had to be better sloped to increase its immunity. This led to the BT-7, which was a great improvement over the previous models. As in the case of the BT-5, there was a commander's model (BT7U) which initially retained the cylindrical turret of the early T-26 tanks, but in 1938, following experience against the Japanese in Manchuria, a new turret with

sloping sides was designed for the T-26 which was also fitted to the BT-7. There was also an artillery fire-support version (BT-7A), that had the same turret as the BT-5A. Other alterations to the BT-7 were the use of a more powerful engine and an improved transmission system. During 1938 a new diesel engine, developed specifically for tank use, became available and was installed in all subsequent BT-7 tanks, which were then designated BT-7M. This new engine gave the tank much greater range and also reduced the fire risk.

Several experimental vehicles were developed from the basic BT tank. One of these was the BT-IS which had heavily sloped armor that shrouded the tracks and which contributed greatly to the eventual development of the T-34 tank. During 1937 several BT-5s were equipped with snorkels, to develop deep-fording of water obstacles; these were designated BT-5PH. As newer BT models entered service, older models were rebuilt for use as special- purpose vehicles such as the BT bridgelayer, smoke tank and chemical tank.

Below: *Black smoke billows from the exhaust, as the driver of this BT-7 revs up to lift his tank out of the water-logged ditch. Designed in the mid-1930s, the BT-7 has all the characteristics of a late 20th century tank.*

Type 95 HA-GO Light Tank

In 1934-35 Mitsubishi built two prototypes of a new light tank, which was then standardized as the Type 95. The hull was of riveted and welded construction with the driver sitting at the front right and the bow machine-gunner on his left; the commander, who also loaded, aimed and fired the gun, was in the turret, and the engine and transmission at the rear. The inside of the tank was lined with asbestos padding to reduce the heat and give the crew some protection against personal injury when the vehicle was traveling cross country. The suspension was of the well-tried bellcrank type, with the drive sprocket at the front and the idler at the rear and two track-return rollers. Some of the Type 95s used in Manchuria had their suspensions modified as it was found that severe pitching occurred when the tank was crossing the local terrain, and these were redesignated the Type 35 (Special). Armament consisted of a turret-mounted 37mm gun and a hull-mounted 6.5mm machine-gun. Later in the war the 37mm gun was replaced by an improved model with a higher muzzle velocity.

The Type 95 saw action throughout World

War II and production amounted to about 1,250 tanks, most built by Mitsubishi. When it entered service the Type 95 compared well with its contemporaries, but by the early part of World War II it was outdated, and the Japanese used it in small units or wasted them as static defenses in various Pacific islands.

Left below: *This Type 95 has had its 37mm gun removed and the gap blanked over, suggesting that it is being used as a supply vehicle, possibly as an ammunition carrier.*

Right below: *Under new ownership, a US Marine in a fire position in front of an abandoned Type 95 on Iwo Jima.*

SPECIFICATIONS

Country of origin: Japan.
Crew: 3.
Armament: One Type 94 37mm gun; Type 91 6.5mm machine-gun in hull front (see text).
Armor: 12mm (0.47in) maximum; 6mm (0.25in) minimum.
Dimensions: Length 14ft 4in (4.38m); width 6ft 9in (2.057m); height 7ft 2in (2.184m).
Weight: Combat 16,314lb (7,400kg).

Engine: Mitsubishi Model NVD 6120 six-cylinder air-cooled diesel developing 120hp at 1,800rpm.
Performance: Road speed 28mph (45km/h); range 156 miles (250km); vertical obstacle 2ft 8in (0.812m); trench 6ft 7in (2m); gradient 60 per cent.

Hotchkiss H-35 and H-39 Light Tanks

WHEN THE FIRST Division Légère Mecanique was formed in 1934, the French cavalry needed a light tank and selected the Hotchkiss H-35, even though it had been built for and turned down by the infantry. This became the Char Léger Hotchkiss Modèle 35H, and was powered by a six-cylinder Hotchkiss petrol engine. The H-35 was followed by the H-38 and H-39, which had a number of modifications, including thicker armor and a more powerful engine.

The hull consisted of cast sections bolted together, with the driver at the front, and a cast turret identical to that fitted to the Renault R-35 and R-40 tanks, mounting a 37mm gun, either 21 or 33 calibers long, with a coaxial 7.5mm machine-gun. The engine and fuel tank were at the rear of the hull, separated from the fighting compartment by a fireproof bulkhead. Like most French tanks of this period, the Hotchkiss had a major drawback - one man had to command, as well as to load and aim the gun.

Production was about 1,000 tanks, of

which 821 were in front-line service when World War II broke out. Many were taken over by the Germans and some were used on the Russian Front. When Israel was formed in 1947 some H-39 tanks were taken into service and rearmed with British 6-pounder anti-tank guns.

Below: *French-built Hotchkiss H-39 in service with the German Wehrmacht as the PzKpfw 39H (f). Many of these French tanks were pressed into service with little or no modifications, while others were fitted with 7.5cm anti-tank guns in open-topped turrets for service as mobile tank destroyers.*

SPECIFICATIONS

Country of origin: France.
Crew: 2.
Armament: One 37mm SA 38 gun; one 7.5mm Model 1931 machine-gun co-axial with main armament.
Armor: 40mm (1.57in) maximum; 12mm (0.47in) minimum.
Dimensions: Length 13ft 10in (4.22m); width 6ft 1in (1.85m) height 6ft 7in (2.14m).
Weight: Combat 26,456lb (12,000kg).

Engine: Hotchkiss six-cylinder water-cooled petrol engine developing 120bhp at 2,800rpm.
Performance: Road speed 22.5mph (36km/h); range 93 miles (150km); vertical obstacle 1ft 8in (0.5m); trench 5ft 11in (1.8m); gradient 60 per cent.

Below: *PzKpfw 39H (f) fitted with the optional skid tail, which was installed in a number of French light tanks as an aid to crossing trenches. The rear turret hatch which doubles as a seat for the commander was another typically French feature, but the vertical antenna mounted on the track guard is a German addition.*

Char B1 Heavy Tank

◆◆

DEVELOPMENT OF THE French Army's four-man Char B1 started in the 1920s. It was large by the standards of the time, weighing 24.6 tons (25,000kg) and armed with a hull-mounted 75mm gun, two fixed machine-guns in the front of the hull, and two turret-mounted machine-guns. Some 35 of the first model, Char B1, were built, but production then switched to an improved version with heavier armor and a more powerful engine. This was designated Char Bl-bis and 365 had been built by the fall of France in 1940.

The hull of the Char Bl-bis was made of cast sections bolted together and could withstand attack from any German anti-tank gun except the infamous 88mm. The driver was seated at the front of the hull on the left and steered the tank with a conventional automobile steering wheel connected to a hydrostatic system. Mounted to the driver's right was the short barreled (17.1 calibers) 75mm gun, which could be elevated between +25° and -15°, but could not be traversed; it was aimed by the driver, who swung the tank until the

gun was lined up with the target. A 7.5mm Chatellerault machine-gun, which could be fired by either the driver or the commander, was fixed in the front of the hull on the right, below the 75mm gun. The turret mounted a 37mm gun and a 7.5mm machine-gun, which was not coaxial but trained independently. The tank carried 74 rounds of 75mm (HE), 50

Below: *Photographed from a passing Wehrmacht staff car, a Char B1 lies abandoned in a street which is little damaged apart from a broken window (in shop front to the left of the tank). This was presumably the work of looters rather than of military action.*

SPECIFICATIONS

Country of origin: France.
Crew: 4.
Armament: One 75mm gun in hull; one 7.5mm machine-gun in hull; one 47mm turret-mounted gun; one 7.5mm machine-gun co-axial with 47mm gun (see text).
Armor: 60mm (2.36in) maximum.
Dimensions: Length 21ft 5in (6.52m); width 8ft 2in (2.5m); height 9ft 2in (2.79m).

Weight: Combat 70,548lb (32,000kg).
Engine: Six-cylinder inline water-cooled petrol engine developing 307bhp at 1,900rpm.
Performance: Road speed 17mph (28km/h); range 93 miles (150km); vertical obstacle 3ft 1in (0.93m); trench 9ft (2.75m); gradient 50 per cent.

rounds of 37mm (AP and HE) and 5,100 rounds of machine-gun ammunition

The commander had to aim, load and fire the turret guns as well as command the tank, while the loader was equally busy, since he had to pass ammunition to the commander as well as load the hull-mounted 75mm gun. The engine, transmission and fuel tanks were at the rear of the hull, and the suspension on

each side consisted of 16 double steel bogie wheels with vertically-mounted coil springs and semi-elliptical leaf springs. There were also three independent bogie wheels forward and one to the rear, with quarter-elliptical leaf springs.

Further development of the Char Bl-bis resulted in the Char Bl-ter. This had additional armor, a fifth crew member (a mechanic) and the 75mm hull gun had a

traverse of 5° left and 5° right. Only five were built and none was used in action. Captured tanks were also used by the German Army for a variety of roles. The driver training model had the turret and hull-mounted gun removed, the latter being replaced by a machine-gun. The type was then known as the PzKpfw B1 (f) Fahrschulewagen. The Germans also modified 24 tanks in 1942-43 for use in

the flamethrower role. These had flame-guns fitted in place of the hull guns and the type was known as the PzKpfwB1-bis (Flamm). The gun turret was retained to give the vehicle some anti-tank capability. Finally there was a self-propelled gun model. This had the hull gun and turret removed, and on top of the tank was mounted a standard German 105mm howitzer. The conversion work was carried out by Rheinmetall Borsig. Very few such conversions were effected and most of those served in France.

The Char B1-bis was one of the best French tank of its time and properly handled by a determined crew it could more than hold its own against the onslaught of the German panzers.

PzKpfw V Experimental Medium Tank

◆❖◆

AFTER WORLD WAR I Germany was banned from possessing tanks, but various stratagems were used to overcome such restrictions, one being to use innocuous names - so heavy tanks became "heavy tractors." In 1934 the army ordered a new medium tank armed with a 75mm gun and several machine-guns. Rheinmetall's winning design used the suspension from their genuine commercial tractor, coupled with an amalgam of contemporary British, French and Soviet ideas, although it included some original German concepts, as well.

The PzKpfw V was multi-turreted, as in other 1930 tanks (see, for example, T-35 entry), with a main turret mounting the 75mm gun and two small turrets mounting 7.92mm machine-guns. The hull design was derived from the Grosstraktor (ie, heavy tank) of 1929, but with a much better suspension, while the turret was well designed with a commander's cupola.

In the event the PzKpfw V only served as a test-bed for the gun and mounting, and never went into full-scale production, six

prototypes being built, five of mild steel and one of armored plate. When they invaded Norway in 1940, however, the Germans shipped at least four of the existing PzKpfw Vs to Oslo, where they were photographed on a jetty, thus misleading Allied intelligence into believing that the type was in full service.

Left below: *Supposed production line of PzKpfw V (Exp), pictured in 1935.*

Right below: *Famous propaganda picture of PzKpfw V (Exp) taken in Oslo in 1940 in order to mislead Allied intelligence.*

SPECIFICATIONS

Country of origin: Germany.
Crew: 7.
Armament: One 7.5cm *KwK* L/24 gun; 3.7cm gun co-axial with main armament; four 7.92mm MG 13 machine-guns in pairs in two sub-turrets.
Armor: 0.57in (14.5mm).
Dimensions: Length about 21ft 4in (6m); width 9ft 6in (2.9m); height 8ft 6in (2.65m).
Weight: 47,950lb (21,750kg).

Engine: Maybach V-12 water-cooled inline petrol engine developing 360bhp.
Performance: Road speed 19mph (30km/h); trench 7ft 2in (2.2m); gradient 30 degrees.

Renault R-35 Light Tank

IN 1934 THE FRENCH INFANTRY issued a requirement for a new light tank to replace the Renault FT-17. This new tank was to weigh 7.9 tons (8,000kg), have a crew of two, a maximum road speed of 12mph (20km/h), to be armed with a single 37mm gun or twin 7.5mm machine-guns, and to have a maximum armor thickness of 1.6in (40mm). The winning design was the Renault R-35; production started in May 1935 and some 945 were in front-line service when the Germans invaded in May 1940. Their role was infantry support, but their slow road speed gave them little strategic mobility.

The hull was of cast sections bolted together, like most French armored vehicles at the time. The driver was seated at the front, slightly offset to the left and the centrally-mounted one-man turret was identical to that of the Hotchkiss H-35 and H-39 tanks. Like many contemporary French tanks, the commander entered through a horizontally-hinged door in the rear of the turret, which could be left open to serve as a seat when not in action. Main

armament was a short-barreled 37mm gun, but later tanks switched to a longer-barreled version. There was a co-axial 7.5mm machine-gun, but no other MGs. The tank carried 100 rounds of 37mm and 2,400 rounds of 7.5mm ammunition.

The engine and self-sealing fuel tank were at the rear, separated from the fighting compartment by a fireproof bulkhead. The suspension consisted of five rubber-lined wheels on each side, the first mounted independently and the others on two bogies, all being mounted on bellcranks with springs. Most tanks had a tail fitted to increase their trench-crossing capabilities. Later production versions were fitted with a radio, which gave even more work for the commander, who already had to command the tank as well as aim, load and fire the armament. Some R-35s were fitted with a frame which ran over the top of the hull and turret, to enable them to be used as fascine carriers. The Germans employed captured R-35s in various roles. The basic tank was used as a

reconnaissance vehicle (PzKpfw R-35 (4.7cm)(f)); some had the turret removed and were used as artillery tractors or for carrying ammunition (Munitionpanzer 35R(f)). An anti-tank variant (4.7cm Pak(t) auf GWR35(f)) carried a Czech 4.7cm anti-tank gun and artillery versions carried either a 10.5cm howitzer (10.5cm leFH 18 auf GW35R(f)) or 80mm mortar (Munitionpanzer 35R(f)).

SPECIFICATIONS

Country of origin: France.
Crew: 2.
Armament: One 37mm gun; one 7.5mm machine-gun co-axial with main armament.
Armor: 1.77in (45mm) maximum.
Dimensions: Length 13ft 10in (4.2m); width 6ft 1in (1.85m); height 7ft 9in (2.37m).
Weight: 22,046lb (10,000kg).
Engine: Renault four-cylinder petrol engine developing 82bhp at 2,200rpm.

Performance: Road speed 12.42mph (20km/h); range 87 miles (140km); vertical obstacle 1ft 10in (0.5m); trench 5ft 3in (1.6m) or 6ft 7in (2m) with tail; gradient 60 per cent.

Opposite: The German Army adapted many captured tanks. This is a French Renault R-35, which has been rebuilt and armed with a Czech 47mm anti-tank gun in a fixed mounting.

Below: French R-35, armed with a 37mm gun and a coaxial 7.5mm machine-gun. This tank's main role was to support the infantry and some 950 were in front-line service at the time of the German invasion in 1940.

Char SOMUA S-35 Medium Tank

IN THE EARLY 1930s the French cavalry issued a requirement for the Automitrailleuse de Combat (AMC) and the winning design came from the SociÈtÈ d'Outillage MÈcanique et d'Usinage d'Artillerie (SOMUA). This was placed in production as the AS-3, but it was then decided to adopt it as the standard medium tank of the French Army, under the designation Char S-35 (S = SOMUA; 35 = 1935). The S-35 had good armor, mobility and firepower. The hull was made of three cast sections - hull floor, front superstructure and rear superstructure - with a maximum thickness of 1.6in (4lmm). These were joined by bolts just above the tops of the tracks, with the vertical join between the front and rear parts near the rear of the turret.

The driver was seated at the front of the hull on the left, with the radio operator to his right. The electric-powered turret, which was identical to that of the Char B1-bis, was also of cast construction and had a maximum thickness of 2.2in

(56mm). Main armament was a 47mm SA 35 gun with a coaxial 7.5mm Model 31 machine-gun, and unusually among French tanks of this era, there was no hull-mounted machine-gun. Ammunition carried comprised 118 rounds of 47mm and 1,250 rounds for the machine-gun. Provision was also made for mounting another 7.5mm machine-gun on the

Below: *Brand-new Char SOMUA at the factory. This was a well-designed tank, which if used with more determination and imagination could have had a much greater effect against the invading Germans in 1940.*

SPECIFICATIONS

Country of origin: France.
Crew: 3.
Armament: One 47mm gun; one 7.5mm Model 31 machine-gun co-axial with main armament.
Armor: 56mm (2.2in) maximum.
Dimensions: Length 17ft 11in (5.46m); width 6ft 11in (2.108m); height 8ft 10in (2.692m).
Weight: Combat 44,2000lb (20,048kg).

Engine: *SOMUA* eight-cylinder water-cooled petrol engine developing 190hp at 2,000rpm.
Performance: Maximum road speed 23mph (37km/h); road range 160 miles (257km); vertical obstacle 1ft 8in (0.508m); trench 7ft 8in (2.336m); gradient 65 per cent.

commander's cupola for use in the anti-aircraft role, although this was seldom mounted, as the commander/gunner already quite enough to do.

The engine, transmission and fuel tanks were at the rear, separated from the fighting compartment by a fireproof bulkhead. The suspension on each side consisted of two assemblies, each of which had four bogie wheels mounted in pairs on

articulated arms, these being controlled by semi-elliptic springs. The ninth bogie wheel at the rear had its own spring. The lower part of the suspension was provided with an armored cover which could be hinged up to allow access to the bogie assemblies.

In 1940 production switched to an improved model, the S-40, which had a more powerful 220hp engine, modified

suspension and various other modifications. However, few of these had been completed by the fall of France. The S-35 was a better tank than history gives it credit for. About 500 had been completed by the fall of France and during the fighting the S-35 proved that, tank-for-tank, it was superior to the PzKpfw IIIs and IVs of the German army, but bad tactics gave them little chance to prove

their worth except in a few isolated actions. It had two major weakness, the first being that, like all French tanks of the period, it had a one-man turret, which placed an impossible load on the commander/gunner in battle. The other was the method of construction using three castings joined by bolts, since an unlucky hit precisely on one of the joint lines tended to split the tank open like a banana.

The S-35 was also used by the Germans for a variety of roles including crew training and internal security; some were even used on the Russian front. The Germans called the type the PzKpfw35C 739 (f). Some were also fitted as command vehicles, and a few were handed over to the Italians.

Inset: *Factory picture of a pristine S-35. The hull was produced in two castings and the join is clear in this picture, with seven recesses for bolts along the top of the track-guard and four across the front. An incoming anti-tank round hitting this join was almost invariably catastrophic.*

Below: *PzKpfw 35C 739(f), a requisitioned SOMUA S-35, leads a patrol on airfield protection duties. Many captured French tanks were used in this way, suggesting that the Germans thought fairly well of them.*

Below: *A humiliating scene for the French as a German tank squadron parades through the streets of Paris, all mounted in captured French tanks. In the lead is a radio-equipped PzKpfw 35C 739(f) (captured S-35 SOMUA) followed by a squadron of PzKpfw 39H (f) (captured Hotchkiss H-39).*

PzKpfw II Light Tank

❖

ONCE GERMANY HAD decided to re-arm, the PzKpfw I was rushed into service and development work on what would become PzKpfw III and IV started. It was soon realized, however, that these last two would take much longer to get into service than had been hoped. It was therefore decided to rush through the development of a 10-ton successor to PzKpfw I which would give the troops something better to train with until the definitive battle tanks were ready. As usual, however, the "interim" vehicle served for much longer than had been expected and played a key role in all military operations until 1942.

The operational requirement was issued in July 1934 and Henschel, Krupp and MAN. submitted designs, which were generally similar except for major differences in the suspension. The design by MAN. was selected and a number of prototypes were built, some of which were sent to Spain for full-scale trials in the Civil War, where they did well, except that vulnerability to anti-tank weapons was

made clear, while the lack of an HE round was a serious tactical limitation. The first production models appeared in 1935, but deliveries were slow as changes were made in the design, including increasing the armor thickness, particularly in the front. Some changes were also made to the suspension and the weight increased by nearly 1.95 tons (2,000kg), so that experiments had to be made to improve

Below: The PzKpfw II was armed with a 20mm cannon and a coaxial 7.92mm machine-gun, which only offered a relatively small improvement over that carried by the PzKpfw I.

SPECIFICATIONS

Country of origin: Germany.
Crew: 3.
Armament: One 2cm *KwK* 30 or 38 gun; one 7.92mm MG 34 machine-gun co-axial with main armament.
Armor: 0.39in (10mm) minimum; 1.18in (30mm) maximum in the *Ausf* A, B and C; 0.57in (14.5mm) minimum; 1.38in (35mm) maximum in the *Ausf* F.
Dimensions: Length: 15ft 9in (4.8m); Width: 7ft 3in (2.2m); Height: 6ft 6in (1.98m).

Weight: 29,944lb (9,500kg).
Engine: Maybach HL 62 TR six-cylinder water-cooled inline petrol engine developing 130hp at 2,600rpm.
Performance: Road speed 25mph (40km/h); range 120 miles (192km); vertical obstacle 1ft 5in (0.43m); trench 5ft 8in (1.72m); fording depth 3ft (0.91m); gradient 50 per cent.

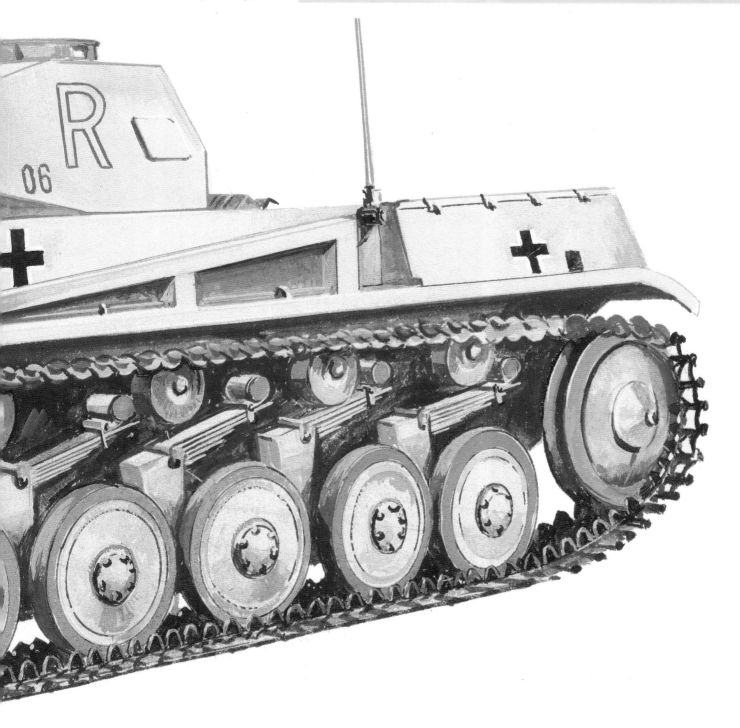

the engine horsepower, and an extra 10hp was squeezed out of the Maybach engine by boring out the cylinders, though the lower power motor appears to have continued to be fitted to some versions.

The hull was built up from welded heat-treated steel, 1.2in (30mm) thick on the front and 0.4in (10mm) on the sides and rear. The turret was made in a similar way, again 1.2in (30mm) thick on the front and 0.6in (16mm) around the sides and back. The engine was in the rear compartment, driving forward through the fighting compartment to a gearbox and final drive in front. The gearbox was a Zahnradfabrik (ZF) crash-type with six forward speeds and one reverse, the steering being by clutches and brakes. The driver sat off-center to the left side. The fighting compartment had the turret above it, again offset slightly to the left.

The armament was an improvement on that of the PzKpfw I, but still not very effective: the 20mm gun had a maximum range of 656 yards (600m), and only fired armor-piercing ammunition. Armor penetration of these 20mm rounds was not impressive, but the gun had a reasonably rapid rate of fire. Secondary armament was a single 7.92mm machine-

gun, coaxial with the main gun. Some 180 20mm and 1,425 7.92mm rounds were carried. As in PzKpfw I, vision from the turret was poor, and fire control when fully closed-down was difficult. Most vehicles were fitted with a high-frequency radio, but used a vertical rod antenna rather than the frame type so popular in the mid-1930s.

The suspension was unusual, with five road wheels hung on quarter-elliptic leaf springs, with the rear idler and front drive sprocket both clear of the ground. This suspension was quite effective, and within the limits of its engine power the PzKpfw II was quite maneuverable and agile. The tracks were narrow, but quite strong.

One unusual variant was the amphibious version, Schwimmpanzer II, which was developed for use in

Below: *PzKpfw II demonstrates its agility on a German training ground. The suspension consisted of five road wheels on quarter elliptic leaf springs, which was simple and gave a relatively smooth ride.*

Inset: *PzKpfw II at war, with soldiers' figures indicating how small this tank was, with an overall height of only 6ft 6in (1.98m). There were constant efforts to improve the design, but it was basically too small, too lightly armed and too inflexible for World War II conditions.*

Unternehmung Seelöwe (= operation sea-lion) the invasion of Britain. For this, the tank was waterproofed and had flotation bags attached to the return rollers; propulsion was provided by a propeller turned by an extension shaft from the engine. One regiment was equipped with these tanks, but they were never to be used.

The three initial variants of the PzKpfw II - Ausf A, B and C - were generally very similar. The Ausf A had the original low power engine and weighed 16,105lb (7,305kg); about 100 were built in 1935 and 1936. The Ausf B featured the higher power engine, new reduction gears and tracks, a commander's cupola, and, as usual, the weight increased. The Ausf C appeared in 1937 and carried thicker front armor, bringing the weight up yet again,

this time to the final figure of 20,944lb (9,500kg). Issues to units began in earnest in 1937 and the type's participation in major campaigns was: Poland (1939) - approximately 1,000; France (1940) - 955; Russia (1941) - 1,067. Manufacture of the general type continued up to late 1942 or early 1943, by which time the basic tank was well outdated.

The Ausf D and E versions, also known

as Luchs (= lynx) were intended to be faster reconnaissance vehicles and were given a new suspension by the makers, Daimler-Benz. This involved five large overlapping road wheels mounted on torsion bars running under the floor, a system that was perfected in the Panther and Tiger tanks. These tanks did not perform satisfactorily and were not in service for very long.

Yet another attempt to improve the performance was made in late 1940 with the F variant. Thicker armor was fitted to the front and sides and a higher velocity gun installed, though its caliber was still only 20mm. However these changes did little to increase the battlefield value of the tank, and the extra 2,204lb (1,000kg) of weight that they entailed put an extra strain on the engine.

Below: A mixed group of tracked and wheeled vehicles are brought to a halt by a river during the invasion of France in 1940. German engineers in inflatable boats are already at work on the far bank and it is clear from the concentration of vehicles on the near bank and the relaxed attitude of the troops that there is no enemy threat. Tanks in view include two PzKpfw 35(t), German commandeered Czech LT-35s in the left foreground, and a single PzKpfw II on the right. There are also several of the ubiquitous motor-cycle combinations.

Ninety-five were converted into flamethrower vehicles. Fitted with two gun-type projectors and designated Flammpanzer II, they were capable of some 80 shots, each of 2 to 3 seconds duration, and remained in service until the end of the war. Despite the many and obvious limitations of the design, the PzKpfw II formed the backbone of the armored divisions of the German Army from 1938 until late 1941, and as late as April 1942 some 860 were still on strength.

Opposite: *A combination which proved highly dangerous for the Commonwealth forces in the Western desert campaign - a tank and an infantry soldier of the panzer grenadiers, both belonging to Rommel's famous Afrika Korps. The occasion was Operation Crusader and smoke from destroyed British tanks billows across the battlefield. The tank is a PzKpfw II, which type enjoyed its greatest successes in the desert, although still under-gunned.*

Below: *An Afrika Korps PzKpfw II. The track sections on the nose were carried as spares, but also provided added protection; the road wheel on the glacis plate is also a spare. Note the wide separation between the 37mm main gun and the coaxial 7.92mm machine-gun, an unusual feature which appeared on a number of German tank designs in the 1930s. The large bin on the track guards was used for spare parts, tools, the crew's personal equipment and rations.*

PzKpfw IV Medium Tank

❖❖

THE PZKPFW IV was a workmanlike but not outstanding design, its main distinction being that it was the only German tank to remain in continuous production throughout World War II. In 1935 the General Staff issued a requirement for two types of battle tank: one mounting a high velocity gun, which led to the PzKpfw III, the other for a support tank mounting a large-caliber gun firing an HE shell. The latter requirement led to the PzKpfw IV armed with the short-barreled (24 caliber) 7.5cm gun, the Ausfall A appearing in 1936. Only 35 were built before the -B model entered production, but the first important model was Ausfall D, which entered service in 1939.

PzKpfw IV had three compartments. The driver and radio operator/ machine-gunner shared the front, with the hull machine-gun on the right; the latter was slightly set back from the driver in early models, but later they were abreast. In the center was the fighting compartment and turret, accommodating the gunner, loader

and the commander, who sat in a prominent cupola at the rear of the turret, where he had excellent all-round vision. The turret was slab sided with a complex shape, with escape hatches in the sides; it was trained under electrical control, an innovation in German tanks. The Maybach V-12 diesel engine was in the

Below: *An early model PzKpfw IV with the original short-barrel 7.5cm gun, traveling at speed along a North African road. There was a five-man crew, and in this picture those taking advantage of the open air are the hull machine gunner (behind the barrel), loader (above "8") and the commander (in cupola).*

SPECIFICATIONS

Country of origin: Germany.
Crew: 5.
Armament: One 7.5cm *KwK* L/24 gun; one 7.92mm MG 34 machine-gun co-axial with main armament; one 7.92mm MG 34 machine-gun in hull.
Armor: 0.79in (20mm) minimum; 3.54in (90mm) maximum.
Dimensions: Length 19ft 5in (5.91m); width 9ft 7in (2.92m); height 8ft 6in (2.59m).
Weight: 43,431lb (19,700kg).

Engine: Maybach HL 120 TRM V-12 inline diesel developing 300hp at 3,000rpm.
Performance: Road speed 25mph (40km/h); cross-country speed 12.5mph (20km/h); range 125 miles (200km); vertical obstacle 2ft (0.6m); trench 7ft 6in (2.3m); fording depth 2ft 7in (0.8m); gradient 30 degrees.
(*Note: Date relate to the PzKpfw IV Ausf D.*)

rear compartment, connected by the driveshaft to a front gearbox and forward-mounted driving sprockets. Suspension was by four coupled bogies on each side, sprung by leaf springs. There was a large idler wheel at the back and four small return rollers. There was room in the hull for 80 rounds of 7.5cm ammunition for the main gun, and 2,800 rounds in belts for the machine-guns.

The Ausfall D was the model which took part in the Polish and French campaigns, as well as the advance into Russia in 1941, but by the latter stage its deficiencies had become too apparent to be ignored further. Battle experience had showed that the tank was basically a sound design and well laid out, but that the armor was much too thin to enable it to perform its designated task of

supporting the PzKpfw IIIs and there followed a steady program of improvement which was to continue until the end of the war.

The next model, Ausfall E, had thicker armor on the nose and turret, and a new cupola, and older models were retrofitted to this new standard. The Ausfall F became the main production version, having been given a new lease of life when

the short-barreled main gun was replaced by the much longer (48 caliber) and more powerful 7.5cm KwK40 L/48, which enabled the PzKpfw IV to take on almost any contemporary tank, and even to give a good account of itself against the T-34. This effectively changed the PzKpfw IV's role from support into a battle tank in its own right. The Ausfall F was built in large numbers and fought on all fronts, as did

the -G which followed it, differing outwardly only in respect of its thicker armor, additional protective plates on the turret, and skirting plates. The latter, intended to protect the tracks and sides of the tank, were 0.2in (5mm) thick and radically altered the look of the tank, making it appear deep and rather clumsy.

The last production model, Ausfall J, appeared in 1944. The design was greatly

simplified to the overcome shortage of many raw materials, although it was still basically the same tank which had started

Below: *An elderly Russian couple, returning home in 1944, pass a destroyed PzKpfw IV Ausf H. Note the tank's long-barrelled 7.5cm gun, armored skirts to protect the running gear, additional armor on turret and the hull machine-gun. With no apparent damage, it is probable that the tank simply ran out of fuel.*

the war five years before. By 1945 over 8,000 had been delivered and many more were built for specialist purposes. A number soldiered on after the war and the last known service versions were with the Syrian Army, who employed them as anti-tank weapons during the Arab-Israeli War of 1967.

Right: *US infantry patrol in the French town of Pontfaroy in August 1944 passes a battle-damaged late model PzKpfw IV. Note that the vertical face of the driving compartment is coated with an anti-magnetic substance called "Zimmerit" which was intended to prevent magnetic mines placed by Soviet infantry (a common tactic on the Eastern Front) from sticking to the surface of the tank.*

Below: *One of the final versions of the PzKpfw IV, the Panzerbefehlswagen mit 7.5 cm KwK L/48 (armored command vehicle with 7.5cm gun, 48 calibers) belonging to SS Panzer Regiment 12 of the Hitlerjugend (Hitler Youth) Division. Note the side skirts, extra armor around the turret, long-barrelled 7.5cm gun with double-baffle muzzle brake, and additional track links on the glacis plate to add to protection against anti-tank rounds.*

Right: *Units of the German 25th Panzer Division take a break during their advance towards the Somme, early during the Battle of France in 1940. The tank on the right is a PzKpfw IV; all the others are PzKpfw 35(t) (requisitioned Czech L-35s).*

Below: *PzKpfw IV with the long-barrelled (48-caliber) gun, which was fitted in all versions from the Ausf F2 on. This resulted in a weapon with much greater muzzle velocity and thus much increased range and hitting power. Note the unusual side door in the turret and the cutaway under the front corner of the turret. The hemispherical dome to the right of the figure "8" houses one end of the cross-turret, stereoscopic rangefinder.*

Right: *This is an early model PzKpfw IV with the short (24-caliber) 75mm gun with which the tank was capable of a support role. It was only with the arrival of the 48-caliber gun (see opposite page) that the PzKpfw IV became capable of taking on Allied tanks. Note also the commander's uniform, with the black coverall and floppy black beret of the pre-war Panzertruppen.*

LT-38

THE LT-38 ENTERED service with the Czech Army in 1938 just before the German occupation, and the German Army not only took over the tanks but also continued production for themselves under the designation PzKpfw 38(t). The tank was used in action by the 7th and 8th Panzer Divisions during the invasion of France in 1940 and continued in production in Czechoslovakia until 1942. The main armament was a Skoda 37.2mm gun, with one 7.92mm co-axial machine-gun and a similar weapon in front of the hull.

The hull was mainly of riveted construction, but with the top of the superstructure bolted in place. The suspension was of the semi-elliptic leaf-spring type, with one spring controlling a pair of road wheels. There were four road wheels, with the idler at the rear and the drive sprocket at the front.

The hull was adapted for a wide range of other roles, including a smokelayer, reconnaissance vehicle, ammunition carrier and artillery prime mover. Its chassis was most widely used to mount

artillery, anti-tank and anti-aircraft weapons, one of the latter being the 2cm Flak 30 or Flak 38, which was armed with a 20mm gun with an elevation of 90° and full traverse through 360°, with 1,040 rounds of 20mm ammunition being carried.

Left below: *The German Army used many LT-38s under the designation PzKpfw-38 (t). It was a very reliable tank and was used in the invasion of Poland in 1939, the invasion of France in 1940 and Operation Barbarossa in 1941. Its 37mm gun was not very powerful and by 1942 the tank was obsolete.*

SPECIFICATIONS

Country of origin: Czechoslovakia.
Crew: 4.
Armament: One 37.2mm gun; one 7.92mm Type 37 machine-gun co-axial with main armament; one 7.92mm Type 32 machine-gun in hull.
Armor: 30mm (1.18in) maximum; 8mm (0.3in) minimum.
Dimensions: Length 14ft 11in (4.546m); width 7ft (2.133m); height 7ft 7in (2.311m).

Weight: Combat 21,385lb (9,700kg).
Engine: Six-cylinder water-cooled inline petrol engine developing 150hp at 2,600rpm.
Performance: Road speed 26mph (42km/h); road range 125 miles (201km); vertical obstacle 2ft 7in (0.787m); trench 6ft 2in (1.879m); gradient 60 per cent

(Data for late production LT-38.)

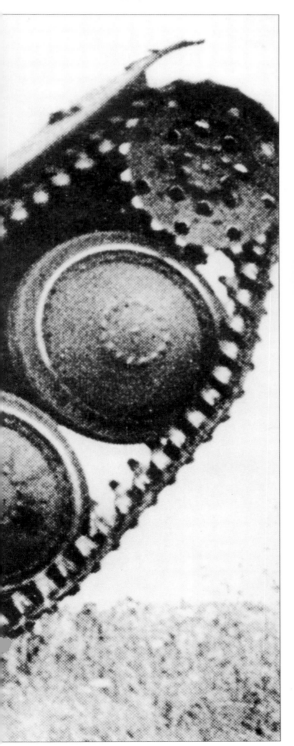

Above: *PzKpfw-38 (t) and motor-cycle combination in November 1940. The tanks agility, speed and reliability made it ideal for the German Army's blitzkrieg tactics.*

Below: *A Fieseler Storch army cooperation aircraft overflies a German unit equipped with PzKpfw-38 (t), which is pausing during its advance into France in 1940.*

A11 Matilda I Infantry Tank

THE ORIGIN OF THE MATILDA I lay in a War Office request for a tank built down to a price; not surprisingly, the result was dismal and one of the most basic armored vehicles ever to enter service. The tactical concept of the "infantry tank" called for good protection, low speed to keep pace with infantry, and limited firepower - machine-guns were considered to be sufficient armament. These limits were bad enough, but the designer was required to make maximum use of existing components, employ a two-man crew, and to adhere to a fixed price - £6,000 for the complete vehicle.

Numerous two-man tanks had appeared in the 1920s and 1930s. It had been shown repeatedly that the one-man turret imposed too great a workload, but the designer was forced to repeat this error. One machine-gun made a mockery of the whole concept of "firepower," and for a tank to carry just one such weapon was a waste of manufacturing resources. The top speed of 8mph (13km/h) was equally derisory. Nevertheless, the design was

accepted and the first vehicles were delivered in 1938 and were operational in France in 1940, where their limitations showed up for all to see. Their crews fought valiantly, and they had one small success, but all were finally lost on the way to, or at, Dunkirk; the end of an unhappy chapter.

Below: *The British Matilda I was built down to a fixed cost, just £6,000 at 1936 prices, and showed it - not even track guards were fitted. Note the suspension and the small turret which accommodated one man, who combined the roles of commander, gunner and loader.*

SPECIFICATIONS

Country of origin: United Kingdom.
Crew: 2.
Armament: One .3in or .5in Vickers machine-gun.
Armor: 60mm (2.36in) maximum, 10mm (0.39in) minimum.
Dimensions: Length 15ft 11in (4.85m); width 7ft 6in (2.28m); height 6ft 1½in (1.86m).
Weight: Combat 24,640lb (11,161kg).

Engine: Ford eight-cylinder petrol engine developing 70bhp at 3,500rpm.
Performance: Road speed 8mph (12.8km/h), range 80 miles (128km); vertical obstacle 2ft 1in (0.63m); trench 7ft (2.133m).

Type 97 CHI-HA Medium Tank

◆◆◆

TWO DESIGNS WERE prepared to replace the Type 89, the Mitsubishi version being declared the winner and put into production as the Type 97 (CHI-HA). This was armed with a short-barreled 57mm cannon and two 7.7mm machine-guns: one in the turret rear, the other in the bow, to the driver's left. There was a four-man crew, which considerably eased the load on the commander. The hull was of riveted and welded construction and the two-man turret was in the center of the hull, but offset to the right and sat on a large diameter ring, which enabled heavier guns to be fitted later. The engine was at the rear of the hull, and power was transmitted to the gearbox in the front of the hull by a propshaft which ran down the centerline of the hull.

There were many variants of the Type 97 medium tank, including one with a 47mm gun, a flail-type mine-clearing tank, bulldozer, various self-propelled guns, a bridge-layer and a number of different engineer and recovery models, to name a few. One of the most unusual was a "ram"

tank which had a steel prow mounted at the front of the hull to clear a path through forests in Manchuria. The Type 97 played a prominent role in 1941-42 and is often seen in newsreel shots of the Japanese entering Singapore.

Left below: *A Japanese Army crew drive their Type 97 down the Bukit Timah Road on Singapore island, having reached the destination known to them as Shon~n.*

Right below: *Type 97 tank on the Bataan Peninsula during the invasion of the Philippines. The rail around the turret is a high frequency radio antenna.*

SPECIFICATIONS

Country of origin: Japan.
Crew: 4.
Armament: One type 90 57mm gun; one 7.7mm Type 97 machine-gun in turret rear; one 7.7mm Type 97 machine-gun in bow.
Armor: 25mm (0.98in) maximum; 8mm (0.3in) minimum.
Dimensions: Length 18ft 1 in (5.516m); width 7ft 8in (2.33m); height 7ft 4in (2.23m).
Weight: Combat 33,069lb (15,000kg).

Engine: Mitsubishi 12-cylinder air-cooled diesel developing 170hp at 2,000rpm.
Performance: Road speed 24mph (38km/h); range 130 miles (210km); vertical obstacle 2ft 6in (0.812m); trench 8ft 3in (2.514m); gradient 57 per cent.

Type 97 TE-KE/KE-KE Tankette

❖

THE TYPE 97 TANKETTE (or TE-KE/KE-KE) was a replacement for the earlier Type 94 tankette which had proved very unreliable. Two different prototypes were completed in 1937 and after trials one was standardized as the Type 97 tankette, entering service with the Japanese Army in 1938. Conceptually, the tankette was already obsolete, but despite this the Type 97 was built in large numbers. The vehicle was one of the neatest designs of any tankette, and had a riveted hull and one-man turret, with the driver at the front left and the commander (who also had to load, aim and fire the gun) in the turret. The diesel engine and transmission were at the rear, and the suspension consisted of two two-wheeled bogies, with the drive sprocket at the front. Armament consisted of a 37mm gun, although some examples were armed with a single 7.7mm machine-gun instead.

There were several variants of the Type 97 tankette, including one with the turret removed, engine moved forward and a fully enclosed cargo area at the rear. This

model was used for a wide variety of roles including those of ammunition carrier, artillery observation post vehicle, barrage balloon mooring vehicle and self-propelled gun, with either a 37mm or a 47mm anti-tank gun mounted at the rear of the hull.

Left below: The Type 97 was a very neat design, perhaps the best of the two-man tankettes made by a number of armies in the 1920s and '30s.

Right below: An abandoned Type 97 on a Pacific island. The picture shows good detail of the suspension system and of the well-sloped armor, which was something of an innovation in the 1930s.

SPECIFICATIONS

Country of origin: Japan.
Crew: 2.
Armament: One 37mm type 94 gun (see text).
Armor: 12mm (0.47in) maximum.
Dimensions: Length 12ft 1in (3.682m); width 5ft 11in (1.803m); height 5ft 10in (1.773m).
Weight: Combat 10,469lb (4,748kg).

Engine: Ikega four-cylinder inline air-cooled diesel developing 65hp at 2,300rpm.
Performance: Maximum road speed 26mph (42km/h); range 155 miles (250km); trench 5ft 7in (1.701m); gradient 60 per cent.

A9 Cruiser Tank Mark I

❖❖

WHEN WORK STARTED on a replacement for the Vickers Medium Mark II there were several difficulties. The first was that, despite the trials with experimental tank units, nobody really knew what they wanted a future tank to do, the second that this was the time of the "Great Depression" and any new equipment project had to designed to a very tight budget. The General Staff Requirement for the new tank was issued in 1934 and the designer tried to combine the best features of the Medium Mark II with as many innovations as possible, but all at the lowest possible price.

Just as the prototype A9 started trials in 1936, the War Office changed its policy on tanks, now requiring three types. "Cruisers" would fulfil the traditional cavalry role, whilst also being capable of fighting it out with other tanks. "Infantry" tanks would move at slow speeds alongside the assaulting infantry, their main task being to destroy enemy infantry and machine-gun nests. Finally, "light"

tanks would perform the reconnaissance role. So, the A9 now became the Cruiser Tank Mark I. The main gun was the 2-pounder, with a secondary armament of three 0.303in machine-guns, one coaxial and two in small, cramped "sub-turrets" on either side of the driver, but their arcs of fire were limited and their tactical value doubtful. The six-man crew, surprisingly

Below: The A9, showing the main turret mounting a 2-pounder gun and one of the two sub-turrets with its 0.303in Vickers machine-gun. The successful suspension design was used again in the Valentine infantry tank.

SPECIFICATIONS

Country of origin: United Kingdom.
Crew: 6.
Armament: One 2pounder gun; three .303in Vickers machine-guns. (CS version had one 3.7in howitzer in place of the 2pounder.)
Armor: 14mm (0.55in) maximum, 6mm (0.25in) minimum.
Dimensions: Length 19ft (5.79m); width 8ft 2in (2.49m); height 8ft 8in (2.64).
Weight: Combat 28,728lb (13,013kg).

Engine: AEC Type 179 six-cylinder water-cooled inline petrol engine developing 150bhp.
Performance: Road speed 25mph (40km/h), cross-country speed 15mph (24km/h); range 150 miles (240km); vertical obstacle 3ft (0.92m); trench 8ft (2.43m).

large for the size of the tank, comprised commander, gunner, loader, driver and two hull machine-gunners. Power was provided by an AEC petrol engine (as used in London buses), giving the tank a road speed of 25mph (40km/h). The suspension was a Vickers multi-bogie design and although the prototype had problems with shedding its track these were soon solved and the system was successful enough to

be incorporated, virtually unaltered, into the later Valentine. Two definite advances were the introduction of hydraulic traverse for the turret and the addition of an auxiliary engine. Once in service, it was realized that the lack of an HE round for the 2-pounder meant that the tank could not deal with strongpoints or pillboxes, so a few were converted to take a short-barreled 3.7in howitzer, in which form they were

known as the A9 (CS) (= close support).

A total of 125 were built, which were issued to three divisions. Some went to 1st Armored Division, which took them to France in 1939 and 1940, and left practically all of them at Dunkirk. The remainder went to 2nd and 7th (Desert Rats) Armored Divisions, which took them to Egypt, where they were used until 1941.

Below left: *An A9 Cruiser of A Squadron, 1st Royal Tank Regiment in the Egyptian desert, 30 May 1940. Note the flat, almost vertical armor plating on the main turret, sub-turret forward, and the sand guards fitted over the rear part of the suspension. These guards were made of light metal and were intended to cut down on the huge dust cloud raised in the desert; they were not protection for the tracks against anti-tank rounds.*

Below right: *The A10 Heavy Cruiser Mark 2, fielded in 1940, was a direct development of the A9, with additional armor plating on the turret and glacis, and with the two sub-turrets removed. It was, in effect, an "infantry" conversion of the cruiser tank.*

Below bottom: *A column of "closed-down" A10, with the lead tank showing additional armor bolted on to the vertical plate, and the absence of machine-gun turrets. The large turret makes the 2-pounder gun appear puny.*

PzKpfw III Battle Tank

❖

IN 1935, THE Germans planned to build two basic types of tank, the first of which would carry a high velocity gun to defeat enemy tanks. The second would provide support for the first, carrying a large-caliber gun capable of firing a destructive HE shell to destroy enemy infantry and artillery. The intention was that tank battalions would consist of three companies of the first type to one company of the support vehicles.

The first of those two vehicles, PzKpfw III, was developed under the cover-name Zugführerwagen (ZW = platoon commander's vehicle), and the original plan was to arm it with a high-velocity 50mm gun. However, the infantry was re-equipping with the 37mm anti-tank gun, and it was decided to standardize in order to ease ammunition supply problems, although the large turret ring for the 50mm weapon was retained. Early versions had relatively minor differences and were built in small numbers as development continued as the designers tested different aspects of the design: Ausf

A - 15; B - 15; C - 15 and D - 30. The first major production version was the Ausf E (and the very similar Ausf F) which was accepted in September 1939 and was planned as the basis of the armored divisions of the Wehrmacht; 98 took part in the invasion of Poland, and 350 in the Battle of France in May 1940.

The PzKpfw III was laid out well, with

Below: British scout car parked beside an abandoned German PzKpfw III in the North African desert, 15 December 1941. The PzKpfw III was used in large numbers by Rommel's famous Afrika Korps.

SPECIFICATIONS

Country of origin: Germany.
Crew: 5.
Armament: *One 5cm KwK 39 L/42 fun; one 7.92mm MG 34 machine-gun co-axial with main armament; one 7.92mm MG 34 machine-gun in hull.*
Armor: 1.18 (30mm) minimum; 3.54in (90mm) maximum.
Dimensions: Length 17ft 8in (5.4m); width 9ft 6in (2.9m); height 8ft (2.4m).
Weight: 42,769lb (19,400kg.

Engine: Maybach HL 120 TRM developing 300hp at 3,000rpm.
Performance: Road speed 25mph (40km/h); cross-country speed all models 11mph (18km/h); range 109 miles (175km); vertical obstacles all models 2ft (0.6m); trench 7ft 6in (2.3m); fording depth 2ft 7in (0.8m); gradient 30 degrees.

(Data for Ausf E)

each of the five man crew having adequate space to do his job, while the prominent "dustbin" cupola at the rear of the turret gave the commander an excellent view. In early versions the driver had a pre-selector gearbox, making driving far less tiring than in many contemporary tanks, but, as always, there was a price and the gearbox was mechanically complicated and maintenance difficult. The 320hp Maybach engine was adequate and cross-country performance reasonably good.

The tank proved not to be entirely successful in action; the 37mm gun could not penetrate the armor of the British infantry tanks encountered in the Battle of France, while the German tank's 1.2in (30mm) of frontal armor could not defeat the British 2-pounder shot, an experience that was repeated in the early days of the Western Desert campaign. The firepower problem was already being addressed and a new 50mm gun was rushed into production and mounted in Ausf E to H. Unfortunately for the tank's crews, even this gun was not entirely satisfactory as it was a low-velocity weapon, although it outranged the British 2-pounder and also fired a useful HE shell. Ausf H introduced extra armor bolted on to the hull and

turret, and wider tracks to carry the extra weight. Also, the easy-to-use but complicated ten-speed gearbox was replaced by a simpler six-speed manual change. Most of these features were subsequently retrofitted to earlier marks.

By 1941 there were nearly 1,500 PzKpfw IIIs in service, and the type was very successful in the first stages of the invasion of Russia, although it then became clear that both the Soviet T-34 and KV-series tanks were impervious to the 50mm low-velocity gun, and in a further crash program a high-velocity version was introduced. Even this failed to penetrate Soviet armor, although it did well in the desert against the British.

The Ausf. J was longer, had better protection and was designed to be easier to produce; some 2,700 were built. The Ausf M went further and deleted many minor items such as hatches and vision ports; some 2,600 were built. Ausf N mounted a low-velocity 7.5cm gun to provide HE support to the heavy tank battalions.

Below: *PzKpfw Ausf C, armed with 3.7cm L/45 main gun, with a coaxial 7.92mm MG34 machine-gun, and a second MG34 in a flexible mount to the right of the driver. Note crew escape hatch above road wheels #2 and #3.*

The most unusual version was Tauchpanzer III (= diving tank), with all 168 PzKpfw IIIs of 18th Panzer Regiment being converted to this standard in mid-1940 for the planned invasion of England. These tanks were intended to travel along the sea-bed, for which the air intakes, turret ring and other apertures were sealed, and non-return valves installed on the exhausts. An air hose, 59ft (18m) long and 8in (20cm) diameter, was attached to a float, enabling the tank to operate to a depth of 50ft (15m) for around 20 minutes, with a command vessel guiding the submerged tanks via radio. It was particularly fortunate for these crews that the operation was cancelled!

Right: *PzKpfw III lies on the burning Russian steppes during Operation Barbarossa, the German invasion of the Soviet Union.*

Below: *Crewman of a PzKpfw III surrenders to two British infantrymen. Note the bracket welded to the rear of the tank which carries numerous extra gasoline cans to extend the tank's range; probably a local modification.*

Far right: *Italian officials and apprehensive-looking local inhabitants watch PzKpfw IIIs of the newly-arrived Afrika Korps parade through their home town in 1941.*

Left: *German infantry climb aboard a PzKpfw III during the advance to Tobruk. The soldier to the left of the tank commander is carrying a flame-thrower, with the fuel cans strapped to his back.*

Below: *A PzKpfw III in the North African desert. As with the example on page 177, it has a large bracket on the rear to carry extra fuel. Note the cloud of sand left behind by even a single tank, a sure give-away to enemy observers that a vehicle was on the move.*

A13 Cruiser Tank Mark IV

◆❖

THE BRITISH ARMY conducted a long period of trials in the inter-war years, trying out various tactics and organizations for the best use of tanks. As a result, by the mid-1930s it had settled on two types of tank: a slow-moving, heavily armored "infantry tank" designed to give integral support to the infantry, and the fast, lightly armored "cruiser tank" which would conduct highly mobile, striking operations. The first of the latter types was the Cruiser Mark I, which entered service in 1938, but was quickly followed by the Cruiser Mark IV, neither of which was ever given a name. The Cruiser Mark IV was derived directly from the designs of the US inventor, J. Walter Christie (see T3 entry) one of whose tanks was purchased by the War Office in 1936. This tank had an excellent suspension system, but was considered lacking in many other respects and Morris Motors were given the task of completely reworking the design to make it battleworthy, to achieve which they had to design a new hull and a much improved turret.

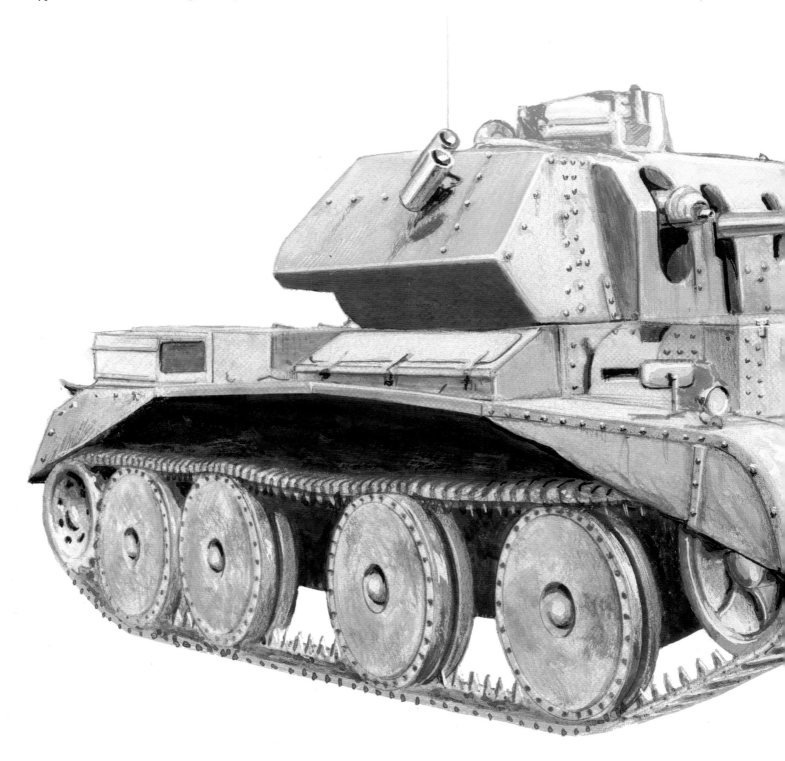

The Christie suspension was excellent and gave an astonishing speed. In the US version the tracks could be removed, enabling it to run along highways on its rubber-rimmed roadwheels at a speed of some 46mph (74km/h), but even with the tracks fitted it was still capable of 27mph (43km/h). The British never anticipated running the tanks without their tracks but

Below: *Cruiser Mark IV of 1st Armoured Division (note rhinoceros badge), 1940.*

Inset: *A13 suspension was derived from the Christie system.*

SPECIFICATIONS

Country of origin: United Kingdom.
Crew: 4.
Armament: One 2pounder gun and one Vickers machine-gun (Mk IVA mounted a 7.92mm BESA).
Armor: 6mm (0.24in) minimum, 38mm (1.5in) maximum.
Dimensions: Length 19ft 9in (6.02m); width 8ft 4in (2.54m); height 8ft 6in (2.59).
Weight: 33,040lb (14,987kg).

Engine: Nuffield Liberty V-12 water-cooled petrol engine developing 340bhp.
Performance: Speed 30mph (48km/h), range 90 miles (144km); vertical obstacle 2ft (0.61m); trench 7ft 6in (2.29m); gradient, 60 per cent.

they found its cross-country performance so good that crew discomfort became a serious problem, because when traveling fast across west European terrain they could be thrown about and injured. The only engine available which could give the necessary power was the American Liberty V-12 aero-engine of World War I, and this was derated to 340hp to improve torque and enhance reliability, and put into production by Nuffield in the UK.

The turret had sloped upper plates, but the undercut sides proved to be shot-traps, and the hull was very box-like. Some extra armored plates were added to the Cruisers employed in the campaign in North Africa, but the design was always under-armored, especially when facing German tanks and anti-tank guns. Also, once it was in service various mechanical weaknesses became apparent and, despite the efforts put into the design, reliability was poor. Despite all these shortcomings, however, the Cruiser Mark IV was a step forward in British tank design and it set the pattern for the later wartime cruisers.

Left: *The obvious debris of defeat as a battle damaged A12 lies in the streets of Tobruk, 4 May 1941. Even though it had only been in service since 1939, the A13 was not up to the standard of modern warfare, especially that practised by its most effective exponents - Rommel's Afrika Korp.*

Left: *In September 1940 a troop of A13s of 3rd Battalion, Royal Tank Regiment patrol a road in East Anglia. This was a time when the threat of invasion was very real and had it taken place, tanks such as these, inadequately armed as they were, would have been thrown into front-line action to repel the invaders.*

A12 Matilda II Infantry Tank

◈

EVEN WHILE THE first infantry tank, Matilda I, was in the prototype stage, a new General Staff requirement was issued stating that such tanks must carry a main gun capable of defeating enemy tanks. This was a fundamental change and meant that an armament solely of machine-guns, as in Matilda I, was inadequate and as that tank could not be modified to take a heavier gun a new design was called for.

That new design was prepared at Woolwich Arsenal, with the wooden mock-up being completed in April 1937. The first mild steel prototype was built by the Vulcan Foundry at Warrington, but war seemed so imminent that an initial order for 65 was placed even before it had been completed. Fortunately, the trials went well and further large orders were placed with various firms.

A brief explanation of the names is necessary. Although both were infantry tanks, there was no relationship between the designs of Matilda I and Matilda II. For a few months in 1939-40 both were in

service at the same time, but after the debacle at Dunkirk no further Matilda Is remained in service, following which the Matilda II simply became the "Matilda," by which name it was known for the rest of the war. To avoid confusion here, however, the suffixes I and II will be retained.

The Matilda II had a conventional

Below: *Matildas of the Royal Tank Regiment in the Western desert. Although it appears impressive, a close-knit advance such as this would have been a tactical disaster, not least because the tanks' top speed was 15mph!*

SPECIFICATIONS

Country of origin: United Kingdom.
Crew: 4.
Armament: One 2pounder gun; one .303in Vickers machine-gun (Mk I); one 2pounder gun; one 7.92mm BESA machine-gun (Mk II); one 3in howitzer; one 7.92mm BESA machine-gun (Mk II CS).
Armor: 0.55in (14mm) minimum; 3in (78mm) maximum,
Dimensions: Length 18ft 5in (5.61m); width 8ft 6in (2.59m); height 8ft 3in (2.51m).

Weight: 59,360lb (26,926kg).
Engine: Two AEC six-cylinder inline diesels developing a total of 174bhp (Mks I and II); two Leyland six-cylinder inline diesels developing a total of 190bhp (Mk III).
Performance: Road speed 15mph (24km/h), cross-country speed 8mph (12.8km/h); range 160 miles (256km); vertical obstacle 2ft (0.61m); trench 7ft (2.13m); fording depth 3ft (0.91m).

British layout with a four-man crew, the driver sitting centrally behind the well-sloped glacis plate, while the remaining three were in a somewhat crowded turret. The commander had his own circular cupola, although it gave him only limited vision; the other two were the gunner and the loader. The turret rotated using hydraulic power, one of the first to use this system which had been developed by the Frazer Nash Company, who also produced turret controls for aircraft.

The main weapon was the standard British 2-pounder, with a coaxial 0.303in Vickers machine-gun in the Mark I and a 7.92mm BESA in the Mark II and successive types. Matilda II was, however, one of the first British tanks not to have a hull machine-gun. The ammunition carried comprised 67 rounds of 2-pounder and 4,000 of machine-gun.

Matilda II was unusual in being powered by two engines, originally made by AEC, but later by Leyland, which were coupled together to drive a Wilson epicyclic gearbox and a rear sprocket. The suspension was somewhat complicated, but worked well, and was covered by side skirts with mud chutes. Various versions were produced, including a close support

(CS) tank in which the 2-pounder was replaced by a 3in howitzer.

Matilda II acquitted itself well in the Dunkirk campaign and was also used in the Western Desert, where it proved to be virtually immune to any anti-tank gun or tank that the Italians could deploy, a happy state of affairs which only ended in mid-1941 with the arrival of the German 88mm, which could knock out the

Matilda II at ranges well outside that of the 2-pounder. Unfortunately, the turret ring was too small to accept the more powerful and longer ranged 6-pounder, so the Matilda II was gradually withdrawn from service, its last major action as a gun tank being the first battle of El Alamein in July 1942. However, most of the surviving Matilda IIs were still in good running order and their thick armor made them

Below: Royal Tank Regiment drivers maneuver their Matilda tanks into a close laager on rocky ground. The cast hull and turret were thickly armored and well shaped for their period, and resisted both Italian and most German anti-tank guns - until the appearance of the dreaded "88."

very useful for a host of special applications, such as flail mine-clearer, bridge-layers, dozers, and flamethrowers. Matilda IIs were supplied to Australian and the Soviet Union, and a few of various types were still in service in 1945, the only British tank to serve right through World War II.

Below: *Western desert 1941, with a squadron of Matilda IIs advancing across open terrain.*

Right: *Ritterkreuzträger (Knight's Cross holder) Schwabach, an Oberleutnant der Flak-Artillerie (senior lieutenant of anti-aircraft artillery) (pointing, left) shows how his 88mm gun knocked-out this battered Matilda II. Note, in particular, the large gouge on the mantlet. At his feet is a pile of stones, an extemporary crucifix and a steel helmet, which mark the grave of one of the soldiers who died in the tank.*

Below: *Matilda IIs in the desert outside Tobruk. Note the chutes in the skirts, which allowed sand which had caked in the upper track to fall away, clear of the lower track. The well-sloped turret is also apparent, as are the twin smoke-grenade dischargers.*

Right: *Smart, cheerful and confident; officers and men of 7th Royal Tank Regiment, with their Matilda IIs after leading all the main attacks during Operation Compass. All their attacks against the Italian fortified positions were a complete success.*

Below left: *A brief respite in the Desert Campaign with a Matilda II forming the backdrop for a hasty conference at El Duda, the temporary regimental headquarters of 1st Royal Tank Regiment. Behind the Matilda is a Mark VI Light Tank.*

Below right: *Efficient and regular maintenance was essential in the desert and this Matilda II crew are taking great care that their tank is in tip-top mechanical condition. The gasoline can (bottom left) is the very bad, thin-skinned and easily damaged British design, which was replaced, to the great relief of crews such as this, by the much stronger and better designed German "jerrican."*

Crusader Cruiser Tank

◆◆

THE CRUSADER WAS designed to meet a General Staff requirement for a "heavy cruiser," which proved to be difficult to meet within the stipulated weight and size limitations. The requirement did, however, amount to a tacit admission that earlier requirements for "cruiser" tanks had been mistaken and had resulted in tanks that were both too lightly armored and inadequately armed.

The design of the Crusader was a development of the Covenanter, which had, in its turn, been based on the A13 Cruiser Mark IV. The hull was similar to that of the Covenanter, with a well-raked glacis plate and long flat upper surface, and a four-man crew. The driver sat at the front right and in the Marks I and II there was a hull machine-gunner to his left. The fighting compartment and turret were none too large, even for their two-man crew of gunner and commander, with the latter also acting as loader and radio operator (although his position was not as bad as that of his opposite number in a two-man tank of the French Army).

Main armament of Crusader I and II was the 2-pounder, with a coaxial 7.92mm BESA machine-gun. There was also a second machine-gun in a small turret alongside the driver, which proved to be of very limited tactical value and many were removed in local workshops. In the Mark III the 2-pounder main gun was replaced by a 6-pounder, and the hull machine-gun

Below: *A famous picture and enduring image of the Desert Campaign, as British Crusader III cruiser tanks advance. Note petrol cans and ammunition boxes on front tanks, suggesting that the enemy is not too close.*

SPECIFICATIONS

Country of origin: United Kingdom.
Crew: 5 in the Mark I; 4 or 5 in the Mark II; 3 in the Mark III.
Armament: Crusader I one 2pounder gun and two 7.92mm BESA machine-guns; Crusader II one 2pounder gun and one or two 7.92mm BESA machine-guns; Crusader III one 6pounder and one 7.92mm BESA machine-gun.
Armor: Crusader II 40mm (1.57in) maximum and 7mm (0.28in) minimum; Crusader II 49mm (1.93in) maximum and 7mm (0.28in) minimum; Crusader III 51mm (2in) maximum and 7mm

(0.28in) minimum.
Dimensions: Length 19ft 8in (5.99m); width 8ft 8in (2.64m); height 7ft 4in (2.23m).
Weight: Combat Crusader I and II 42,560lb (19,279kg); Crusader III 44,240lb (20,040kg).
Engine: Nuffield Liberty 12-cylinder water-cooled inline petrol engine developing 340bhp.
Performance: Road speed 27mph (43.2km/h), range 100 miles (160km); vertical obstacle 2ft 3in (0.685m); trench 8ft 2in (2.59m); gradient 60 per cent.

was deleted, giving extra space for ammunition stowage.

The engine was the elderly but well tried Nuffield-Liberty, basically a World War I aero-engine de-rated from 400 to 240hp. Early Crusaders had considerable trouble with their engines, mainly from the cooling arrangements, as the large cooling fan often broke its drive shafts, while the aircleaners were difficult to keep clean, but after some experience and modification the engine went very well.

The Crusader used the Christie suspension with five roadwheels, and, unlike the Covenanter, the spring units were contained inside the hull for extra protection. This suspension was, in fact, the strongest point of the Crusader, which had an official top speed of 27mph (43.2km/h), although in the Western

Below top: *A Crusader II leads two of the later M4 Shermans. Note the machine-gun turret on the right side of the glacis plate of the Crusader.*

Below bottom: *Following the great victory at El Alamein, a Crusader leads M4 Shermans through the ruined town of Mersa Matruh; note the German helmet below the turret.*

Right: *An official cameraman films Crusader I. Note the Bren light machine-gun on the turret anti-aircraft mounting of the further Crusader.*

Desert drivers and fitters opened up the engine governors to let the Nuffield-Liberty engine operate at maximum revolutions; the result was a speed of some 40mph (64km/h), which both the suspension and the crew could handle well, although it somewhat shortened the life of the engine.

The Crusader was unquestionably rushed into service before all its development troubles had been ironed out, and in its first engagement, Operation Battleaxe (June 1941), more Crusaders fell into enemy hands through mechanical failure than through battle damage. Nevertheless, the tank went on to fight in all the major actions throughout the Desert Campaign, and by the time of the Battle of Alamein the Crusader III with the 6-pounder gun had arrived. The Crusader was outdated by the end of the North African campaign, although a few went on to fight in Italy. In the desert the Crusader became popular, and its speed was liked, but the armor was too thin, and the armament always too weak.

A number of variants were produced, including a close-support (CS) tank with a 3in howitzer, an AA version, and a gun tractor. The Crusader was built by a

consortium of firms under the leadership of Nuffield Mechanisations Ltd, and a grand total of 5,300 was built before production ceased.

Below: *The crews of two Crusader Is hold a conference, 26 November 1941. The flat surface makes excellent "going" and is ideal for tank warfare. On the right-hand tank note the driver's position on the left and the machine-gun on the right.*

Below top: *Late on the first day of the Battle of Alamein a group of Crusaders and M4 Shermans advance against the Afrika Korps. The nearest Crusader has a jettisonable auxiliary fuel tank.*

Below bottom: *It was vital to recover repairable tanks and here a team from the Royal Electrical and Mechanical Engineers (REME) works hard under enemy artillery fire to load a Crusader III on to a tank transporter.*

M2 Medium Tank

THE M2 MEDIUM TANK was never used in action, its main significance being that it was widely used in training and was the first US tank to be designed specifically for mass production. The M2 was of straightforward design and in most respects was simply a slightly enlarged version of the M2 light tank, with which it shared many components. The turret and parts of the hull were welded face-hardened armor, while the remainder was riveted, but all surfaces were flat.

The main weapon was a 37mm gun in a small turret with sloping sides, but the secondary armament was most unusual. This consisted of no less than six 0.3in machine-guns, two of which were in fixed mounts in the glacis plate, two (for anti-aircraft use) on pintles attached to the sides of the turret and the remaining four in barbettes in vertical walls of the octagonal fighting compartment.

Power came from a Wright nine-cylinder radial aero engine. The suspension was derived from the earlier M2 light tank with vertical volute springing and six rubber-tired bogie wheels on each side; officially known as the Vertical Volute Suspension System (VVSS), this was soon to become very familiar on the M3 Grant/Lee tank. The tracks had rubber pads for quietness and smooth running, as well as to reduce wear on both the tracks and the roads they were running on. An unexpected and unwanted side effect was that these pads, combined with the rubber bushes of the track pins, caused a build-up of static electricity, which not only made using the radio difficult when the tank was on the move but also gave anyone standing on the ground who touched the tank a distinct shock.

Complaints that the tank was underpowered led to the M2A1, in which the Wright engine was supercharged to deliver another 50hp. Among the other measures were that the tracks were widened, the armored protection was increased and the turret was given vertical walls, considerably increasing the internal

volume. The Rock Island Arsenal produced some 94 M2A1 tanks, most of which were used for training until sufficient numbers of the M3 became available.

Even as the first production M2s became available, it was clear that they would not stand a chance against the latest German tanks; as a result, the type was quickly relegated to the training role and none ever saw active combat. As well as being the forerunner of the M3, the M2 formed the basis of several experimental vehicles.

The M2 also formed the basis of the experimental T9 medium tractor, which was later standardized as the M4 and then served as a very effective prime mover throughout World War II. In one remarkable instance the M4 remained in service with the Spanish Army well into the 1980s.

SPECIFICATIONS

Country of origin: USA.
Crew: 6.
Armament: One 37mm M6 gun with a co-axial .3in M1919A4 machine-gun in turret; four .3in machine-guns, one at each corner of barbette superstructure; two .3in machine-guns in hull, firing forward in fixed mount.
Armor: 9.5mm to 32mm (0.37–1.26in).
Dimensions: Length 17ft 8in (5.38m); width 8ft 7in (2.62m); height 9ft 4½in (2.86m).
Weight: Combat 47,040lb (21,337kg).

Engine: Wright nine-cylinder air-cooled radial petrol engine, supercharged, developing 400hp at 2,400rpm.
Performance: Road speed 26mph (43km/h), cross country speed 17mph (27km/h); road range 130 miles (209km); vertical obstacle 2ft (0.6m); trench 7ft 6in (3.54m); gradient 25 per cent.

Opposite: *The M2 had an extraordinary array of machine-guns: two in the front hull, one coaxial, two in each sponson, and two on flexible mounts each side of the turret. This total of nine is almost certainly a record.*

Below: *A preserved M2. By the time it appeared, its concept was archaic and it was as well no US soldiers were obliged to use it in combat. The only good feature was the excellent vertical volute suspension system.*

KV-1 Heavy Tank

◆◆

AT THE OUTBREAK OF WORLD WAR II, the Soviet Army was the only one in the world equipped with heavy tanks, the first of which, the KV-1 (Klim Voroshilov) had been designed at the Kirov Factory in Leningrad. Progress was very rapid: design work began in February 1939, the mock-up was inspected and approved in April, the first prototype ran in September, acceptance was issued on 19 December 1939 and production started in February 1940. A platoon of KV-1s was sent to Finland, where they took part in the breakthrough of the Finnish main position, not one being destroyed.

The KV-1 hull was constructed of well-sloped armor, varying in thickness from 4in (100mm) to 3in (75mm). The turret mounted a 76.2mm main gun (the same as the T-34), with a varying number of 7.62mm machine-guns. All had a machine-gun in the left front of the hull, beside the driver, and some had a machine-gun in the turret overhand, facing the rear. Power was provided by a Model V-2-K 12-cylinder water-cooled diesel.

The German advance forced the transfer of production to a new factory further east at Chelyabinsk, later named "Tankograd," which became the sole Soviet industrial establishment producing heavy tanks and heavy self-propelled guns for the remainder of the war, by the end of which some 13,500 heavy tanks and self-propelled guns on this chassis had been built.

Below left: *Proud Moscow farmers present KV-1 tanks they have paid for to their crews.*

Below: *KV-1s operating outside Stalingrad during the epic siege of that city.*

SPECIFICATIONS

Country of origin: Russia.
Crew: 5.
Armament: One 76.2mm gun (various types); three 7.62mm DT machine-guns. (Some vehicles had an additional machine-gun in the turret rear and a P-40 AA machine-gun.)
Armor: 100mm (3.94in) to 75mm (2.95in), varying with model.
Dimensions: Length 20ft 7in (6.273m); width 10ft 2in (3.098m); height 7ft 11in (2.413m). (Dimensions varied slightly according to models.)
Weight: 104,719lb (47,500kg), varying slightly with model.
Engine: One Model V-2-K 12-cylinder water-cooled diesel developing 600hp at 2,000rpm.
Performance: Road speed 22mph (35km/h); range 156 miles (250km); vertical obstacle 3ft 8in (1.2m); trench 8ft 6in (2.8m); gradient 70 per cent.

T-34 Medium Tank

THE SOVIET ARMY'S T-34 would feature near the very top of any list of the greatest tanks, being a truly masterly design. It had its origins in the mid-1930s when work was being done on a successor to the BT-series (q.v); there were two versions, the A-20 with a 45mm gun and the A-30 with a 76.2mm gun, but both used the Christie wheeled/track arrangement. The chief designer of the Kharkov factory pointed out that the Red Army seldom, if ever, used the BT tank in the wheeled mode, while incorporating this facility complicated the design and incurred severe weight penalties. So, he proposed a purely tracked vehicle and this was agreed by the Main Military Council, which authorized construction of a prototype under the designation A-32 (later T-32). This conducted and won trials against the A-20, but the Armor Directorate requested an increase in armament and armor on the T-32, which the designers achieved, and the new tank then went into production as the T-34.

The international situation was so

serious that the design was accepted "off the drawing-board" in December 1939, and the prototype T-34s left the factory in late January 1940, with full production starting in June 1940. The T-34, which was known as "Prinadiezhit-Chetverkior" (= thirty-four) to its crews, had excellently shaped armor, which considerably increased its resistance to shell

Below: The T-34 revolutionized tank design and the 76mm gun mounted in early models defeated all except the German Panther and Tiger tanks. Note the sloping armor, low silhouette and Christie-type suspension.

SPECIFICATIONS

Country of origin: Russia.
Crew: 5.
Armament: One 85mm M1944 Z1S S53 L/51 gun; two 7.62mm DT machine-guns.
Armor: 18mm to 60mm (0.71in to 2.36in).
Dimensions: Length (including gun) 24ft 7in (7.5m); width 9ft 7in (2.92m,); height 7ft 10in (2.39m).
Weight: 70,547lb (32,000kg).

Engine: One V-2-34 12-cylinder water-cooled diesel developing 500hp at 1,800rpm.
Performance: Road speed 31mph (50km/h); range 186 miles (300km); vertical obstacle 2ft 7in (0.79m); trench 8ft 2in (2.49m); gradient 60 per cent.

penetration. The armament, a 76.2mm long-barreled high-velocity gun, was also an innovation for tanks of this class, while the use of the new 500hp diesel engine (already in service on the BT-7M tank) reduced the fire risk and greatly increased the tank's operational range. The modified Christie suspension permitted high speeds, even on rough terrain, and the wide tracks reduced the ground pressure to a minimum. On top of all this, the overall design facilitated rapid mass production, and lent itself to simple maintenance and repair in the field.

By the end of 1940 115 T-34s had been produced, some of which were sent to Finland for combat tests but arrived too late to participate in operations. By June 1941, when the Germans attacked, a total of 1,225 had been produced and by the time of the Battle of Moscow, 1,853 had been delivered to units. The T-34 made its combat debut on 22 June 1941, in thevicinity of Grondno in Belorussia, and it came as a total surprise to the German Army, which quickly learned to treat this tank with the greatest respect. It was seriously proposed that it should be "reverse-engineered" and placed in production in Germany but this was

turned down and the Panther produced instead, although the latter's design owed a great deal to that of the T-34.

When the Soviet tank industry was evacuated to the east, production of the T-34 was moved to the Uralmashzavod (Ural Machine-Building Plant) in the Urals, as well as a number of subsidiary plants, generally safe from German bombing. The T-34 tank was originally armed with the 76.2mm Model 1939 gun mounted in a welded turret of rolled plate, but in order to accelerate production a new cast turret was soon introduced. During mid-1941 a new Model 40 F-34 gun was adopted, which had a longer barrel and higher muzzle velocity. A multiplicity of minor and major changes were made to the T-34 during production, but the most significant took place in autumn 1943,

Below top: *The Soviet Army trained special infantry "tank rider" units which went into battle on the backs of tanks such as these T-34s in the Battle of the Kursk Bulge. Losses were very high but so was the success rate.*

Below bottom: *T-34/76s engage targets in the Kursk battles. The T-34 came as a terrible shock to the Germans who had assumed that their tank designs were superior to anything the Soviet could produce; they were wrong.*

when the 85mm 215 S-53 or D-5T gun, with 55 rounds, was adopted. This new tank was designated T-34/85 and was approved for mass production on 15 December 1943. By the end of the year 283 had been built, and in the following year a further 11,000 were produced.

The T-34/85 remained in production until the mid-1950s, when the Soviet Army adopted the T-54, but the T-34 remained in service throughout the second half of the 20th century and in 2002 a few still remained in smaller African and Asian armies.

Below top: *Fresh from the factory at Tankograd, T-34/76s are loaded for a railroad journey to the front line far to the west. The crews had helped on the production line and were fully trained prior to departure; it was a very efficient system.*

Below bottom: *The goal is reached and a Soviet T-34/85 crew is greeted by British allies in Germany. Note the finish in the turret; somewhat rough by Western standards but the armor was sufficiently thick to defeat German anti-tank rounds except at very close range.*

Below top: *A tank workshops in besieged Leningrad, with workers preparing T-34/76s for return to the front-line. Among the many advantages of the T-34 were its excellent reliability and simple maintenance, which minimized time out of action.*

Below bottom: *Near Kharkov in 1942, a T-34-equipped armored unit accepts the surrender of a large number of Germans. The T-34 was a key factor in the defeat of Germany in what the Soviets termed the Great Patriotic War.*

Below: *T-34/76s advance in tactical formation across an almost featureless countryside, although a solitary traffic-sign suggests a road underneath the snow. Western Russia's open terrain was ideal tank country and immense battle were fought here.*

Below top: *T-34/76s attack through wooded country near Vitebsk in 1943. The powerful but simple 12-cylinder, 500hp diesel engine, wide tracks and efficient Christie-type five-wheel suspension gave the T-34 excellent battlefield mobility under all conditions.*

Right: *A T-34 tank and infantry in the final stages of an attack in the Oryol-Kursk salient in 1943. The combination of good soldiers, rugged but effective equipment, and vast numbers was to overwhelm the German armed forces on the Eastern front.*

Below top: *German troops examine three captured Soviet T-34s which have become bogged down in a swamp, thus enabling them to be captured. Such German successes were few.*

Below bottom: *After World War II T-34s were exported in large numbers, where their ruggedness, reliability and ease of operation made them very popular with Third World armies. These T-34/85s are being operated by Cuban troops in the Angolan city of Huambo.*

Carro Armato M 13/40 Medium Tank

❖❖

THE M13/40 WAS DESIGNED to overcome the deficiencies in the M11/39, whose 37mm main gun was mounted in the hull, a very unsatisfactory arrangement. The new tank was armed with a 47mm gun mounted in a conventional, rotating turret. Secondary armament comprised four 8mm machine-guns: one coaxial with the main armament, a second, pintle-mounted on the turret roof for anti-aircraft use, and two in the hull front. The hull was of bolted construction with the driver and bow machine-gunner seated in the front, and the loader and commander in the turret, where the latter had to aim and fire the main armament in addition to his other duties.

The M13/40 was used in North Africa in 1941 but proved very unreliable as, somewhat surprisingly, it had not been designed to operate in desert conditions. As a result it was soon replaced in production by the M14/41 which had a more powerful engine and sand filters. The last model in the series was the M15/42, which had a slightly longer hull

and was powered by an eight-cylinder petrol engine.

The M13/40 (799 built) and M14/41 (1,203 built) were the most important Italian tanks of World War 11 and were used in North Africa, Greece and Yugoslavia. Many were captured when they ran out of fuel and at least two Allied units, the British 6th Royal Tank Regiment and the Australian 6th Cavalry, were briefly equipped with these tanks when British tanks were in short supply in 1941.

SPECIFICATIONS

Country of origin: Italy.
Crew: 4.
Armament: One 47mm gun; one 8mm machine-gun co-axial with main armament; one 8mm anti-aircraft machine-gun; twin 8mm machine-guns in hull front.
Armor: 42mm (1.65in) maximum; 6mm (0.24in) minimum.
Dimensions: Length 16ft 2in (4.92m); width 7ft 3in (2.2m); height 7ft 10in (2.38m).

Weight: Combat 30,865lb (14,000kg).
Engine: SPA 8 TMO40 eight-cylinder diesel developing 125hp.
Performance: Road speed 20mph (32km/h); road range 125 miles (200km); vertical obstacle 2ft 8in (0.8m); trench 6ft 11in (2.1m); gradient 70 per cent.

Left: *British officers examine an M13/40, while its disconsolate crew looks on.*

Above: *General Rommel (with field glasses) uses M13/40 for a grandstand view.*

Valentine Infantry Tank Mark III

❖

THE VALENTINE ORIGINATED as a private venture by Vickers-Armstrong, built to meet the War Office specification for an "infantry tank". The design was submitted to the War Office in early 1938, but nothing was done until July 1939, when Vickers was suddenly ordered to produce 275 in the shortest possible time. The tank's name does not fit into the usual pattern of British tank names and originated because the design was delivered to the War Office on 14 February, an unusually romantic touch in the materialistic world of armored warfare!

In some ways the Valentine was a well-armored cruiser rather than a pure infantry tank, although its low speed was a handicap when used in open warfare. The driver sat on the centerline in a cramped compartment, with the other two men (three from Mark III onwards) in the turret. In all versions the turret was too small and in the three-man crew the commander had a particularly difficult time, as he had to load the main

armament, command the vehicle, select targets for the gunner, and operate two radio sets. The pressure on the commander was eased a little with the four-man crew, although since there were now three men in the same turret space they tended to get in each other's way.

Main armament was the 2-pounder, an accurate weapon, but which could not

Below: *The Valentine had all the attributes of a cruiser tank, with two exceptions. It was better armored, and it was much slower, its maximum speed of 15mph being all that was necessary for it to accompany the infantry.*

SPECIFICATIONS

Country of origin: United Kingdom.
Crew: 3 (4 in Mks III and IV).
Armament: One 2pdr and one 7.92mm BESA machine-gun (Mks I-VII); one 6prd and one 7.92mm BESA machine-gun (Mks VIII-X); and one 75mm gun and one 7.92mm BESA machine-gun (Mk XI).
Armor: 8mm (0.31in) minimum; 65mm (2.56in) maximum.
Dimensions: Length (overall) 17ft 9in (5.41m); width 8ft 7½in (2.63m); height 7ft

5½in (2.27m).
Weight: 35,840lb (16,257kg).
Engine: AEC petrol engine developing 135hp (Mk I); AEC diesel developing 131hp (Mks II, III, VIII); GM diesel developing 138hp (Mks IV, IX); and GM diesel developing 165hp (Mks X, XI).
Performance: Road speed 15mph (24km/h), range 90 miles (144km); vertical obstacle 3ft (0.91m); trench 7ft 9in (2.36m); gradient 60 per cent.

Left: *Two Valentine tanks, destroyed in the Western desert. The top tank has had a hit on the muzzle of its 2-pounder gun an extraordinary "fluke" while the lower tank (in rear of top picture) has been hit in the side, the passage of*

the shell clearly marked by the large dent in the track guard.

Below: *The Valentine was progressively upgunned. The Valentine Mark VIII (lower*

picture) was armed with the 6-pounder main gun in place of the original 2-pounder, but the final Valentine Mark XI (top picture) mounted the even more powerful 75mm main gun with a muzzle brake.

defeat the latest German armors and lacked an HE shell for general targets. A total of 79 rounds were carried for the 2-pounder, plus 2,000 rounds for the coaxial 7.92mm BESA machine-gun. Valentine Mark VIII introduced the 6-pounder, but, to compensate for the extra space occupied by the breech, no coaxial machine-gun was fitted, leaving the crew with no option but to use the main gun against infantry and other soft targets. This very unsatisfactory solution was repeated in the Mark IX, but from the Mark X on the machine-gun was restored. As with the Matilda II and Crusader, the Valentine turret was traversed using a hydraulic motor controlled by a spade grip.

The Mark I was powered by an AEC petrol engine, but all successive marks used AEC diesels, which were remarkably reliable and easy to maintain. The suspension was the "slow-motion type" consisting, as in the Cruiser Mark I, with two three-wheeled bogies on each side. The hull was built with riveted plate armor, although Canadian Valentines and some British-built Mks X and XI were given cast nose plates, which were both stronger and cheaper.

There were eleven distinct marks of gun

tank, as well as separate versions for amphibious landings, bridgelaying, flamethrowing and minefield clearance. The Valentine also proved to be a valuable platform for many experiments, one of which would have involved a stripped-down chassis fitted with a rotor so that it could be towed behind an aircraft and then descend to the ground. A jeep was fitted with the system, which proved

Below: *Valentine Mark V in factory condition. Armament is a 2-pounder main gun with a 7.92mm coaxial BESA machine-gun, but unlike many contemporary tanks, there was no hull machine-gun. The suspension was derived from that used on the Mark I Cruiser, but was not used on any further designs.*

perfectly feasible, but the tank was a different matter and the project, quite literally, never got off the ground.

Valentines were issued to cavalry units to replace tanks lost at Dunkirk, only later did they reach the tank brigades for their proper role of infantry support. Valentines gained a great reputation for reliability with the British 8th Army and in the pursuit after El Alamein some motored over 3,000 miles (4,830km) on their own tracks. Others took part in theMadagascar and Pacific campaigns, while a few operated in the Arakan jungles during the Burma campaign. By the time production ceased in early 1944 8,275 Valentines of all marks had been built in the UK and Canada, of which 2,690 were supplied to the Soviet Union.

Below top: *Valentine Mark V leads a supply convoy in Tunisia, 18 January 1943 towing a "Rotatrailer" with additional fuel and ammunition.*

Below bottom: *Disabled British tanks, including a Valentine (foreground), litter the desert in 1942; disconsolate prisoners begin the trek to Italy.*

Right: *A Valentine leads a troop of A9 Cruisers Mark Is, through a Libyan town. For reasons not explained, the Valentine lacks its main gun, so the enemy cannot be nearby!*

M3 Light Tank

◆◆

THE STANDARD US LIGHT TANK in June 1940 was the M2A4, which had been standardized in 1939, and which was the culmination of a line of development stretching back to the M2A1 of 1935. The M2A4 weighed some 12 tons (12,193kg),

had a 37mm turret-mounted gun and was constructed from riveted armor plate. A requirement to increase the thickness of the armor of the M2A4 necessitated changes to the suspension system, and this, together with improved protection

from aircraft attack, led to the design being standardized in July 1940 under a new designation the M3 Light Tank. Initially, the M3 was completed with the same Continental W-670 seven-cylinder, air-cooled, 250hp radial engine as the M2A4, but in 1941 shortages of this engine resulted in the Guiberson 7-1020 diesel engine authorized for installation in 500 M3 light tanks. Also, as a result of British battle experience in North Africa, additional fuel capacity was provided in the form of two externally-mounted, jettisonable fuel tanks. Main armament

was a 37mm cannon, with a 0.3in machine-gun mounted coaxially, and two further 0.3in machine-guns in fixed, forward-facing mounts in sponsons above the track guards.

Below left: *Morning maintenance parade on a British-operated M3. Its official name was the Stuart, but its great reliability and exceptional mobility led to it being nicknamed the "Honey."*

Below right: *An M3 Stuart leads an M4 Sherman in a training exercise across padi fields, conducted by 1st Regiment, 5332nd Brigade of the Chinese Nationalist Army, Kibani, Burma, mid-1944.*

SPECIFICATIONS

Country of origin: USA.
Crew: 4.
Armament: One 37mm M5 gun; one .3in M1919A4 machine-gun co-axial with main armament; two .3in machine-guns in hull sponsons; one M3in machine-gun on turret roof.
Armor: 44.5mm (1.75in) maximum; 10mm (0.375in) minimum.
Dimensions: Length 14ft 10½in (4.53m); width 7ft 4in (2.23m); height 8ft 3in (2.51m).

Weight: Combat 27,400lb (12,428kg).
Engine: Continental W-670 seven-cylinder air-cooled radial petrol engine developing 250hp at 2,400rpm.
Performance: Road speed 36mph (58km/h), cross-country speed 20mph (32km/h); road range 70 miles (112km); vertical obstacle 2ft (0.6m); trench 6ft (1.8m); gradient 60 per cent.

The basic M3 was produced in quantity by the American Car and Foundry Company, who had delivered 5,811 by August 1942. The next version, the M3A1 light tank, used the same hull as the M3, which was still constructed from riveted plate, but incorporated an improved turret of welded homogeneous plate (as opposed to the earlier, brittle, face-hardened armor) with power traverse for the turret, a gyrostabiliser to permit more accurate firing of the 37mm gun on the move, and a turret basket. The M3A1 was standardized in August 1941 and the American Car and Foundry Company produced 4,621, of which 211 were powered by Guiberson diesels.

A pilot, which had both hull and turret formed of welded armor, was originally designated the M3A1El, but this led, through a separate line of development, to the M5 light tank. The next model in the M3-series was the M3A2, which was also to be of welded construction but otherwise similar to the M3A1 in all respects; in the event none were built. The M3A3, however, did reach production. This was a much more comprehensive redesign of the M3A2, including changes in the turret, hull and sponsons, and it was considered

so worthwhile that it continued to be built even after the production line for its successor, the M5, had been established. Some 3,427 M3A3s were built.

In British service the M3 was designated the Stuart Mark 1 and provided a much-needed addition to the tank strength of the Eighth Army in the Western Desert in 1941 and 1942. It subsequently appeared in all theaters of World War II, but is chiefly remembered for its service in the desert, with empire forces in Burma, in the capture of Antwerp, and with American forces in the Pacific. It was under-gunned and poorly armored, but was also highly mobile and very reliable, so much so that it was affectionately known as the "Honey" by British cavalry regiments, many of which preferred it to the Daimler armored car for reconnaissance.

Below: *Australian infantry, supported by an Australian-manned M3A1 Stuart, advance through palm trees on a Pacific island. The two men nearest the camera are armed with Bren 0.303in Bren light machine-guns, an excellent weapon widely used by Commonwealth forces in World War II.*

Although it was fast and had good ground-crossing ability for the "cavalry" scouting role for which it had been designed, the M3 had limited scope for development or adaptation. The hull was too narrow, setting an absolute maximum on the diameter of the turret ring and thus limiting the size of the main armament to well below the 75mm which was necessary for an effective tank gun in the second half of the war. The M3 was also too high and angular, offering a high silhouette and many shot traps, and was declared obsolete in July 1943. Nevertheless, the M3 was the most widely used light tank in any army during World War II, a total of 13,859 having been built by the time production ended in October 1943, and it fought in virtually every theater.

Below: *A British cavalry regiment, the King's Royal Irish Hussars, tries out its newly-delivered M3 Stuarts in the Western Desert in September 1941. M3s were found to be ideal reconnaissance vehicles and were preferred to British Daimler armored cars.*

Below: *M3 Stuarts of the US Army at a depot awaiting issue to front-line units. The 37mm main gun was not really adequate and the armour was thin and contained many shot traps; nevertheless, this was a very popular vehicle, produced in very large numbers, and used by numerous armies.*

Inset: *Advancing across Normandy, following the invasion on 6 June 1944, a US Army M3 Stuart breaks through a road-block, made from farmers' carts and farming implements. Quite what such a very amateurish barrier was expected to achieve against modern armored vehicles is not clear.*

Left: *A knocked-out M3 in the desert campaign, circa 1942. This vehicle belonged to the famous 7th Armored Division, nick-named the "Desert Rats" from their divisional sign, the jerboa, which is depicted on the right-hand track-guard of this tank. This tank has been immobilized by the loss of its right track, possibly caused by an anti-tank mine, known technically as a "mobility kill."*

M3 Grant/Lee Medium Tank

❖

EARLY REPORTS TO THE United States from the European battlefields of 1939-40 quickly showed that the then current 37mm gun of the American M2 medium tank would not be sufficiently powerful for modern conditions. It was then suggested that, in what would be described today as a "quick fix," the M2 could be improved by increasing its armor and mounting the existing 75mm M1 gun in a sponson. The design was quickly finalized, the new tank was designated the M3 Medium Tank in July 1940 and on 28 Augus 1940 the contract for 1,000 M2A1 medium tanks, which had been signed only 15 days previously, was summarily terminated in favor of the M3.

Up to this point, America's tank production needs had been met largely by the heavy engineering industry, which built each vehicle by hand, but it was now decided that wartime conditions required the application of mass production techniques as used as in the automobile industry. Thus, production of the M3 started in August 1941 and by the time it

ended only 16 months later 6,258 M3s had been built (Chrysler 3,352. Alco 685, Baldwin 1,220, Pressed Steel S 501 and Pullman 500), which demonstrates the effectiveness of this decision.

During this production run various modifications were implemented to either overcome shortages or to improve the tank. The M3 had a riveted hull, but

Below: A typical sight from the Desert Campaign, as M3 Grants advance in February 1942. The exceptional height 10ft 3in (3.1m) and bulkiness are obvious, but they were popular with their crews.

SPECIFICATIONS

Country of origin: USA.
Crew: 6.
Armament: One 75mm M2 or M3 gun in hull sponson; one 37mm M5 or M6 gun in turret; one .3in M1919A4 machine-gun co-axial with turret gun; one .3in machine-gun in cupola on turret; two .3in machine-gun in bow.
Armor: 12mm to 37mm (0.47–1.46in).
Dimensions: Length 18ft 6in (5.64m); width 8ft 11in (2.72m); height 10ft 3in (3.12m).

Weight: Combat 60,000lb (27,216kg).
Engine: Continental R-975-EC2 nine-cylinder air-cooled radial petrol engine developing 340hp at 2,400rpm.
Performance: Road speed 26mph (42km/h), cross-country speed 16mph (26km/h); road range 120 miles (193km); vertical obstacle 2ft (0.6m); trench 6ft 3in (1.9m); gradient 60 per cent.

M3A1 had a cast hull produced by Alco, in which the side doors were eliminated for additional strength. Baldwin built 12 M3A2 with welded hulls, which were followed by 322 M3A3s, also with welded hulls, but powered by two coupled General Motors 6-71 diesel bus engines as an alternative to the Wright radial engine. Some M3s, M3A1s and M3A2s were fitted with Guiberson diesels, in which

case the designation was suffixed "(Diesel);" e.g., M3A1 (Diesel). Another answer to the shortage of Wright aero engines was produced by Chrysler, who combined five standard automobile engines to produce a powerpack known as the "Eggbeater." This required modifications to the hull and suspension, resulting in the M3A4, but the hull was riveted as in the original M3; 109 were

built. The M3A5 resulted from the installation of twin GM diesels of the M3A3 in the riveted hull of the M3.

A British Tank Commission visited the United States in June 1940, intending to

Below: *Despite the rain and water, this is a scene in the desert as an M3 advances after Alamein. The black object in the turret is the commander, wrapped in a blanket, who is observing something behind his tank.*

order British-designed tanks from American firms, but with British defeat apparently imminent this was turned down by the US Government, so the Commission placed orders for the M3, instead, all of which were supplied under the terms of the 1941 Lend-Lease Act. Some of these tanks were built with a British-designed turret and were designated Grant I (after Civil War Union general, Ulysses S.

Grant). Others were identical with those built for the US Army and were given the name Lee (after Civil War Confederate general, Robert E. Lee). Thus, standard M3 Lee I, M3A1 Lee II, M3A3 Lee IV, M3A3 (Diesel) Lee V, and M2A4 Lee VI (only 12 M3A2s were ever built and none went to Britain, but the designation Lee III appears to have been kept open for it). The M3A5s became the Grant II.

The Grant I had its first impact at the battle of Gazala on 27 May 1942, the first time the 8th Army had managed to achieve any degree of parity with the 75mm gun of the PzKpfw IV, although it was some time

Below: *A very cheerful looking group of 8th Army soldiers. The sponson-mounted 75mm was added to the design at a late stage in order to get a large calibre weapon into service with units as quickly as possible.*

before problems associated with fuses for the HE shell could be resolved. By October 1942 a further 350 M3s of various sub-types had reached the Eighth Army and these tanks made a significant contribution to the success at El Alamein in November of that year. Some M3s were shipped to the UK for training units, but the majority were used in North Africa and the Middle East. By April 1943 the M4 Sherman was in full production, and the M3 was finally declared obsolete on 16 March 1944. Its appearance on World War II battlefields was relatively brief, but it played a major role, especially in the Desert Campaign.

Below: *M3 Grant in service with the British Army, during the Arakan campaign. It was long thought that tanks had no role to play in jungle warfare but this was disproved time and again by General Slim's XIVth Army.*

Right top: *Two M3 Grants. The front-line operational life of the M3 was relatively brief S from mid-1942 to March 1944 S but it played a significant role, especially with the British Eighth Army at the Battle of Alamein. Compare the turret with the M3 Lee overleaf.*

Right bottom: *A British M3 Grant crew surrenders to German infantry during the Battle of Alamein, one of the few Axis successes during this battle. The white object is from a piece of paper on the picture during developing and is not a flag.*

Right: *A striking picture of an Eighth Army M3 Lee, belonging to the 4th Queen's Own Hussars. The only significant difference with the Grant was that while the latter had a British-designed turret, the Lee's turret was of American design. Note also the all-rivetted hull, the side door, the simple but effective suspension system, rubber-padded tracks, and the jerricans just visible on the rear bracket. The height of the commander above ground level is also very obvious.*

Carro Armato L6/40 Light Tank

❖

THE L 6/40 WAS DEVELOPED from a series of 5 ton (5,000kg) tracked vehicles developed by FIAT-Ansaldo for export. Two prototypes were completed in 1936; one was armed with twin 8mm Breda machine-guns, whilst the other had a 37mm gun and a co-axial 8mm machine-gun. The Italian Army ordered 283 L 6/40s, which were delivered between 1941 and 1942, but some of this number were completed as Semovente L40 47mm self-propelled anti-tank guns.

The riveted hull varied in thickness between 1.3in (30mm) and 0.24in (6mm) with the driver at the front of the hull on the right, the turret offset to the left, and the engine located at the rear.

The main armament consisted of a 20mm cannon with an elevation of +20° and a depression of -12°, and also an 8mm machine-gun mounted co-axially. The suspension consisted of two bogies, each with two road wheels, with the drive sprocket at the front, and the idler at the rear, and three track-return rollers were also provided.

The L 6/40 was designed to replace the CV33 tankette, but it was already obsolete by the time it entered service with the Italian Army in 1941. It was used in Italy, North Africa and Russia. A flamethrower model was developed but it did not enter service. The command model was fitted with radios and had an open roof. The Semovente L40 was armed with a 47mm anti-tank gun mounted in the front of the superstructure, to the left of the driver. It had a crew of three. Some 296 rounds of 20mm and 1,560 rounds of 8mm machine-gun ammunition were carried.

SPECIFICATIONS

Country of origin: Italy.
Crew: 2.
Armament: One Breda Model 35 20mm gun; one Breda Model 38 8mm machine-gun co-axial with main armament.
Armor: 30mm (1.26in) maximum; 6mm (0.24in) minimum.
Dimensions: Length 12ft 5in (3.78m); width 6ft 4in (1.92m); height 6ft 8in (2.03m).

Weight: 14,991lb (6,800kg).
Engine: SPA 180 four-cylinder inline petrol engine developing 70hp.
Performance: Road speed 26mph (42km/h); road range 124 miles (200km); vertical obstacle 2ft 4in (0.7m); trench 5ft 7in (1.7m); gradient 60 per cent.

Left: *Despite having developed and built tanks since 1918, the Italy never produced a world-class design. The L6/40 was no exception, being underpowered, thinly armored and poorly armed; when it entered service in 1941 it was already obsolete.*

A22 Churchill Infantry Tank

◆◆

BEFORE THE MATILDA II infantry tank had even entered service, plans were being made for its successor, which was given the designation A20. Design work started at Harland & Wolff in September 1939 and four prototypes were running by June 1940, but the project was then cancelled, and a different company, Vauxhall, was directed to start work on an entirely new design, the A22, which had to be in production within 12 months. With a German invasion apparently imminent, the company had a pilot model running within seven months and the first 14 production tanks had been completed by June 1941, just 11 months after the start of design work.

The Churchill was exceptionally well armored for its day, with particularly thick frontal plates, which were repeatedly upgraded by the addition of welded on appliqué plates. The turret was increased in size and complexity, and for the first time in a British tank the commander's cupola in the Mark VII was given an all-round vision capability when closed down

a great step forward, though it was common enough in contemporary German tanks. The hull was also comparatively spacious and the ammunition stowage was particularly generous, with the Mark I capable of carrying 150 rounds of 2-pounder and 58 of 3in howitzer ammunition, whilst still leaving room for five men. The hull was sufficiently wide to

Below: *Churchill I with a turret-mounted 2-pounder and a hull-mounted 3in howitzer, whose barrel can be seen jutting past the right-hand horn. This had a limited field-of-fire and was not repeated in later versions.*

SPECIFICATIONS

Country of origin: United Kingdom.
Crew: 5.
Armament: One 6pounder gun and two 7.92mm BESA machine-guns.
Armor: 102mm (4in) maximum and 16mm (0.63in) minimum.
Dimensions: Length 24ft 5in (7.44m); width 10ft 8in (3.25m); height 8ft 2in (2.49m).
Weight: Combat 87,360lb (39,574kg).

Engine: Two 6-cylinder Bedford water-cooled inline developing 350bhp.
Performance: Road speed 15.5mph (24.8km/h); cross-country speed 8mph (12.8km/h); range 90 miles (144km); vertical obstacle 2ft 6in (0.812m); trench 10ft (3.048m).

(Data for Churchill III)

enable a 6-pounder to be mounted in the Mark III without too much trouble, though the later 75mm and 95mm weapons caused some difficulties and the turret-ring was smaller than ideal.

The Churchill Mark I was armed with the then standard British 2-pounder gun, even though it was already clear that it was inadequate for modern conditions, but the problem was that the government-owned Royal Ordnance Factories were tooled up for 2-pounders, and in the desperate days after Dunkirk there was no time to switch over. The Mark I also mounted a 3in (76.2mm) howitzer low down in the front of the hull, alongside the driver, an arrangement very similar to that in the French Char B (q.v.). There was also a specialized Close Support version of the Mark I which not only had the hull-mounted 3in howitzer but also a second 3in howitzer, which replaced the 2-pounder gun in the turret; a few were produced only and the idea was pursued no further. In the Churchill Mark II and later marks this hull-mounted howitzer was replaced by a BESA machine-gun.

By March 1942 the 6-pounder was available and was fitted to the turret of the Churchill III in that month. Further

improvements followed and the Mark VII had a 75mm gun, the Mark VIII a 95mm Close Support howitzer, and some North African Mark IVs were reworked in Egypt to accommodate a 75mm gun and 0.3in Browning machine-gun in the turret, both of which were taken from Shermans and perhaps Grants.

The engine was created by laying two Bedford truck engines on their sides and joining them to a common crankcase; this resulted in a powerful and compact unit, but which. proved to be very unreliable and difficult to maintain or repair. As a result, the engine gained a bad reputation which, despite major improvements, it never quite lived down. The Churchill was the first British tank to use both the Merritt-Brown regenerative steering system, which not only saved a great deal

Left below: *Royal Tank Regiment squadron commander (2nd from right) holds an "orders group" with troop commanders on a Churchill II. The lieutenant on the left wears the correct pattern webbing and revolver for an armored officer.*

Right below: *One of many Churchill conversions was this Armored Vehicle Royal Engineers (AVRE) belonging to 1st Assault Brigade, 79th Armored Division. It was armed with a Petard 11.4in (29cm) mortar, which fired a 40lb (18kg) bomb 80yd (73m).*

of power, but also enabled the driver to make much sharper turns, as well as hydraulically-assisted steering and clutch controls. The suspension used 11 small bogies on each side, each with its own vertical coil spring; movement was limited and the ride harsh, but it was simple, cheap, and absorbed a fair degree of battle damage.

Variants included vehicles for bridging, mine clearing, armored recovery, and flamethrowing. There was also a particularly successful Armored Vehicle Royal Engineers (AVRE) which fulfilled numerous engineer roles until replaced by the Centurion AVRE in the early 1960s.

A total of 5,460 Churchills was produced, and went into action for the first time during the Dieppe raid (August 1942); several Marks I, II and III took

Below: *Churchill IIs go into battle at El Alamein. The Churchill was one of the better British tank designs of the war, but was hampered, as were all "infantry" tanks, by its low maximum speed of 15mph (25km/h).*

Right: *A Churchill of 7th Royal Tank Regiment, of 31 Tank Brigade at Maltot, France on 26 July 1944. This tank is armed with the 6-pounder, a considerable improvement on the earlier 2-pounder.*

part, but virtually all either sank after leaving the landing craft, or were captured. A number of Churchills were sent to the Soviet Union, and a few Mark IIIs reached North Africa in time to take part in the battle of Alamein. Churchills were used in Tunisia and Italy, and several brigades were deployed in North-West Europe, where their thick armor proved very useful, although they were hampered by being outgunned by German armor. The tank remained in service in diminishing numbers until the 1950s.

Left: *The bocage countryside, immediately inland from the Normandy beaches, is broken up by innumerable hedges, which made it very hard going for the infantry. As a result, tanks such as this Churchill were called in to help them fight their way through. The date is 28 June 1944 and the troops belong to 15th (Scottish) Infantry Division. The Churchill is operated by 7th Royal Tank Regiment of 31st Armored Brigade and an unusual weapon on the turret is a 0.303in Bren light machine-gun, which is fitted with a 100-round drum magazine for anti-aircraft duties.*

Left: *Churchill crashes its way through a hedgerow. Although it had a low top speed, the Churchill was very agile and proved capable of climbing slopes or crossing obstacles which defeated other tanks.*

Below: *Factory picture of a Churchill I. Note the hull-mounted 3in (76mm) howitzer and the strap-on auxiliary fuel drums at the rear. The tools and fire extinguishers on the rear decking were standard equipment for all tanks.*

Left: *Most tanks were used as the basis of special versions, known as "funnies" in the British Army. A number of examples are seen here on Juno beach, Normandy, shortly after D-day, 6 June, 1944. Tank "34" is a flail-version of the M4 Sherman in which a metal roller is rotated so that the attached chains beat the ground, thus exploding any anti-tank mines. Closest to the camera is a Churchill bridgelayer, which carried and laid a 30ft (9.1m) bridge, which were issued on a scale of three to each tank (armored) brigade.*

T-60 Light Tank

◆◆

THE T-60 LIGHT TANK appeared in 1941 as the replacement for the T-40 light tank, but, unlike its predecessor, was not amphibious. The T-40 was armed with a 12.7mm machine-gun and one of the needs in the new tank was for a powerful gun. Soviet engineers initially attempted to mount the standard 37mm weapon, but, even with a reduced charge round, the turret ring was incapable of absorbing the recoil of this weapon. Accordingly, the designers took an alternative approach by developing a new high-powered weapon and round specially for the T-60. The outcome was the 20mm SWAK-20 cannon, firing a new armor-piercing incendiary (API) round with a heavy, soft core incorporating a sub-caliber slug, which possessed the same armor-penetrating capabilities as the original 37mm round.

T-60's hull front and turret had 0.8in (20mm) frontal armor, giving improved protection against heavy-caliber machine-gun rounds, but both were welded rather than cast. The turret was offset to the left, with the engine mounted alongside it on the right and the driver was placed centrally in the front.

The improved T-60A had increased armor and solid roadwheels replacing the previous solid pressings. Over 6,000 T-60s were built before the type was supplanted by its successor, the T-70 light tank, after which T-60 chassis were employed as mountings for M-8 and M-1 3 (Katyusha) rocket-launchers, and also as artillery tractors for 57mm anti-tank guns.

Below: *The Soviet Army's T-60; note how the turret is offset to the left.*

Inset: *A parade of T-60s; the crews show how small these two-man tanks actually were.*

SPECIFICATIONS

Country of origin: Russia.
Crew: 2.
Armament: One 20mm ShVAK cannon; one 7.62mm DT machine-gun.
Armor: 7mm to 20mm (0.28in to 0.79in).
Dimensions: Length (overall) 14ft 1in (4.3m); width 8ft 1in (2.46m); height 6ft 2in (1.89m).

Weight: 11,354lb (5,150kg).
Engine: GAZ-202 six-cylinder water-cooled petrol engine developing 70hp at 2,800rpm.
Performance: Road speed 28mph (45km/h); range 382 miles (615km); vertical obstacle 1ft 9in (0.54m); trench 6ft 1in (1.85m); gradient 60 per cent.

T-70 Light Tank

IN THE EARLY STAGES of the Great Patriotic War the Soviet generals realized that light tanks were ineffective in modern conditions. Nevertheless, by early 1942 tank losses had been tremendous and production was slowed by transferring tank factories eastwards. So, since light tanks were relatively easy to produce, an order was placed for the T-70, which began to replace the T-60s in January, on the principle that even a light tank was preferable to no tank at all.

The T-70 had the same chassis as the T-60, but with front instead of rear drive, the 37mm gun was replaced by a 45mm weapon, the hull armor was modified to give a cleaner outline and better protection, and the driver was provided with an armored visor. Power was doubled by the simple expedient of installing two engines in place of the one in the T-60, and finally the suspension was reinforced to take the extra weight. In mid-1943 production switched to the T-70A, which had increased armor and more powerful engines. The turret shape was also improved. Production

of T-70/T-70A was discontinued in the autumn of 1943 as medium tank output increased, although no less than 8,226 had been produced. In 1944 all surviving chassis were modified by installing an extra bogie wheel on each side and converted to self-propelled gun mountings.

Below: *The T-70 was one of the best light, two-man tanks of World War II; a total of 8,226 were completed in 1942 and 1944.*

Inset: *Soviet Army T-70A in action. The 45mm main gun was quite large for tanks of this size, but the T-70 was only a substitute until sufficient T-34s became available.*

SPECIFICATIONS

Country of origin: Russia.
Crew: 2.
Armament: One 45mm L/46 gun; one 7.62mm DT machine-gun.
Armor: 0.39in (10mm) minimum; 2.36in (60mm) maximum.
Dimensions: Length 15ft 3in (6m); width 7ft 8in (2.52m); height 6ft 9in (2.22m).

Weight: 21,958lb (9,960kg).
Engine: Two Z1S-202 six-cylinder water-cooled petrol engines each developing 70hp at 2,800rpm.
Performance: Road speed 32mph (51km/h); range 279 miles (446km); vertical obstacle 2ft 2in (0.71m); trench 9ft 6in (3.12m); gradient 70 per cent.

M4 Sherman Medium Tank

❖

THE M3 WAS RUSHED INTO PRODUCTION with a 75mm gun mounted in a sponson on the side of the tank, which was acceptable as an interim solution, but its tactical limitations were clear from the start. Thus, on the day following the decision to authorize production of the M3 in August 1940 design work started on yet another new medium tank, but one which would, this time, mount the 75mm gun in a conventional turret with a full 360° traverse. The new project was provisionally designated the T6 Medium Tank, and one of the design criteria was that it would reuse the maximum amount of components from the M3. The T6 was standardized in September 1941 under the official title of M4 Medium Tank, but in all its many models it was more widely and popularly known simply as the "Sherman," after the Civil War Union general, William Tecumseh Sherman.

As adopted, the Sherman weighed about 30 tons (30,482kg) and was armed with the 75mm M3 gun. The turret was a one-piece rounded casting, 3in (76.2mm) thick

at the front, and power operated, with a gyrostabilizer controlling the gun in elevation. The lower hull was welded, while the construction of the upper hull

Left below: Infantrymen of 55th Armored Infantry Battalion of the US Third Army run past an M4 Sherman during the attack on the German village of Wernberg, April 22, 1945.

Right below: During the advance across France in 1944 the crew of an M4 Sherman watch pensively as two engineers unearth an anti-tank mine. Such hidden menaces caused many casualties and frequent delays.

SPECIFICATIONS

Country of origin: USA.
Crew: 5.
Armament: One 75mm M3 gun; one .3in M1919A4 machine-gun co-axial with main armament; one .3in M1919A4 machine-gun ball mount in bow; one .5in M2 machine-gun on turret roof; one 2in M3 smoke mortar in turret roof.
Armor: 15mm (0.6in) minimum; 100m (3.94in) maximum.
Dimensions: Length 20ft 7in (6.27m); width 8ft 11in (2.67m); height 11ft 1in (3.37m).
Weight: Combat 69,565lb (31,554kg).
Engine: Ford GAA V-8 water-cooled inline petrol engine developing 500hp at 2,600rpm.
Performance: Road speed 26mph (42km/h), road range 100 miles (160km); vertical obstacle 2ft (0.61m); trench 7ft 6in (2.29m); fording depth 3ft (0.91m); gradient 60 per cent.
(*Note: Data relate to a typical M4A3.*)

provided a certain degree of identification of the various models. The original M4 had a welded upper hull, while the M4A1 had a cast, rounded upper hull, both of which were approximately 2in (50.8mm) thick. Variations between the major models in the M4 series were mainly due to different engine installations, apart from the difference in hull construction in the case of the M4 and M4Al.

Production of the Sherman was authorized to replace the M3 as soon as possible. At least seven factories were involved in building the M3 with a grand total of 49,230 of all types being eventually completed. Product improvement was a continuous process throughout, and indeed after production had ceased, the most significant improvements centering on armament,

stowage of ammunition, and suspension.

The gun conceived for the T6 medium tank prototype was the unsatisfactory 75mm T6 gun (the identical designations were a coincidence). The next model, the T7, was better and was standardized as the 75mm M2 gun in May 1941, but was still relatively short-barreled and had a muzzle velocity of only 1,850ft/s (564m/s). Early model Shermans mounted this M2

gun, but even as early as September 1940 the Armored Force was asking for a higher muzzle velocity, this request being met in the 75mm M3 gun, adopted in June 1941. This gun fired armor-piercing shot at a muzzle velocity of 2,030ft/s (619m/s) and was also more suited to tank use. The longer barrel was better balanced for installation in a gyrostabilizer mount while rotation of the breech to allow the block to open horizontally permitted greater depression of the gun in a turret mount.

Although the 75mm gun was accepted as the standard weapon, the Ordnance Department felt (correctly) that greater penetrating power would be required and set to work to provide it. During all this activity concerning medium tanks, a heavy tank, the M6, had been under development, with some twelve being

Left below: *One of the greatest armored commanders of all time, Lieutenant-General George Patton, Commanding General, Third US Army, takes a picture of an M4 flame-thrower demonstration; France, October 1944.*

Right below: *An M4 Sherman of 1st Polish Armored Regiment of the Polish Armored Division, maneuvring on the Mulberry floating harbor off the Normandy beaches on 1 August 1944.*

produced in 1942 before the project was shelved. This tank was armed with a 3in (76mm) and it was found that when fitted with the 75mm breech from the M2 gun the result was a most satisfactory weapon. This was designated the 76mm T1 gun, and was mounted on a Sherman in a project which began in August 1942, but, to the astonishment of the Ordnance Committee it found no support and

further development ceased in November 1942. This was, however, later rescinded and by July 1944 over 2,000 76mm gun tanks had been produced.

Another innovation in armament concerned the 105mm howitzer. In April 1941 officials at the Aberdeen Proving Ground suggested that the Sherman would conveniently mount the 105mm howitzer, but it was not until over a year later that

two M4A4s were modified for this purpose. Further tests were carried out on a similarly modified vehicle, the M4E5, and the howitzer in the M52 mount was adopted as a standard item. These vehicles were used in headquarter companies to provide fire support and some 4,680 were built on the M4 and M4A3 hulls.

Early models of the Sherman had an unfortunate reputation for "brewing-up"

(ie, catching fire) when hit by anti-tank rounds. To overcome this stowage racks were provided in the lower hull, those for 75mm and 76mm ammunition being surrounded by water jackets, while the semi-fixed 105mm howitzer ammunition was protected by armor plate.

To improve the ride and stability, and at the same time reduce the tank's specific ground pressure, experiments were made with different suspensions and tracks. The original and highly characteristic vertical volute spring suspension (VVSS) of the Sherman series had originated with the M2 medium tank, as had the 16in (0.4m) track, but both were more suited to a 20 ton (20,321kg) vehicle than the 30-plus tons of the M4. Eventually a new horizontal volute spring suspension (HVSS) and 23in (0.58m) track were

Left below: *An M4 Sherman of the Chinese Nationalist's 1st Provisional Tank Group motors along the Burma Road, southwards towards Lashio Hsenwi. (For security reasons, the censor has deleted all background)*

Right below: *Dramatic picture of a US Army M4 Sherman motoring across the North African desert in November 1942. As with many World War Two pictures, the censor has scratched out the unit and formation signs.*

perfected and incorporated in production.

More Shermans were manufactured than any other single tank, but critics were (and remain) keen to highlight its deficiencies, particularly in comparison with the German Panther. The M4 certainly had shortcomings, but it more than made up for them by its reliability, endurance and, in the final analysis, sheer weight of numbers, and when the war ended in the West it was the Sherman that was master of the battlefield.

Below: *M4 Shermans of the Free French 2nd Armored Division in their marshalling area "somewhere in France" on D+45 (July 21, 1944). The Sherman was a good tank, although it may not have been the best tank in the war, but US industry was capable of producing it in vast quantities, which the Germans had no hope of matching.*

Right: *Captured by the Germans, this Sherman has been painted with crosses and put into service. It is the British "Firefly" version fitted with a 17-pounder gun.*

Below: *The infantry fighting from the tank is a pose for the cameraman; in practice US Army infantry advanced on foot, although this technique was used by the Red Army.*

Opposite: *M4 Shermans of the Polish Armored Division prepare to go into battle in support of the British 51st Highland Division, south of Caen, France, August 8, 1944. The picture not only emphasizes the huge numbers of tanks available to the Allies, but also shows the extraordinary degree of air supremacy over the Luftwaffe, which enabled such forces to assemble in the open with impunity.*

Left: *British infantry aboard a Sherman, in an orchard east of Caen, France, 18 July 1944. They will dismount before nearing the enemy and go into battle on foot, leaving the tanks free to maneuver on their own.*

Below: *An M4 of a Canadian armored regiment, in the bocage country at Vaucelles, France, shortly after the D-day landings. The Sherman had a fine reputation for reliability and performance, but its gun was not powerful enough to defeat Panthers and it tended to "brew-up" (ie, ignite) if hit by a German 88mm shell.*

A27M Cromwell Infantry Tank

◆◆◆

In late 1940 the Leyland company and Rolls-Royce decided that a modified Merlin aircraft engine would make an excellent tank engine. De-rated to 600hp and named the Meteor, this engine was sufficient to power heavy cruiser tanks, but as it would take time to get it into production and the need for tanks was very pressing, Leyland's next tank design was initially powered by the Nuffield Liberty engine. However, the engine compartment was sized and outfitted to accept the Meteor in due course. This tank, designated A27(L) Centaur (L = Liberty), was armed with the new British 6 pounder gun and was also fitted with the new Merritt-Brown gearbox, a substantial improvement over previous types. The Centaur was subjected to extensive trials and the first production models did not appear until January 1943.

The General Staff then changed armament policy and now required cruiser tanks to have an HE round to attack anti-tank guns, infantry positions and bunkers, in addition to the existing anti-tank

rounds. A new gun was rapidly developed, based on the American 75mm, but utilizing as many parts of the British 6-pounder as possible. Meanwhile, the 6-pounder was installed in Centaurs and early Cromwells, but the new 75mm gun was installed in Cromwell Mark IV onwards and then retrofitted to earlier marks. Secondary armament consisted of

Below: *British Cromwell tank in action in the French town of Vernon on 27 August 1944. It is using HE shells from its 6-pounder (57mm) main gun to destroy a German machine-gun post that is holding up the advance.*

SPECIFICATIONS

Country of origin: United Kingdom.
Crew: 5.
Armament: One 6pounder gun; one 7.92mm BESA machine-gun to co-axial with main armament; one 7.92mm BESA machine-gun in hull (Marks 1 to III); one 75mm QF Mark V or VA gun; two 7.92mm machine-guns (Marks IV, V and VII); one 95mm howitzer; two 7.92mm BESA machine-guns (Marks VI and VIII).
Armor: 0.31in (8mm) minimum; 3in (76mm) maximum; 0.4in (10mm) minimum; 3in (76mm) maximum in welded variants; 4in (102mm) appliqué armor.
Dimensions: Length 20ft 10in (6.35m); width 10ft (3.04m); height 9ft 3in (2.84m).
Weight: 61,600lb (27,942kg).
Engine: Rolls-Royce Meteor V-12 water-cooled petrol engine developing 600hp at 2.250rpm.
Performance: Road speed 40mph (64km/h); cross-country speed 18mph (29km/h); range 173 miles (277km); vertical obstacle 3ft (0.92m); trench 7ft 6in (2.28m).

two 0.3in BESA machine-guns, one coaxial with the 75mm, the other in the hull to the driver's left. Later in the war most of these machine-guns were removed, with the hole blanked over by an armored plate. Ammunition comprised 64 rounds of 75mm and 4,950 rounds of 0.3in.

The suspension was Christie-type, adapted from the A13, but strengthened and widened and gave an excellent ride. However, it was not capable of the planned 40mph (64km/h) and from the Mark V onwards the drive was geared down to hold maximum speed to 32mph (52km/h).

The Meteor engine gave little trouble, the first engines were built by Rolls-Royce to get the design right, but production then switched to other companies. As soon as

these engines became available they were installed in new production tanks and retrofitted into the Liberty-powered tanks. All these tanks were then designated A27(M) Cromwell (M = Meteor).

Cromwell was fast, agile and popular with its crews. Maintenance was not too difficult, with the reliability of the Meteor being particularly appreciated by those who had had to wrestle the vagaries of overstrained Liberty and inaccessible AEC engines in previous designs. They were used for training during 1943-44, the opportunity for action not coming until the Normandy invasion, when the British 7th Armoured Division and some reconnaissance regiments took it to France. After the breakout they were able to use

the Cromwell as it had been intended - exploiting the breakout. Supported by 95mm Howitzer CS versions, Cromwell squadrons out-maneuvered the heavier German tanks. Although they were always outgunned by their opponents, Cromwell crews relied on superior training and maneuverability for their success.

Below: *British Cromwell crew relax in a field, June 15, 1944; their unit, HQ 22 Armoured Brigade, had been cut-off for three days.*

Right above: *British Cromwell; note driver's hatch and port (both open), hull machine-gun and coaxial machine-gun (right of main gun).*

Right below: *Cromwell III armed with 6pounder main gun; note blanked-off machine-gun mounting to the right of driver's position.*

PzKpfw VI Tiger I Heavy Battle Tank

❖

IN 1937, AND DESPITE that fact that PzKpfw IIIs and IVs were starting to reach front-line units, the General Staff issued a new requirement for an even larger and heavier "breakthrough" tank, which would lead armored assaults. After some design work had been done, the project was allowed to lapse. But, when PzKpfw IIIs and IVs proved less successful than had been expected against the heavily armored French and British tanks in 1940, and were then thoroughly outclassed by Soviet T-34s and KV-1s in Russia, a new requirement for a heavy tank was issued. This had to mount the successful 8.8cm high-velocity gun and to be sufficiently well armored to defeat present and future anti-tank weapons. Porsche and Henschel submitted designs, both based on the work done in 1937, and both designs shared the same Krupp-designed turret. However, the Porsche was rejected and the Henschel tank was ordered into production in August 1942. as PzKpfw VI Tiger.

The Tiger's hull was a simple, box-like unit with a one-piece superstructure on

top, all welded. Most surfaces were vertical, but the armor was thick: front 3.94in (100mm); sides 3.15in (80mm); and decks 1.02in (26mm). Shapes were kept simple to assist production. Inside, were four compartments, the driver and hull gunner being separated in front, with the gearbox between them. The fighting compartment was fairly normal, although

Below: *Tiger I of SS-Division Leibstandarte in Normandy, 1944. Note the long barrel of the 88mm gun, interleaved roadwheel suspension, and Zimmerit anti-magnetic coating on all vertical surfaces.*

SPECIFICATIONS

Country of origin: Germany.
Crew: 5.
Armament: One 8.8cm *KwK* 36 L/56 gun; one 7.92mm MG 34 machine-gun co-axial with main armament; one 7.92mm MG 34 machine-gun in hull.
Armor: 1.02in (26mm) minimum; 4.33in (100mm) maximum.
Dimensions: Length 27ft (8.25m); width 12ft 3in (3.73m); height 9ft 4in (2.85m).
Weight: 121,253lb (55,000kg).

Engine: Maybach HL 230 P 45 V-12 water-cooled inline petrol engine developing 700bhp at 3,000rpm.
Performance: Road speed 24mph (38km/h); cross-country speed 12mph (20km/h); range 62 miles (100km); vertical obstacle 2ft 7in (0.8m); trench 5ft 11in (1.8m); fording depth 4ft (1.2m); gradient 35 degrees. (*Note: Data relate to t he Tiger I Ausf E.*)

there was little room to spare when the full load of 92 rounds of 8.8cm ammunition was stowed. These shells could penetrate 4.4in (112mm) of armor at 492 yards (450m) - more than enough for enemy tanks of the day.

The suspension consisted of eight interleaved road wheels, giving a comfortable ride, but it was very complicated, with 16 torsion-bars beneath the floor. But the major difficulty was that they froze together in the Russian winter nights, jamming the track, and having discovered this, the Russians often timed their attacks for dawn, when they could be reasonably sure that the Tigers would be immobilized. A further complication was that the tracks were too wide for rail transport, so that the outer roadwheels had to be removed and narrower tracks fitted.

The fourth compartment housed the Maybach engine, which was changed in late 1943 to one of slightly greater power, but in general it was sufficiently reliable and powerful. The difficulty was that the tank's range was always too limited, while top speed was low because of the need to gear down the transmission. The weight was too great for the usual German clutch-and-brake steering, so Henschel adapted

the British Merritt-Brown regenerative system and coupled it to a pre-selector Maybach gearbox with eight forward speeds. The result was a set of controls which were very light for the driver, but difficult to maintain and repair.

It was intended that the Tiger would be deployed in special battalions of 30 vehicles, each under the control of an army or corps headquarters, and, in general, this was done, although some armored divisions were given their own Tiger battalions, particularly those of the Waffen-SS. Hitler took a personal interest in this impressive new tank and ordered it to be used at the earliest opportunity. As a result, Tigers were thrown into battle for the first time in the late summer of 1942, when they were committed near Leningrad, thinly spread out, in small

Left below: Crews of a Tiger I (right) and PzKpfw IV (left) stop for a chat in Normandy, 1944. Note the massive mantlet at the base of the barrel, designed to prevent incoming anti-tank rounds entering the turret.

Right below: Tiger I of SS-Panzer Abteilung 101 passes through a Normandy village in 1944, with the crew appearing remarkably formal. Note the track sections on the bow-plate, which enhanced anti-tank protection.

numbers, and on difficult ground; the result was a fiasco, as was the Kursk battle next year. When used in ambush, however, where its gun could inflict the most damage, the Tiger was supreme; indeed, in 1944 a single Tiger held up an entire division in France, knocking out 25 Allied tanks before it was destroyed.

The Tiger was fearsome but had its problems and was phased out of production in August 1944, by which time some 1,300 had been completed.

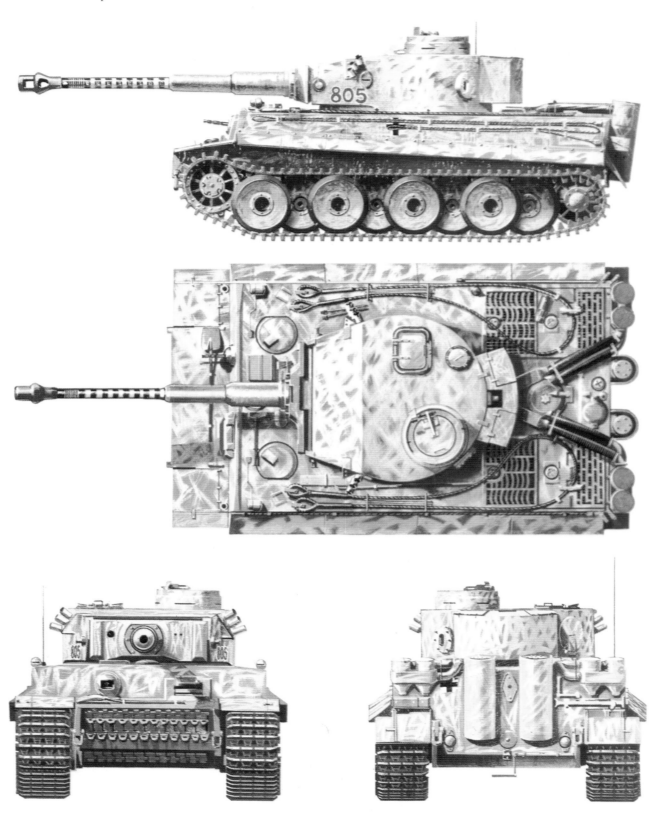

Opposite: *Views of the PzKpfw VI Tiger I (Ausf H) of the 1st SS Panzer Division, "Leibstandarte Adolf Hitler," as used on the Russian Front. The bands around the barrel of the 88mm KwK L/56 gun indicate the number of enemy tanks killed.*

Below: *Tiger I (Ausf E) captured by the British in Tunisia. The British first encountered the Tiger in February 1943 near Pont du Fahs in Tunisia, when 6-pounders engaged two Tigers and nine PzKpfw IIIs and IVs. Both Tigers were knocked out at 500 yards.*

Below bottom: *An unusual combination, with a Tiger I tank passing an Italian Army machine-gun team, which is armed with a tripod-mounted German MG 42 light machine-gun. This picture was almost certainly taken in Russia, where German tank units often had to support the Italians, whose own tanks were very second-rate compared to the latest German and Russian types.*

Left: *A British infantryman takes cover and pauses for breath, totally ignoring the debris of war to his left. The boots belong to a dead SS-trooper, while just beyond him lies a German 51mm mortar. On the right is the nose of an abandoned Tiger I, giving a good close-up view of the Zimmerit anti-magnetic coating and the hull machine-gun position.*

Below: *The Tiger I was first seen by the British in North Africa, where this specimen is being examined by a group of obviously impressed officers and soldiers near Tunis. For its day, it was huge in size, while its armament - the legendary 88mm gun - was the most powerful tank gun in the world.*

Left: *Men of the famous Durham Light Infantry - the "DLI" - pause to take cover behind a wrecked Tiger I in the bocage country of Normandy, just inland from the D-day invasion beaches on 28 June 1944. The soldier on the left holds a Lee-Enfield 0.303in No 4 rifle, with spike bayonet "fixed." His comrade is carrying a Bren 0.303in light machine-gun, and is clearly looking for an opportunity to use it.*

Ram I/II Cruiser Tanks

❖

A T THE START OF WORLD WAR II the Canadian Army had a few antique tanks for training and urgently sought a modern design. It was decided to use the chassis of the American M3 Grant, but redesigned to accept a new turret. The prototype Ram I was completed in June 1941; production started later that year, but only 50 were built before production switched to the improved Ram II.

Ram I had an all-cast hull, with the driver seated at the front right, with a machine-gun turret to his left, armed with a 0.3in machine-gun. The turret contained the other three crew members. Main armament was a 2-pounder gun with a 0.3in M1919A4 machine-gun mounted co-axially. A second machine-gun was mounted on the commander's cupola for use in the anti-aircraft role. Ram I carried 171 rounds of 2-pounder and 4,275 rounds of 0.3in machine-gun ammunition.

Ram II was armed with a 6-pounder gun, and the small turret on the hull front was replaced by a ball-type mounting. Ammunition comprised 92 rounds

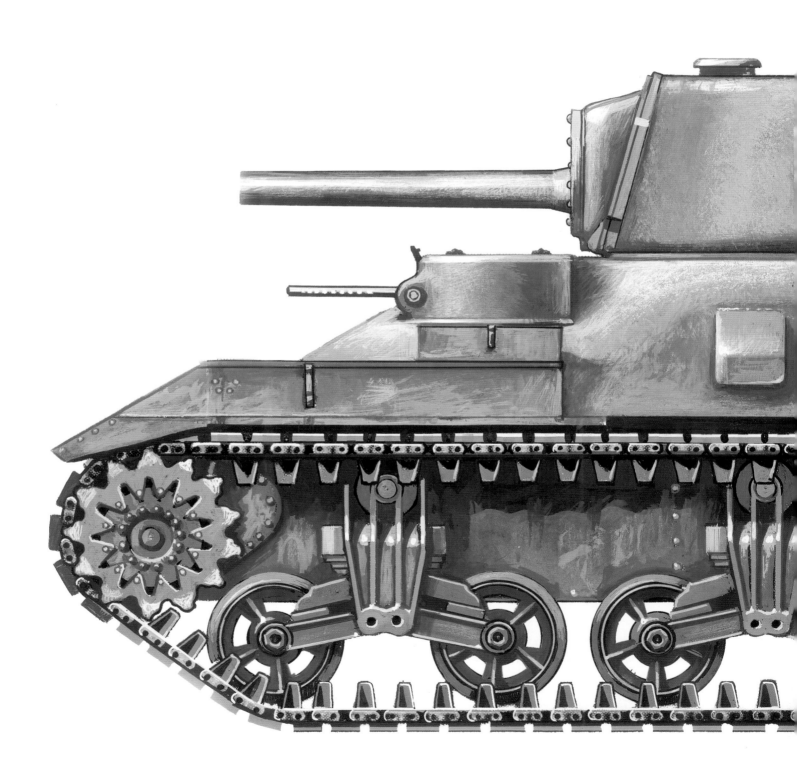

6-pounder and 4,000 rounds 0.3in. Other modifications included elimination of the side doors in the hull, and new suspension, clutch and air cleaners. Production ended in July 1943, with 1,899 completed. Most Rams were shipped to Britain for use by the Canadian armored divisions, but these formations were re-equipped with Shermans before D-day; the Ram never saw combat.

Below: This Canadian Ram I was based on the Grant chassis, but with the sponson-mounted 75mm deleted, a much larger turret mounting a British 2pounder, and a small 0.3in machine-gun turret on the driver's left.

SPECIFICATIONS

Country of origin: Canada.
Crew: 5.
Armament: One 2pounder gun; one .3in machine-gun co-axial with main armament; one .3in machine-gun in cupola on hull top; one .3in machine-gun for anti-aircraft use.
Armor: 90mm (3.56in) maximum.
Dimensions: Length 19ft (5.971m); width 9ft 5in (2.87m); height 8ft 9in (2.667m).

Weight: Combat 64,000lb (29,030kg).
Engine: Continental R975-EC2 nine-cylinder radial developing 400bhp at 2,400rpm.
Performance: Road speed 25mph (40.2km/h); ro   range 144 miles (232km); vertical obstacl   ft (0.609m); trench 7ft 5in (2.26m); grad   60 per cent.

PzKpfw V Panther Battle Tank

Until the invasion of Soviet Russia, the PzKpfw IV was the heaviest German tank and had proved reasonably adequate, but when it first met the Soviet T-34 in October 1941 it was totally outclassed. The Soviet concept of sloped armor, high speed and maneuverability brought about a profound change in German thinking and a new staff requirement was hastily prepared. Initially, and in order to save time, consideration was given to producing a direct copy of the T-34, but national pride prevented this and the requirement issued in January 1942 simply incorporated all the T-34 features.

Progress was rapid, with designs submitted in April 1942 and the first prototypes running in September. The MAN design was chosen for production and after the usual multitude of modifications resulting from testing the prototypes, the first production tank was rolled-out in January 1943. From then on production forged ahead, but never reached the ambitious target of 600

vehicles a month set by Hitler. There were many difficulties, among them the engine and transmission were overstressed to cope with the weight, cooling was inadequate, engines caught fire, and the wheel rims gave trouble.

Once again, Hitler's enthusiasm resulted in another fiasco, this time at Kursk in July

Left below: *A batch of brand-new Panther tanks leaving the MAN factory en route for front-line units.*

Right below: *Ground action is in front, but commander and loader of this camouflaged Panther are watching for Allied aircraft.*

SPECIFICATIONS

Country of origin: Germany.
Crew: 5.
Armament: One 7.5cm *KwK* 42 L/70 gun; two 7.92mm MG 34 machine-guns.
Armor: 0.6in (20mm) minimum; 4.72in (120mm) maximum.
Dimensions: Length 22ft 6in (6.68m); width 10ft 10in (3.3m); height 9ft 8in (2.95m). (Dimensional data relate to the *Ausf* G.)

Weight: 98,766lb (44,800kg).
Engine: Maybach HL 230 P 30 V-12 water-cooled petrol engine developing 700bhp at 3,000rpm.
Performance: Road speed 29mph (46km/h); cross-country speed 15mph (24km/h); range 110 miles (177km); vertical obstacle 3ft (0.9m); trench 6ft3in (1.9m); fording depth 4ft 7in (1.4m); gradient 35 degrees.

1943. Most Panthers broke down on the journey from the railhead, few survived the first day and those that did had to be sent back to the factory to be rebuilt. Later models corrected these faults, and the Panther soon became a fine tank which was superior to the T-34/76 and very popular with its crews.

There was a large one-piece glacis plate in which were originally two apertures, one for the gunner and one for the driver, but in the Ausfall G the driver used a periscope, reducing the holes to one. Frontal protection was excellent. The turret was well sloped, although rather cramped inside, but the commander had a good cupola. The mantlet was massive, with tiny holes for the machine-gun and the gunner's binocular sight.

The suspension used interleaved bogies sprung on torsion bars, giving the Panther the best ride of any German tank during the war, but, as with Tiger I and II, the bogies could freeze up when clogged with snow in Russian winters, immobilizing the vehicle. Maintenance was also difficult since the outer wheels had to be removed to allow access to the inner ones. Steering was by hydraulically operated disk brakes and epicyclic gears to each track, which allowed the tracks to be stopped separately when required without loss of power. It was an adaption of the Merritt-Brown system,

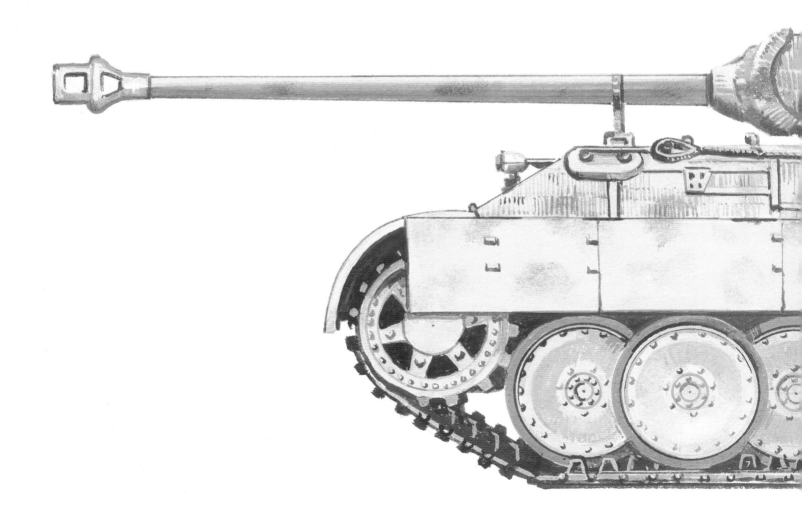

but rather more complicated in design.

The long 75mm gun (with 79 rounds) could penetrate 4.72in (120mm) of sloped plate at 1,094 yards (100m) and this, together with the protection of the thick frontal armor, meant that the Panther could stand-off from Allied tanks and knock them out without being harmed itself. The US Army reckoned that it took five Shermans to knock out one Panther and over 5,000 Panthers had been built by the end of the war. After 1943 the Germans needed numbers of tanks rather than improved designs, and the Panther was simplified to ease production. The hull sides were sloped more, the mantlet was thickened to prevent shot being deflected into the decking, and the gearbox was improved to cope with the weight problem.

Despite its complexity and high manufacturing cost, the Panther was a

Below: *Panther was an outstanding design, although, with a combat weight of 44.3 tons (45 tonnes), it was at the very top end of what could be described as a "medium" tank. The interleaved roadwheels, sprung on torsion bars, gave the best ride of any German World War II tank, but it was a complicated system and liable to seize solid when clogged with snow in a Russian winter and left for any length of time, such as overnight.*

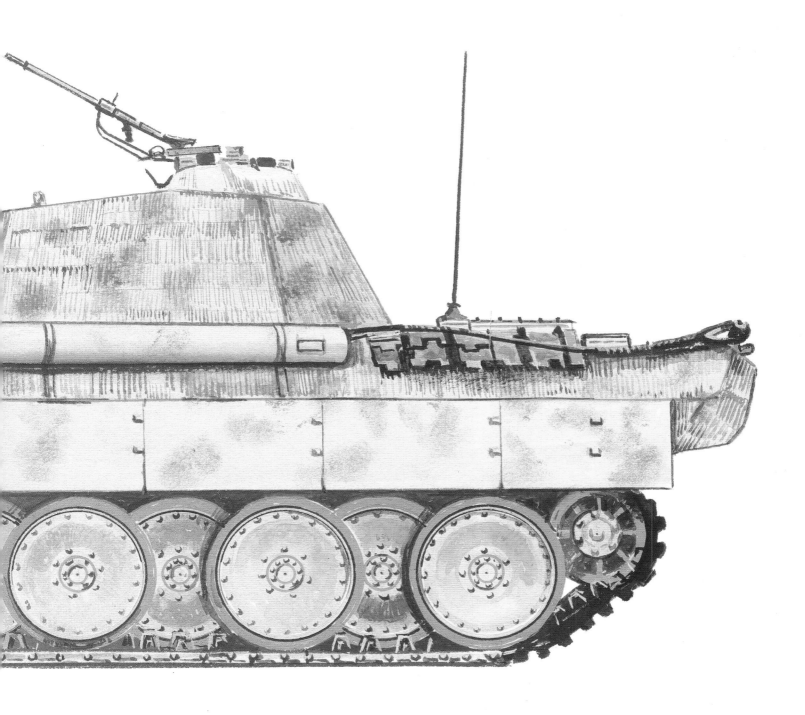

successful design and many consider it to have been one of the best tanks produced during the war. Towards the end of the war its petrol engine and complications were distinct disadvantages, but it was a powerful supplement to the PzKpfw IVs of the armored formations, and it was really only defeated by the overwhelming Allied air strength.

Left below: *PzKpfw V Panther in hull-down fire position during defense of Rome, Italy in 1944.*

Right below: *A very tired funker (radio operator) takes a breather. Note the thick coating of Zim-merit on the mantlet behind him; this was applied as a paste, and when almost dry was patterned with a large "comb" in order to ensure that magnetic mines could not adhere to the tank's outer skin.*

Below: *In action on the Russia steppes, a PzKpfw V Panther and a panzer grenadier machine-gun crew. Although other armies in the 1930s studied the combination of tanks and infantry on the battlefield, it was the Germans who brought it to its highest standard of perfection in the early campaigns of World War II but they were later matched by the Allies.*

Inset: *Although designed in a rush to counter the Soviet Army's T-34, the Panther was also a remarkable design. This picture shows how the glacis plate was very well angled to ensure that incoming, flat trajectory anti-tank rounds would bounce-off. Note also the smooth, well-sloped lines of the turret, and the huge mantlet which added to the frontal protection for the crew.*

A34 Comet Cruiser Tank

❖

BY 1942 IT WAS CLEAR that British tank guns could not defeat the latest German tanks and the 6-pounder, which had entered service in mid-1942, was too small and lacked an HE shell. Thus, in early 1943 it was decided to find a suitable gun which would then be mounted in a new tank using as many Cromwell components as possible. To achieve this, Vickers modified the successful 17-pounder anti-tank gun, producing a lighter, more compact weapon, firing the same projectile, but using a shorter, wider cartridge case. The gun was slightly less powerful than the original 17-pounder, but far ahead of any gun carried on Allied battle tanks at that time. To avoid confusion in names and ammunition supply, the new gun was designated the Vickers HV (= high velocity) 77mm.

The mock-up of the new tank, the A34 Comet, was ready in September 1943 followed by the first prototypes in early 1944, but much redesign was found necessary, and what started as an up-gunned Cromwell soon became a virtually

new vehicle. The hull was largely untouched, leading to criticism that the unnecessary hull machine-gun had been retained and with it the vertical (as opposed to sloped) glacis plate. Despite front line pressures to get the tank into service, continual modifications meant that the first production models were not delivered until September 1944, not reaching the first units until just before Christmas. The 11th Armoured Division was reequipped in early 1945, but the pace slowed as the war ended.

The hull was welded, as was the turret, although the latter also had a cast mantlet and frontal armor. Internal space was adequate and access fairly easy, while ammunition was stowed in armored bins, a major advance. The turret was electrically traversed, with the generator driven by the main engine. It had been intended that the suspension would be identical with Cromwell's, but this was inadequate for the extra weight, so it was strengthened and given four return rollers. With this suspension the Comet was remarkably agile and its cross-country

SPECIFICATIONS

Country of origin: United Kingdom.
Crew: 5.
Armament: One 77mm gun; one 7.92mm BESA machine-gun co-axial with main armament; one 7.92mm BESA machine-gun.
Armor: 102mm (4in) maximum; 14mm (0.55in) minimum.
Dimensions: Length 25ft 1½in (7.66m); width 10ft (3.04m); height 8ft 9½in (2.98m).

Weight: Combat 78,800lb (35,696kg).
Engine: Rolls-Royce Meteor Mark 3 V-12 water-cooled petrol engine developing 600bhp at 2,550rpm.
Performance: Road speed 32mph (51km/h), range 123 miles (196km); vertical obstacle 3ft (0.92m); trench 8ft (2.43m); gradient 35 per cent.

speed could often be more than the crew could tolerate with comfort. The Meteor engine had adequate power for all needs and on a cross-country training course a good driver could handle a Comet like a sports car - and frequently did. There was only one mark of Comet, with just one minor variant which involved a minor change to the exhaust cowls.

The Comet was the last fully developed British tank to take part in World War II. It was criticized strongly at first, but most

of the users' exasperation sprang from frustration the best tank Britain had ever produced came so late that it never had a chance to prove itself properly.

Left below: *Comet was the tank the British Army had wanted throughout the war; fast, agile, and well-armed, with good protection.*

Right below: *In service at last a Comet cooperating with infantry during the final advance into Germany in early 1945; it had some faults but was overall very satisfactory.*

PzKpfw VI Tiger II Heavy Battle Tank

◆◆

The Tiger I had hardly entered service before the German General Staff requested a bigger and better successor, which had to be superior in armor and hitting power to anything that the Soviet Army was likely to produce. Once again Porsche and Henschel were asked for designs which were to incorporate the latest sloped armor and the latest 71-caliber 8.8cm gun. Porsche updated its Tiger I design, but its ideas of electric transmission were once again rejected, in part because supplies of copper were far too limited. As a result, the contract again went to Henschel, but unfortunately Porsche had been so convinced that it would win that it had already started work on the turret and actually put casting in hand. As a result, 50 Porsche turrets were completed and installed in the first models, following which Henschel fitted its own turret, which was both simpler and had better protection. Another requirement was that Henschel should liaise with MAN in order to standardize as many parts as possible with the proposed

Panther II, which never appeared, although the consultations meant that production of Tiger II did not get under way until December 1943.

The Tiger II, known to the Germans as Königstiger and to the Allies as the Royal Tiger, was a massive and formidable vehicle. It was intended to dominate the battlefield, which it could do, providing that it was used sensibly. It was the

Below: *US troops examine a Tiger II which ran out of fuel during the Battle of the Bulge. The Allies had nothing to compare with these huge, well-armed and well-protected heavy tanks.*

SPECIFICATIONS

Country of origin: Germany.
Crew: 5.
Armament: One 8.8cm *KwK* 43 L/71 gun; two 7.92mm MG 34 machine-guns.
Armor: 1.57in (40mm) minimum; 7.28in (185mm) maximum.
Dimensions: Length 23ft 9in (7.25m); width 12ft 3in (4.27m); height 10ft 1in (3.27m).
Weight: 153,000lb (69,400kg).

Engine: Maybach HL 230 P 30 V-12 water-cooled inline petrol engine developing 600bhp at 3,000rpm.
Performance: Road speed 24mph (38km/h); cross-country speed 11mph (17km/h); range 68 miles (110km); vertical obstacle 2ft 9in (0.85m); trench 8ft 2 in (2.5m); fording depth 5ft 3in (1.6m); gradient 35 degrees.

heaviest, best protected and most powerfully armed tank to go into production during World War II, and its armor and gun would do justice to a main battle tank today. The price paid for all this superiority was considerable size, great weight and low performance. Ground pressure was high and agility was poor, the inevitable consequence being that the engine and transmission were overstressed, reliability decreased, and demands on the maintenance system increased.

The hull was welded, as it had been in Tiger I, but, as a result of experience fighting T-34, the armor was much better sloped. Hull layout was similar to that of the Panther, and the large turret was roomy although the gun came right back to the rear wall and made a complete partition longitudinally. Some 80 rounds of ammunition were stowed round the turret sides and floor and there were plenty of racks and shelves for the minor equipment. The commander's cupola allowed an excellent view, though he usually chose to have his head out of the top. The long, powerful 8.8cm gun outranged and out-shot the main armament of nearly all Allied tanks,

enabling the Tiger II to stand-off and engage targets, as it chose. Barrel wear was a difficulty with this high velocity gun, and the later models had a two-piece barrel which allowed the faster-wearing part to be changed easily.

Only one model was built, and altogether no more than 485 examples were completed. Production never suffered, despite the heaviest Allied bombing, and Henschel always had at least 60 vehicles in construction on its shop floors at any one time. At the peak it was taking only 14 days to complete a Tiger II. Severe fuel shortages forced the factory to use bottled gas for testing, though petrol was supplied for operations.

The Tiger II was introduced into service in the autumn of 1944, on the same distribution as the Tiger I, and again in

Below: *A Tiger II (known to the Western Allies as "Royal Tiger") carrying Waffen-SS Panzer Grenadiers during the Battle of the Bulge, the attempted German breakthrough in December 1944. Note the size of the tank, and the very well-sloped glacis plate, which is broken only by the port for the hull machine-gun, a weapon whose role had virtually disappeared by this time in the war.*

small platoons of four or five. Its enormous size and weight made it a ponderous vehicle, often difficult to conceal; in a fast moving battle it was quickly left behind, and this fate did occur to several in Russia. But when used properly it was enormously effective and could engage many times its own numbers of enemy, and knock them all out without damage to itself.

Right: *The Tiger II was not suitable for highly mobile armored warfare of the type conducted on the plains of eastern Europe by German Panthers and Soviet T-34s. It was, however, an immensely successful ambush weapon, and a small number of Tiger IIs, suitably sited, particularly in close country and urban areas, could hold up large numbers of enemy, using the combination of the very powerful 88mm gun and the thick, well-sloped armored protection.*

Left: *Tiger II in a square in the Hungarian capital, Budapest, in the summer of 1944. The figures show just how large this tank was: some 10ft (3.2m) high and 24ft (7.3m) long and weighing 68 tons (69.4 tonnes). The gun was the famous 88mm, with a crewman fitting a cover to protect the inside of the barrel.*

Left: *The turret of the Tiger II was very narrow, thus greatly reducing the frontal area exposed to the enemy. Note also the thickness of the armor plating and the Zimmerit coating.*

Below: *A Tiger II which ran out of fuel on the Stavelot road, during the Battle of the Bulge, leaving its crew no option but to surrender.*

M22 Locust Light Tank (Airborne)

❖

IN FEBRUARY 1941 THE US Army issued an operational requirement for an airportable tank, weighing no more than 7.5 tons (7,620kg). The winning design came from Marmon-Herrington with a pilot model being ordered in May 1941 under the designation Light Tank T9 (Airborne). The first T9 had a welded hull, cast turret, vertical volute spring suspension and weighed 7.9 tons (8,027kg). The improved T9E1 had a modified turret, with added power traverse and a gyrostabilizer; the front plate was modified and the two bow machine-guns removed. The tank was also fitted with brackets to enable it to be slung beneath a C-54 cargo aircraft, although this involved removing the turret, a system which was tested and worked, but never used operationally. A total of 1,900 was ordered, although when production was ended in February 1944 only 830 had been delivered.

The M22 Locust was also supplied to the British who used it in small numbers in the crossing of the Rhine in March 1945,

the tanks being carried in the Hamilcar glider. The Locust was an unsatisfactory design, primarily because its thin armor could be defeated by 0 .5in AP rounds. It was also underpowered and, with a 37mm cannon, was also undergunned. A proposed modification using a breechloading 81mm mortar was tested but not produced.

Left below: *British-manned M22 Locust light tank emerging from a Hamilcar transport glider.*

Right below: *The M22 Locust looked like a good design, but the armor was thin, it was underpowered and also undergunned.*

SPECIFICATIONS

Country of origin: USA.
Crew: 3.
Armament: One 37mm M6 gun; one 37mm M1919A4 co-axial machine-gun.
Armor: 9mm to 25mm (0.35–0.98in).
Dimensions: Length 12ft 11in (3.32m); width 7ft 4in (2.23m); height 5ft 8in (1.74m).
Weight: Combat 17,024lb (7,722kg).

Engine: Lycoming 0-435T six-cylinder horizontally-opposed petrol engine developing 162hp at 3,000rpm.
Performance: Road speed 40mph (64km/h), cross-country speed 27mph (43km/h); road range 135 miles (216km); vertical obstacle 1ft 4in (0.4m); trench 5ft 5in (1.65m); gradient 52 per cent; fording depth 3ft 6in (1.1m).

M24 Chaffee Light Tank

T HE M24 WAS AN EXCELLENT DESIGN, combining outstanding firepower and protection, with very good agility. Its 75mm gun was almost the equal of that of the Sherman while the careful shaping and sloping of the hull and turret resulted in the elimination of shot traps and reduction of the silhouette. Ease of maintenance was another attribute.

The M5A1, an improved version of the M3 Stuart (q.v.) had entered service in 1942 but such was the pace of wartime development that it was already obsolete and attention had already moved to a new light tank. This was required to be a substantial improvement on the M5A1 and, in particular, that it should mount a 75mm gun and the suspension improved. The power train of the M5A1 was to be retained, gross weight should not exceed 16 tons (16,257kg), and the armor should be a maximum of 1in (25mm) thickness and acutely angled to the horizontal.

Cadillac (a division of General Motors) delivered pilot models, designated T24, to meet the stated requirements in October

1943 and 1,000 were ordered before service tests had even begun. Main armament was the M6 75mm lightweight gun, which had been developed from an aircraft weapon. Power was provided by twin Cadillac engines mounted on rails for ease of maintenance, but otherwise identical with those of the M5Al. A major

Left below: US Army M24 Chaffee light tank in Belgium in 1944. Main gun was 75mm, a heavy weapon for a light tank at that time.

Right below: An M24 Chaffee in post-war service with the French Army, who used large numbers in the Indochina war.

SPECIFICATIONS

Country of origin: USA.
Crew: 5, sometimes reduced to 4.
Armament: One 75mm M6 gun; one .3in M1919A4 machine-gun co-axial with main armament; one .3in M1919A4 machine-gun; one .5in M2 machine-gun; one 2in M3 smoke mortar.
Armor: 109mm (0.375in) minimum; 38mm (1.5in) maximum.
Dimensions: Length 18ft (5.49m); width 9ft 8in (2.95m); height 8ft 2in (2.77m).

Weight: Combat 40,500lb (18,370kg).
Engine: Two Cadillac 44T24 V-8 water-cooled petrol engines each developing 110hp at 3,400rpm.
Performance: Road speed 34mph (54km/h), road range 100 miles (160km); vertical obstacle 3ft (0.91m); trench 8ft (2.44m); fording depth 3ft 4in (1.02m) unprepared and 6ft 6in (1.98m) prepared; gradient 60 per cent.

innovation was that the new tank had torsion-bar suspension, with five pairs of stamped disk, rubber-tired 25in (63.5cm) diameter wheels, mounted on each side, with the drive sprocket at the front (It is often thought that torsion-bar suspension was a German World War II invention; in fact a US patent was taken out in 1936). The hull was of all welded construction, reaching a maximum thickness on frontal surfaces of 2.5in (63.5mm) although thinner in less critical places. In July 1944 the T24 was standardized as the M24 Light Tank, popularly known as the "Chaffee," and by June 1945 a total of 4,070 had been produced. Other vehicles using the M24 chassis were designed for specialist applications, including gun and mortar carriages, an anti-aircraft version, cargo carriers, and also an armored recovery vehicle.

The M-24 was used by many armies, one of its most remarkable adventures being with the French, who, in 1954, flew ten tanks into the remote fortress of Dien Bien Phu. Each tank had to be completely broken down into its basic components which were then flown to the fortress in five C-47 and two Bristol Freighter aircraft, and then re-assembled.

Below: *An M24 Chaffee conducts a range-firing exercise with its 75mm main gun. Note that the outer edges of the tracks of this tank have been extended by approximately 12in (30cm) to improve performance over soft ground (compare with standard tracks on the tank on pages 312-313).*

PzKpfw VIII Maus Heavy Tank

❖

DURING THE COURSE OF World War II the Germans directed considerable effort and resources to developing super-heavy AFVs, only making significant progress with the PzKpfw VIII Maus (= mouse). In June 1942, a suggestion was made to Dr Porsche, the car designer and then head of the German Tank Commission, concerning the possibility of producing a tank mounting a 128mm or even 150mm gun in a revolving turret, which would also include a co-axial 75mm gun. Porsche passed this proposal on to Hitler, even though the majority of German tank designers and the leading theoreticians of tank warfare were totally opposed to it, and the Fuhrer agreed. At that time the project was referred to as Mammut (= mammoth), and the Alkett company began assembly of the first tank in August 1943.

The new tank, now referred to, somewhat ironically, as Maus, made its first trial run on 23 December 1943 and then went to Böblingen for further trials which, apart from a few suspension problems, were also successful. In October

the tank went to the proving ground at Kummersdorf, where it was joined by the second prototype (Maus II) which had a different (and very troublesome) engine. By the end of the war a further nine prototypes were in various stages of construction, and production plans had been made for 150.

Below: *Several prototypes of this massive vehicle were running by May 1945, but it was all a waste of effort and resources.*

Inset: *Designed by Hitler's favorite designer, Porsche, the Maus weighed some 185 tons and was armed with a 128mm gun.*

SPECIFICATIONS

Country of origin: Germany.
Crew: 6.
Armament: One 12.8cm *KwK* L/55 gun; one 7.5cm L/36.5 gun co-axial with main armament; one 2cm cannon.
Armor: 1.57in (40mm) minimum; 13.78in (350mm) maximum.
Dimensions: Length (including gun) 30ft 10in (10.1m); width 11ft 2 in (3.67m); height 11ft 9in (3.63m).

Weight: 414,465lb (188,000kg).
Engine: Daimler-Benz MB 509 V-12 water-cooled inline petrol engine developing 1,080hp at 2,400rpm.
Performance: Road speed 12.5mph (20km/h); range 116 miles (186km); vertical obstacle 2ft 2in (0.72m); trench 13ft 9in (4.5m); gradient 30 degrees.

M26 Pershing Heavy Tank

❖

DEVELOPMENT OF THE M26 began in 1942 with the T20 medium tank, which was intended to test improvements for a successor to the M4 Sherman, such as different armaments, transmissions and suspensions. These led on to two experimental heavy tanks, T25 and T26, and of the two, the T26 was given a higher priority. In the T26E1 a Ford engine drove the vehicle through a hydraulic torque converter in series with planetary reduction gearing; known as the "torquematic" transmission, this gave three forward ratios and one reverse gear. The hull was fabricated from a combination of castings and rolled plate, the turret was cast, and the tank used a torsion-bar suspension.

In 1943-44, roughly the mid-point of the war, there was some disagreement over what would be required in a new tank. Armored Command, the highest HQ in the army's professional tank corps, objected to heavy tanks in general, on the grounds of their weight and size, but did want a tank capable of mounting the new

and urgently needed 90mm gun. Army Ground Forces headquarters, the senior army HQ in the Continental United States, wanted 1,000 T26s armed with the 90mm gun, together with 7,000 of the generally similar but lighter T25s armed with the 75mm gun. Headquarters European Theater, however, which was located in England, foresaw no requirement for

Below: *The M26 Pershing was heavy by US World War II standards and mounted what was then thought to be a big gun - a 90mm - today 120mm and 125mm are standard and there are trials with 140mm guns.*

SPECIFICATIONS

Country of origin: USA.
Crew: 5, sometimes reduced to 4.
Armament: One 90mm M3 gun; one .3in M1919A4 machine-gun co-axial with main armament; one .3in M1919A4 machine-gun in hull front; one .5in M2 machine-gun on turret roof.
Armor: 13mm (0.51in) minimum; 102mm (4in) maximum.
Dimensions: Length 28ft 5in (8.65m); width 11ft 6in (3.51m); height 9ft 1in (2.78m).

Weight: Combat 92,355lb (41,891kg).
Engine: Ford GAF V-8 water-cooled petrol engine developing 500hp at 2,600rpm.
Performance: Road speed 30mph (48km/h), road range 100 miles (160km); vertical obstacle 3ft 10in (1.17m); trench 8ft (2.44m); fording depth 4ft (1.22m); gradient 60 per cent.

either the 75mm or 76mm guns but wanted tanks armed with a mix of 90mm guns for the anti-tank role and 105mm howitzers for "close support," in the ratio of one 90mm-armed tank to three 105mm close support tanks. Such different perceptions of the role of the tank were quite normal and the outcome was a decision to produce 20 of the T26E3 mounting the 90mm gun and to send them to Europe for a combat trial. Known as the "Zebra Mission" this trial proved the battleworthiness of the T26E3 in combat, and led to the type being placed in production as the M26 Pershing Heavy Tank.

The M26 was armed with the M3 90mm gun, which was fitted with a large, double-baffle muzzle brake. When traveling for any distance out of contact with the enemy the turret was reversed and the barrel supported on a strut mounted on the rear deck. There was also a coaxial 0.3in machine-gun, with a second in a flexible mounting in the glacis plate, and a 0.5in heavy machine-gun on the turret roof.

At the same time the T26E2, armed with the 105mm howitzer, was adopted as the M45 for the close-support role. This had

the same hull and running gear as the M26, but was armed with the M4 105mm howitzer. The original enthusiasm for such a "close support" tank quickly waned, however, and in the event only 185 were procured and these saw only limited service. Such was the pace of progress in tank design that although it had been introduced as a heavy tank, the M26, which had a combat weight of 92,355lb (41,891kg), was soon reclassified as a medium tank.

The M26 entered service too late to make any real contribution to the campaign in Europe, although one did succeed in killing one Tiger and two PzKpfw IV during the 1945 advance into Germany. Production continued well past the end of World War II and the type was widely used in the Korean War and also

Below: *The M45 was a close support version of the M26, with the same hull and running gear and a very similar turret, but armed with a 105mm howitzer. It is important to note that this was seen as a tank and not as a self-propelled artillery piece.*

Inset: *The M26 had a cast turret with a large bustle (overhang) and mounted an M3 90mm gun with a large, double-baffle muzzle-brake. One of these tanks arrived in Europe in time to destroy one Tiger and two PzKpfw IV.*

supplied to many armies in the Free World.

As was usually the case, the M26 Pershing led to a family of specialist vehicles, including a flamethrower tank, cargo tractor and combat engineer vehicle. Consideration was also given to a mine resistant vehicle, based on the M26 chassis, but with considerably enhanced armored protection, which would have been used to breach anti-tank minefields.

The M26 effectively marked the first in a new line of tanks for the US Army, the next being the M47, which was, in essence, an M26 chassis with the turret of the experimental T42 and a new model 90mm gun. This led, in its turn, to the M48, and ultimately to the M60, following which a new line started with the current M1 Abrams.

Below: *A platoon of M26s engage a North Korean target on the far side of the Maktong River in Korea in September 1950. The M26 was the first in a completely new line of US tank development, which led via the M47 and M48 to the M60. When it entered service at the end of World War II, the M26 was classified as a heavy tank, but so rapid was the increase in tank weights that by 1950 it had been reclassified as a medium tank.*

A39 Tortoise Heavy Tank

❖

THE TORTOISE EPITOMIZES the triumph of protection over all else and was actually an assault gun, since it could never have been a "battle tank" in the accepted sense. The main armament was the "32-pounder," which was another name for the well-established 3.7in AA gun. With a caliber of 94mm this was an even more powerful weapon than the German "88," and capable of penetrating any known World War II armor. Indeed, had the gun been mounted in a revolving turret on a proper tank chassis (and there seems no reason why it could not have been), it would have been a world-beater, but in the Tortoise it never stood a chance. This massive vehicle carried a crew of seven and there were three secondary BESA machine-guns, one in the hull front and two in a small turret on the hull roof. There were also 12 smoke dischargers.

The tracks were carried on multi-wheeled bogies with heavy skirting plates, which also acted as carriers for the outward ends of the axles. The geared-down Meteor engine could produce a top

speed of only 12mph (19.2km/h), which was virtually useless. The entire exercise was a great waste of effort and talent, and it is difficult, some 60 years later, to understand what purpose it was intended to fulfill and how the designers thought that it would be moved to, from and around the battlefield.

Below: Tortoise was developed from 1942 as an assault tank. Weighing 78 tons and armed with a 32-pounder (3.7in [94mm]) gun, it was a massive and powerful machine, but whether of any tactical value is another matter.

SPECIFICATIONS

Country of origin: United Kingdom.
Crew: 7.
Armament: One 32pounder gun; three 7.92mm BESA machine-guns.
Armor: 225mm (8.86in) maximum; 35mm (1.38in) minimum.
Dimensions: Length (hull) 23ft 9in (7.24m); length (over gun) 33ft (10.1m); width 12ft 10in (3.91m); height 10ft (3.05m).

Weight: Combat 174,720lb (79,252kg).
Engine: Rolls-Royce Meteor 12-cylinder liquid-cooled petrol engine developing 600hp.
Performance: Speed 12mph (19.2km/h).

ARL-44 Heavy Tank

◆

IN 1938 ATELIER de Construction de Rueil (ARL) started a project to mount a 75mm gun in a new turret on a modified Char B1 chassis. This project was still on the drawing board when France fell in 1940, but design work continued in secret throughout the occupation, and as soon as Paris was liberated in 1944 it was immediately put into production. The first tank was completed in 1946, which, given the state of France, was a considerable achievement. Designated ARL-44 Char de Transition, at one time it was initially intended to build 300.

Tracks and suspension were similar to those of the Char B1bis, but the hull, turret, gun and engine were all completely new. The driver and co-driver were seated at the front with the other three crew members - commander, gunner and loader - in the turret, while the Maybach engine was at the rear. The ARL-44 was to have been followed by the AMX-50, but although prototypes of this later tank were built and tested, the type was not placed in production as large quantities of M47

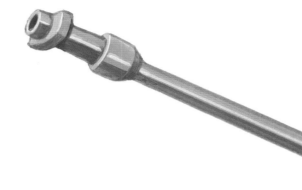

Below: *An ARL-44 on its only public outing during the French 1951 National Day parade. It was armed with a 90mm gun and was essentially a marginally updated 1940 design.*

tanks were available from the USA.

Production of the ARL-44 was undertaken by Renault and Forges et Aciènnies de la Marine et d'Homecourt (FAMH) with turrets supplied by Schneider. Only 60 were built, all being issued to 503rd Armored Regiment; they made one public appearance on the National Day parade on 14 July 1951.

Below: *The ARL-44 was the first French-designed AFV to enter service after World War II. It would have been replaced by the improved ARL-50, but large numbers of US M47 tanks became available under the MDAP and accepting them was the cheaper option.*

SPECIFICATIONS

Country of origin: France.
Crew: 5.
Armament: One 90mm gun; one 7.5mm machine-gun co-axial with main armament; one 7.5mm anti-aircraft machine-gun.
Armor: Not known.
Dimensions: Length 34ft 6in (10.52m); width 11ft 2in (3.4m); height 10ft 6in (3.2m).

Weight: About 105,820lb (48,000kg).
Engine: Maybach petrol engine developing 700hp.
Performance: Road speed 23mph (37.3km/h); range 93 miles (150km); vertical obstacle 3ft (0.93m); trench 9ft (2.75m); gradient 50 per cent.

A41 Centurion Main Battle Tank

Development of the A41 Cruiser started in 1944 and six prototypes were completed before the end of the war, although they arrived in Germany too late to see any combat. With the easing of international tensions and very tight defense budgets, the tank, now named Centurion, did not enter service with the British Army until 1949, with production being undertaken at the Royal Ordnance Factory, Leeds; Vickers, Elswick; and Leyland Motors, Leyland. A total of 4,423 were produced, of which 2,500 were for export and the type saw combat in Korea, India, South Arabia, Vietnam, the Anglo-French Suez campaign, and many Arab-Israeli wars. It proved to be one of the outstanding tanks of the second half of the 20th century.

Centurion had an all-welded steel hull, with a turret of cast armor with the top welded into position. The driver sat at the front of the hull on the right, with the other three crew members in the turret, the commander and gunner on the right and the loader on the left. The engine and

transmission were at the rear, the Meteor engine being a development of the Rolls-Royce Merlin aircraft engine which had powered the World War II Spitfire fighter. The suspension was of the Horstmann type, with three units on each side, each mounting two large road wheels. The drive sprocket was at the rear and the idler at the front, with six track-return rollers, but the top half of the tracks and

Below: *Israeli Armored Corps Centurions advance on the Golan Heights in the 1973 Yom Kippur War. Over 4,000 Centurions were built and served with over 20 armies.*

SPECIFICATIONS

Country of origin: United Kingdom.
Crew: 4.
Armament: One L7 series 105mm gun; one .3in machine-gun co-axial with main armament; one .5in ranging machine-gun; one .3in machine-gun on commander's cupola, six smoke dischargers on each side of the turret.
Armor: 19mm-152mm (0.67in-6.08in) maximum.
Dimensions: Length (gun forward) 32ft 4in (9.85m); length (hull) 25ft 8in (7.82m); width (including skirts) 11ft 1 1/2in (3.39m); height 9ft 10 1/2in (3.01m).
Weight: Combat 114,250lb (51,820kg).
Engine: Rolls-Royce Meteor Mark IVB 12-cylinder liquid-cooled petrol engine developing 650bhp at 2,550rpm.
Performance: Road speed 21.5mph (34.6km/h), range 118 miles (190km); vertical obstacle 3ft (0.91m); trench 11ft (3.35m); gradient 60 per cent.

suspension were concealed from view by armored track skirts, intended to provide protection against HEAT attack.

There were some 25 marks of Centurion, with the early marks armed with a 20-pounder gun and all later marks with the outstanding L7 105mm gun. One of the most important versions was the Mark 13, armed with the fully stabilized L7 105mm gun, which had an elevation of ±20° and a depression of -10∞ in a turret with 360° traverse. A 0.3in machine-gun was mounted co-axially with the main armament, with a similar weapon, pintle-mounted, on the commander's cupola. The Mark 13 also had a 0 .5in machine-gun for the ranging system The tank carried 64 rounds of 105mm, 600 rounds of 0.5in and 4,750 rounds of 0.3in ammunition. When first introduced into service, the Centurion had no night-vision equipment, but later marks had infra-red driving lights and an infra-red searchlight mounted to the left of the main armament.

Those which entered service with the British Army were withdrawn when Chieftain (q.v.) entered service and most were then sold abroad. The major foreign user of Centurions was the Israeli Army, which repeatedly upgraded its fleet, installing more powerful guns, more

powerful and fuel-efficient engines, and additional armor. Surplus Centurion hulls were also converted for use as armored personnel carriers.

South Africa received a number of early model Centurions before the United Nations imposed its defense equipment embargo. During that embargo, the entire South Africa Centurion fleet was upgraded to produce the Olifant Mark 1A, which had a V-12 diesel engine, the South African version of the British L7 105mm gun, and other improvements. These were all subsequently upgraded a second time to the Olifant Mk 1B standard, which involved a complete rebuild, and the installation of a new powerpack, suspension system and electronics, together with appliqué armor on the glacis plate and turret.

Other users scrapped their Centurion fleets in the 1980s and 1990s, but some still remain. A few Swedish Centurions (designated Strv-101 and-102) are deployed on the island of Gotland, while the Austrian Army has scrapped its Centurion hulls, but retained the turrets, which are emplaced as static anti-tank defenses. The Centurion was an outstanding design, its one major weakness being the Meteor petrol engine

which was extremely thirsty. In fact in the 1950s British Centurions used to tow a monowheel fuel trailer, in order to give a reasonable range.

Left: *An early model A41 Centurion with the 20-pounder (83.4mm) gun. Note the well-sloped glacis plate and the large protective mantlet on the gun. Just too late for World War II, the Centurion performed very well in many subsequent wars.*

Below: *During the Korean War, a 20-pounder armed Centurion Mark III negotiates a temporary bridge built by US Army engineers. The Centurion established an excellent reputation in Korea, which led to many foreign sales.*

Below: *A Centurion tank, operated by the Royal Canadian Dragoons, during Exercise Certain Shield in West Germany in November 1973. The bore evacuator mid-way along the barrel and the thermal sleeve denote a 105mm gun. The large "bin" is an infra-red searchlight.*

Opposite top: *A Centurion of the Royal Danish Army. Unusually, the 105mm gun does not have a thermal sleeve. The large object to the right of the gun is an IR searchlight.*

Opposite bottom: *The Centurion served for many years with the South African Army, who regularly upgraded their tanks and also produced their own version, the Olifant.*

Below: *A Centurion gun tank fitted with an experimental mine plough, designed to push the mines to one side, thus enabling the tank to move down a cleared lane.*

T-54/T-55 Main Battle Tanks

❖

THE T-54 AND T-55 main battle tanks are the most widely-used tank of all time; with over 65,000 produced in factories in the Soviet Union, Czechoslovakia and Poland, plus a further 7,000 Type 59s in China. This beats the approximately 50,000-unit production figures of the Soviet T-34 by a handsome margin, and is a record which is unlikely to be broken in the future.

During and in the years immediately following World War II, the Soviet Army's main tank design was the T-34 (q.v.), which when armed with the M1944 85mm gun (as the T-34/85) is generally accepted to have been the finest all-round tank of the war. The T-34 was developed into the T-44, which was produced in small numbers (approximately 200); most were armed with the same 85mm gun, although a few of the last to be built had the new 100mm gun. A significant feature of T-44, repeated in all subsequent Soviet tanks, was that the engine was mounted transversely, reducing overall length and thus saving weight. Nevertheless, T-44 had

many problems, mostly due to a rushed development program, and turned out to be an interim design.

The totally new T-54 appeared in 1949 and was used not only by the Soviet Army, but also by the armies of the newly-formed Warsaw Pact. The T-54 was armed with the D-10T 100mm gun, which fired APHE, HEAT and HE rounds, and was

Below: A platoon of Soviet Army T-55 tanks on a training area in East Germany in August 1979. Note the long-barrelled 100m gun, long-range auxiliary fuel tanks, rounded turret and low, sleek silhouette.

SPECIFICATIONS

Country of origin: Russia.
Crew: 4
Armament: One 100mm gun; one SGMT 7.62mm co-axial machine-gun, two SGMT 7.62mm anti-aircraft machine-guns.
Armor: 150mm (5.9in) maximum.
Dimensions: Length (including main armament) 29ft 6in (9.0m); length (hull) 21ft 2in (6.45m); width 10ft 9in (3.27m); height 7ft 10in (2.4m).

Weight: Combat 91,410lb (41,500kg).
Engine: 12-cylinder four-stroke water-cooled diesel engine developing 630hp at 2,000rpm.
Performance: Road speed 31mph (50km/h); road range with two additional 200l fuel tanks 340 miles (545km); vertical obstacle 2ft 8in (0.8m); trench 8ft 10in (2.7m); gradient 60 per cent.
(Data apply to T-55 AM2B.)

capable of an elevation of +17° and a depression of -4°, the latter being significantly less than in Western tanks and taken as evidence of a primarily attacking role. The turret was virtually hemispherical in shape, which gave good ballistic protection, but made it somewhat cramped inside by Western standards, although crew comfort was never a significant factor in Soviet tank design.

The T-54 was subjected to a constant process of modification and upgrading, and by 1958 it had become sufficiently different to warrant being redesignated the T-55.

First known to the West in 1960, T-55 incorporated many improvements. There was a more powerful engine which not only gave enhanced agility but also gave very long range endurance - 310 miles (500km) with normal fuel but increased to

444 miles (715km) with two 44 gallon (200l) jettisonable tanks mounted on the rear deck. It used the same 100mm main gun as T-54, but with full stabilization and increased the ammunition carried from 34 to 43 rounds. The first production model also retained the bow-mounted machine-gun, although this was deleted from the T-55A onwards.

There were many modified versions of

the T-54/55 series and sophisticated retrofit programs have been undertaken by the Israeli Army, the British firm of Royal Ordnance and the US firm of Teledyne Continental. Russian Federation armies also continued to update versions in service well into the 1990s, of which one of the most recent was the T-55 AM2B. This had a new turret, appliqué armor on both turret and hull, a new and more powerful engine, much improved electronics and vision devices, and the same tracks as the T-72 MBT. Another variant was the Iranian Safir-74, in which T-54/55 captured from Iraq received a major upgrade including the M68 105mm rifled tank gun and a new power pack.

T-54s and T-55s were the main tank force of the Warsaw Pact for many years, and were used in the invasion of Hungary

Below: According to the Novosti News Agency, these T-55 tanks have arrived by air transport and are deploying to their battle stations.

Left below: T-55 crossing a river using a snorkel. These thin tubes would not have allowed anyone to escape whilst underwater, which made such river-crossing exercises very unpopular.

Right below: An Egyptian Army T-55 in a hull-down position during Exercise Bright Star 1985, conducted in conjunction with US Army units.

in 1956, and of Czechoslovakia in 1968. It was the main battle tank in the Arab armies in the 1967 and 1973 wars, and has also been used in combat in Indochina and Africa.

From the Western point-of-view, T-54 and T-55 had shortcomings, including relatively thin armor, main fuel tanks outside the armor envelope, no turret basket, and the lack of a collective NBC system, which meant that individual crew members had to wear their NBC suits. However, it was sufficiently good and available in such vast numbers that these drawbacks would have been of minor significance had war ever broken out in Europe.

Below: *North Vietnamese Army (NVA) driver of T-55 tank. The NVA used tanks against US forces, and later deployed them in very large numbers to sweep the South Vietnamese army aside in the drive for Saigon.*

Right: *T-55s of the Soviet Army. Soviet tanks were of good quality, but it was their sheer numbers which gave NATO Cold War planners such a problem; over 10,000 were available for an attack into western Europe.*

Below: *North Vietnamese T-55s hit by South Vietnamese forces during the final attack on the South. To turn the left-hand tank on its side would have required a very powerful explosion. Despite such successes, the North won by sheer weight of numbers.*

Inset right: *The Israelis captured large numbers of T-55s in the 1970s and many, as seen here, were converted to mount the Israeli-made 105mm gun. This was more effective than the Soviet 100mm gun and also greatly reduced ammunition supply problems.*

Below: *A carefully staged picture, showing close cooperation between Soviet Army infantry (left), armored forces (represented by T-55 tanks) and attack helicopters (Hinds, overhead). The Soviet Army was a great proponent of such "combined arms" warfare.*

Below: *The Soviet Army, both by the nature of its history and climate, designed its equipment and trained its soldiers to fight in the snow. These were major factors in defeating the French Army in 1812 and the German Army in World War II, and could have played a major role in a war against NATO. The kneeling figures show just how low was the turret on the T-55.*

Left: *Having been brought close to the action on these T-55s, Soviet Army infantry troops debus in order to carry out the last part of the attack on skis. The tanks have been whitewashed to help their camouflage. Note the infra-red projector above the main gun.*

M41 Walker Bulldog Light Tank

❖❖

THE STANDARD LIGHT TANK in use with the United States Army at the end of World War II was the M24 Chaffee (q.v.), which weighed 40,500lb (18,370kg) and was armed with a 75mm gun. Shortly after the end of the war work started on a new light tank, designated the T37; the first prototype was completed in 1949 as the T37 Phase I. This was followed by the T37 Phase II, which had a redesigned turret and different fire-control system. This model was then redesignated as the T41 and a slightly modified version of this, the T41E1, was standardized as the M41, which was authorized for production in 1949. The original name for the M41 was the "Little Bulldog," which was unusual since tanks were normally named after successful generals, but the name was subsequently changed to the even more unusual combination of "Walker Bulldog" after General W. W. Walker, who was killed in a jeep accident in South Korea in 1951.

Production of the M41 was undertaken by the Cadillac Car Division of the

General Motors Corporation at the Cleveland Tank Plant, with the first production models being completed in 1951. Further models were the M41A1, M41A2 and the M41A3, all of which had a slightly different gun control system, whilst the M41A2 and M41A3 had a fuel-injection system for the engine.

The hull of the M41 was of all-welded steel construction, whilst the turret was of

Below: M41 Walker Bulldog in the Korean War, 10 January 1952. Platoon commander, First Lieutenant Don S. Brimball, crouches as he directs the fire of one of his tanks.

SPECIFICATIONS

Country of origin: USA.
Crew: 4.
Armament: One 76mm gun; one 7.62mm machine-gun co-axial with main armament; one 12.7mm anti-aircraft machine-gun.
Armor: 9.25mm-38mm (0.36in-1.49in).
Dimensions: Length (gun forward) 26ft 11in (8.21m); length (hull) 19ft 1in (5.82mm); width 10ft 6in (3.12m); height (including 12.7mm machine-gun) 10ft 1in (3.07m).

Weight: Combat 51,800lb (23,495kg).
Engine: Continental or Lycoming AOS-895-3 6-cylinder petrol engine developing 500bhp at 2,800rpm.
Performance: Road speed 45mph (72km/h), range 100 miles (160km); vertical obstacle 2ft 4in (0.71m); trench 6ft (1.83m); gradient 60 per cent.

welded and cast construction. The driver was seated at the front of the hull on the left, with the other three crew members in the turret, the commander and gunner on the right and the loader on the left. The engine and transmission were at the rear of the hull, separated from the fighting compartment by a fireproof bulkhead. Like most American AFVs of that period, the M41 was provided with a hull escape

hatch, thus enabling the crew to leave the vehicle with a better chance of survival than if they baled out via the turret or driver's hatch. The suspension was of the torsion-bar type and consisted of five road wheels, with the drive sprocket at the rear and the idler at the front. There were three track return rollers.

The main armament of the M41 was a 76mm gun with an elevation of +19° and

a depression of -9°, traverse being 360°. A coaxial 7.62mm machine-gun was mounted to the left of the main armament and a 12.7mm Browning machine-gun on the commander's cupola. Some 65 rounds of 76mm, 2,175 rounds of 12.7mm and 5,000 rounds of 7.62 ammunition were carried. The barrel of the 76mm gun was provided with a bore evacuator and a "T" type blast-deflector, the latter's function

being to reduce the effects of blast and obstruction caused by the flow of propellant gases into the atmosphere. These gases otherwise raised a dust cloud and made aiming the weapon more difficult.

The M41 was one of the three main tanks developed for the US Army in the early 1950s, the others being the M47 medium and the M103 heavy tanks, and

was the first member in a whole family of vehicles sharing many common components. That family included the M42 self-propelled antiaircraft gun, the M44 and M52 self-propelled howitzers, and the M75 armored personnel carrier. In addition there were many trials variations in the 1950s. Some M42s were also used as targets by the United States Navy; designated QM41, they were fitted with

Left below: *M41 Walker Bulldog operated by the Royal Laotian Army in 1961. Note the bow machine-gun in ball-mounting in glacis.*

Right below: *The empty ammunition cases are evidence of a heavy fighting on the road to Quang Tri in South Vietnam; one victim was this burnt-out M41 Walker Bulldog.*

remote-control equipment and used as mobile targets for new air-to-ground missiles.

The M41 was replaced by the M551 Sheridan in US Army service. A large number were exported and many armies, such as those of Brazil, Taiwan and Denmark, liked them so much that they regularly upgraded them to keep them in service. Various upgrade packages were offered to other users, most of which involved replacing the 76mm gun with a 90mm (or even 105mm) weapon and replacing the original six-cylinder petrol engine with a more fuel-efficient diesel powerplant.

Left below: *The M41 was a very neat, compact design. With a weight of 26 US tons (23.5 tonnes) and armed with a 76mm gun.*

Right: *The tank was originally to have been named the Bulldog, but it was then decided to include the name of General Walker who died in the Korean War, and, unusually for a US Tank name, the two were combined.*

Left: *The M41 served with the US Army from the early 1950s until replaced by the M551 Sheridan. With an combat weight of 26 tons it was hardly a light tank by traditional standards, but it was developed in parallel with M48 and M103 and in comparison with them it certainly was "light."*

PT-76 Light Amphibious Tank

❖

Throughout the Cold War the Soviet Army's main battle plan was for a very rapid armored thrust across NATO territory, sweeping through West Germany and the Low Countries and on into France in an attempt to reach the Atlantic coast and thus achieve victory on the ground before NATO forces could mobilize properly. One of the major natural obstacles to such a thrust were the many rivers and lakes, of widely varying sizes which lay across their proposed path; all were crossed by bridges, but the Soviet general staff knew that NATO had elaborate plans to demolish them.

This led to a Soviet preoccupation with river-crossing operations and the development of a vast range of amphibious equipment, bridges, and combat boats. One important item in this for many years was the Plavayushtshiy Tank-76 (= amphibious tank - 76mm gun [PT-76]) which, despite its name, was regarded by the Soviet and other Warsaw pact armies as a reconnaissance vehicle and not as a fighting tank, and whose

amphibious capability was intended to enable it to press ahead with its scouting missions. One aspect which set it apart was that the great majority of other tracked vehicles with an amphibious capability needed to erect screens or snorkels, whereas the PT-76 required just two very minor preparations and could then drive straight into the water.

Below: Many tanks can either swim or wade across rivers with some preparation, but the PT-76 was unique in its ability to enter the water immediately. But, there is always a price; in this case it was the tank's bulk.

SPECIFICATIONS

Country of origin: Russia.
Crew: 3.
Armament: One 76.2mm gun; one SGMT 7.62mm machine-gun co-axial with main armament.
Armor: 0.55in (14mm) maximum.
Dimensions: Length (gun forward)25ft (7.62m); length (hull) 22ft 8in (6.91m); width 10ft 4in (3.14m); height 7ft 2in (2.19m).

Weight: 30,865lb (15,000kg).
Engine: Model V6 B; 6-cylinder diesel; 240bhp.
Performance: Road speed 27.34mph (44km/h); water speed 6.2mph (10km/h); range 162 miles (260km); vertical obstacle 3ft 8in (1.1m); trench 9ft 2in (2.8m); gradient 60 per cent.

The PT-76 had a hull of all-welded steel construction and a three-man crew, with the driver seated at the front center, and the commander/gunner and loader in the large, dish-shaped turret, which was mounted well forward. The engine and transmission were at the rear, driving either the tracks or two hydrojets. With typical Soviet ingenuity, the engine was simply one half of the Model V-54 used in the T-54 main battle tank, with six cylinders instead of twelve. Armor was thin, a maximum 0.5in (14mm), which could be penetrated by heavy machine-guns firing armor-piercing (AP) rounds.

Main armament was a 76.2mm gun, the D-56T on early PT-76s and DT-56TM on later versions, which differed only in the design of the muzzle brake. Both had a cylindrical bore extractor half way along the barrel. There was a 7.62mm coaxial machine-gun but, unusually, no additional machine-gun on a rooftop mounting. The 76mm gun had an elevation of +30° but like virtually all Soviet tanks had a depression of only -4° which limited its use in a hull-down (defilade) fire position. The PT-76 carried 40 rounds of 76.2mm and 1.000 rounds of 7.62 ammunition.

The most outstanding feature of the PT-

76 was its amphibious capability, and the hull needed to have a large volume to make this possible. Propulsion in water was by two hydrojets mounted in the rear of the hull, with their intakes above the sixth roadwheel and outlet ports in the rear plate of the hull, where they were normally covered by swivelling masking plates. Steering when waterborne was by means of differential control of the vanes on the hydrojet intakes, a somewhat "rough-and-ready" but nevertheless effective solution. The only preparations required prior to entering the water was to raise the trim vane, which normally lay flat across the glacis plate, and to fit a periscope above the driver's hatch to enable him to see over the top of the vane. Maximum water speed was about 6mph (10km/h) which meant that it could cope with river speeds of about 5mph (8km/h). The vehicle had considerable reserve buoyancy as a result of which it floated well clear of the surface; this meant that either the 76mm gun or the coaxial

Below: *PT-76 was armed with a low-pressure 90mm gun, fitted with a bore-evacuator and double-baffle muzzle brake. It was powered in the water by two hydrojets and one louvered intake can be seen above the driving sprocket.*

machine-gun could be fired while afloat, although presumably without any degree of accuracy.

PT-76 was replaced in Warsaw Pact armies by reconnaissance versions of the BMP-1 and BMP-76 vehicles. However, it continued to be used by the Soviet Naval Infantry for seaborne amphibious landings well into the 1990s. In this case it was definitely used as a light tank, being employed to swim ashore in the first wave of an assault and then provide mobile firepower ashore in the vulnerable early hours of the operation, until heavier vehicles were available, after which it would have reverted to its reconnaissance role.

The basic chassis, suspension system and tracks were used for a wide variety of other vehicles, including missile carriers, armored personnel carriers, anti-aircraft guns, gun tractors and anti-tank guns, to name but a few. A virtually identical vehicle was built in Poland. In China a direct copy, the Type 60, was initially built, but production then switched to the Type 63, which had a completely new turret mounting an 85mm gun and a co-axial 7.62mm machine-gun; but in this case, with the addition of a 12.7mm anti-aircraft machine-gun on the turret roof. These changes increased the overall weight, so the hull had to be modified to provide the extra flotation.

Production ended in 1967 after some 7,000 had been built of which well over 2,000 were exported. Israel has developed an upgrade package with a 90mm gun, new fire control and a 300-hp engine. The basic PT-76 was very popular with Third World armies, because it was very cheap to buy and to operate and was very reliable. For many of these armies the amphibious capability was of little importance compared to its firepower, mobility and "tank-like" appearance.

Below: *PT-76 was exported in large numbers, many recipients using it as a light tank rather than as a reconnaissance vehicle. This example is in service with the Finnish Army.*

Opposite top: *The PT-76 was powered by two hydrojets; one intake can be seen above the left trackguard and the two outlets are under the covers on the rear plate.*

Opposite bottom: *This PT-76 has the bow hydro-vane in the waterborne position. Raising this and opening the rear outlet plates were the only preparations needed before swimming.*

M47 Medium Tank

WHEN THE KOREAN WAR broke out a new medium tank was needed urgently. This was partially solved by mounting the turret from the T42 experimental tank on the hull of the existing M26 Pershing. The new tank, considered an interim design by the US Army, became the M47 Patton and 8,676 were built in 1950-53 - not bad for a "stop-gap!" Both hull and turret are of all-cast construction. The driver is seated at the front left, with the bow machine-gunner to his right, and the usual turret crew of commander, gunner and loader. Main armament is the M36 90mm gun, with a T-shaped blast deflector. This fires a variety of rounds, including HEAT and HEAT (Fin-Stabilized) and several companies developed 90mm APFSDS rounds. There is a co-axial 7.62mm machine-gun, a 12.7mm anti-aircraft machine-gun, and a 7.62mm bow machine-gun.

The USA Army relegated the M47 to reserve status after only a few years, but many were supplied to NATO countries and remained in service for many years,

until displaced by more modern tanks "cascaded" at the end of the Cold War. A new tank factory was built in Iran between 1970 and 1972 and the first tank to be produced there was a developed version of M47 designated M47M. This retained the 90mm main gun, but had several components from the M48 and M60 series, including engine, transmission, electrics and optical equipment, resulting in a much superior vehicle.

Below: *Three M47s of the US Army's 714th Tank Battalion in night live-firing during Exercise Snow Storm, April 1953.*

SPECIFICATIONS

Country of origin: USA.
Crew: 5.
Armament: One M63 90mm gun; one M1919A4E .3in machine-gun in bow; one M1919A4E1 machine-gun co-axial with main armament; one M2 .5in machine-gun on commander's cupola.
Armor: 12.7mm-112mm (0.50in-4.60in).
Dimensions: Length (gun forward) 28ft 1in (8.1m); length (hull) 20ft 8in (6.1mm); width 10ft 6in (3.51m); height (including anti-aircraft machine-gun) 11ft (3.35m).
Weight: Combat 101,775lb (46,170kg).
Engine: Continental AV-1790-5B 12-cylinder air-cooled petrol engine developing 810hp at 2,800rpm.
Performance: Road speed 30mph (48km/h), range 80 miles (130km); vertical obstacle 3ft (0.914m); trench 8ft 6in (2.59m); gradient 60 per cent.

M48 Medium Tank

❖❖

As SOON AS THE M47 "interim tank" had been authorized for production, Detroit Arsenal started design work on a new medium tank armed with a 90mm gun. Two months later, in December 1950, Chrysler was awarded a contract to build six prototypes under the designation T48, the first of which had to be completed by December 1951. But, in March 1951 - and well before the prototypes were even completed - both the Ford and the Fisher Division of General Motors were given production orders for the M48, as it was now known. Production started in 1952 and first deliveries were made to the US Army the following year. M48s were also built by Alco at Schenectady, New York, and production was finally completed by Chrysler at its Delaware plant in 1960. The M48 was followed in production by the M60, essentially an M48A3 with a 105mm gun and other detailed changes, production of this model being undertaken at the US Government's Detroit Tank Plant.

The M48 hull and turret were both of cast armor construction. The driver was

seated at the front of the hull with the other three crew members located in the turret, with the commander and gunner on the right and the loader on the left. The engine and transmission were at the rear of the hull, separated from the fighting compartment by a fireproof bulkhead. The suspension was of the torsion-bar type and consisted of six road wheels, with the

Below: M48A3s of the US Marine Corps' A Company, 3rd Tank Battalion, 9th MEB, 3rd Marine Division, move out on a routine mission; Da Nang, South Vietnam. This version had the M41 90mm main gun.

SPECIFICATIONS

Country of origin: USA.
Crew: 4.
Armament: One 90mm gun M41; one .3in M1919A-4E machine-gun co-axial with the main armament (some have a 7.62mm M73 MG); one .5in machine-gun in commander's cupola.
Armor: 12.7mm-120mm (0.50in-4.80in).
Dimensions: Length (including main armament) 24ft 5in (7.442m); length (hull) 22ft 7in (6.882mm); width 11ft 11in (3.631m); height (including cupola) 10ft 3in (3.124m).

Weight: Combat 104.000lb (47,173kg).
Engine: Continental AVDS-1790-2A 12-cylinder air-cooled diesel engine developing 750hp at 2,400rpm.
Performance: Road speed 30mph (48km/h), range 288 miles (463km); vertical obstacle 3ft (0.915m); trench 8ft 6in (2.59m); gradient 60 per cent.

drive sprocket at the rear and the idler at the front. Depending on the model, there are between three and five track-return rollers, and some models have a small track-tensioning wheel between the sixth road wheel and the drive sprocket.

The main armament on the early versions was the M41 90mm gun, while secondary armament comprised a coaxial machine-gun of either 0.3in or 7.62mm caliber and a 0.5in M2HB machine-gun in the commander's cupola (except on the M48A1 which had a simple mount). The M48 could be fitted with a dozer blade, if required, at the front of the hull, and all M48s had infra-red driving lights and some an infra-red/white light searchlight above the main armament.

The first model to enter service was the M48, which had a simple cupola for the commander, with the machine-gun mounted externally, which was followed by the M48A1 which had relatively minor improvements. Next came M48A2, which had many improvements including a fuel-injection system for the engine and larger capacity fuel tanks. The M48A2C was a slightly modified M48A2. The M48A3 was a significant improvement as this had a diesel engine, which increased the

vehicle's operational range considerably, and a number of other modifications including a different fire-control system; all earlier models were upgraded to this standard.

The M48A4 was to have had the turrets removed from M60 tanks when they were refitted with a new turret with the 152mm gun/missile launcher system (see M551 Sheridan), but with the failure of this system this plan was dropped. The second and more successful attempt to provide the M48 with a 105mm gun came with the M48A5. This was achieved but involved so many changes that the result was almost a new tank, which, so it transpired, was little different from the M60 (which itself had originally been simply an M48A3 with a 105mm gun). Another version, the M48C, was for training use

Below: *A Marine Corps M67A2 flamethrower tank attacks a Viet Cong position in South Vietnam; January 1966. There were three versions: M67 on the M48A1 chassis, M67A1 on the M48A2 chassis and M67A2 the M48A3 chassis. The differences lay in the chassis, but the flamegun was the same and unusually for such vehicles the flamegun tube ran up the 90mm barrel.*

only and had a mild steel hull. The M48 was exported in very large numbers and remains in service with a number of armies. A small number of these are M48A2 or -A3s which retain their 90mm guns, but the vast majority have been upgraded to take the 105mm. Apart from the US Army's M48A5 conversions, one of the biggest of these programs was undertaken by Wegmann in Germany, which converted 650 German Army tanks to a new M48A2GA2 standard, with a L7A3 105mm rifled 105mm gun, and improved optical and fire control equipment. Other similar programs were undertaken in Turkey, Iran and Israel. Israel has also fitted its M48 fleet with large arrays of explosive reactive armor (ERA).

Below: *A scene on the streets of the city of Huè in South Vietnam during the Communist Tet offensive in February 1968. A Marine Corps M48A3 is used as shelter by a group of Marines who have come under sudden sniper fire. On the right, a courageous Marine pulls his wounded comrades into the temporary sanctuary offered by the tank. The Marines eventually defeated the Viet Cong and drove them out of the city but it was a long and bloody battle.*

Left: *M48A5 of the US Army. This version had the 105mm gun, Xenon searchlight, M1 cupola and many other improvements, which made it virtually identical with the M60. The M48A5 was issued exclusively to National Guard armored units.*

Inset above: *An M48 of the Israeli Army armed with the 105mm gun and protected by add-on blocks of Blazer explosive reactive armor (ERA). These explode when hit by an incoming round, thus deflecting it and negating its effect. The reason for the small blocks is that only a few are detonated at a time and can be easily replaced.*

Below: *A Marine Corps tank company commander holds a morning briefing, prior to moving out on a new day's operations. The tanks are M48A3s; note the T-shaped muzzle brake and the Xenon white-light searchlights.*

Inset: *Blazer ERA-equipped M48s of the Israeli. As a result of the numerous wars and the constant state of conflict with most of its Arab neighbors, the Israeli army has more experience of the combat use of tanks than any other army in the past 50 years.*

Below: *A Marine Corps M48 demonstrates the smoke-generating device developed by Corps engineers, which operates using the tank's engine.*

AMX- 13 Light Tank

❖

THE AMX-13 WAS designed by the Atelier de Construction d'lssy-les-Moulineaux (AMX) near Paris, for use as a tank destroyer and reconnaissance vehicle, and was the standard light tank of the French Army for many years.

The first prototype was completed in 1948 and following trials, the type entered production at the Atelier de Construction Roanne in 1952, with production continuing at that plant until the early 1960s when it was transferred to the civilian Creusot-Loire plant at Chalons-sur-Saône. The AMX-13 remained in production until the late 1980s during which time no fewer than 7,700 light tanks, self-propelled guns and armored personnel carriers (APCs) in this family of armored fighting vehicles (AFVs) were constructed.

The hull was of all-welded steel construction, with a maximum thickness of 1.6in (40mm). The driver sat at the front of the hull on the left, with the front-mounted engine to his right. The turret was at the rear of the hull, with the

commander on the left and the gunner to his right. To keep the hull as low as possible the tank was designed for crew members no taller than 5ft 8in 1.73m). One of the most unusual features was "oscillating" turret, which consisted of two parts, the lower one, which was mounted on the turret, having two trunnions. The gun was mounted rigidly in the upper part, which sat on the two

Below: *The AMX-13 was a very successful light tank. Most were armed with a 90mm gun, but the example seen here mounts a Creusot-Loire 105mm gun.*

SPECIFICATIONS

Country of origin: France.
Crew: 3.
Armament: One 90mm gun; one 7.5mm or 7.62mm machine-gun co-axial with main armament; two smoke discharges on each side of turret.
Armor: 0.4in-1.6in (10mm-40mm).
Dimensions: Length (gun forward) 20ft 10in (6.36m); length (hull) 15ft (4.88m); width 8ft 2in (2.50m); height 7ft 7in (2.30m).

Weight: Combat 33,069lb (15,000kg).
Engine: SOFAM Model 8 GXb eight-cylinder water-cooled petrol engine developing 250hp at 3,200rpm.
Performance: Road speed 37mph (60km/h); range 218 miles (350km); vertical obstacle 2ft 2in (0.65m); trench 5ft 3in (1.6m); gradient 60 per cent.

trunnions, and elevated as a complete unit, which enabled an automatic loader to be installed and thus to reduce the crew from the usual four to three.

The gun is fed from two revolving, six-round magazines, the only disadvantage being that once 12 rounds have been expended a crew member must physically leave the tank to reload. The first AMX-13s were armed with a 75mm gun, but later models were armed with either a 90mm or a 105mm gun and many were fitted with SS-11 anti-tank missiles, although these were removed from surviving tanks in the 1980s. There was a co-axial machinegun of either 7.5mm or 7.62mm caliber and a mounting on the turret roof for an optional anti-aircraft machinegun. The chassis served as a basis for many variants.

The AMX-13 is no longer in use with its two former, largest users, the French and Dutch armies, but many remain in service around the world, with the Singapore Army the largest single operator. The Singapore Automotive Engineering company converted their vehicles to the new AMX-13 SM1 standard, which included a completely new automotive package, with a diesel engine and a fully

automatic transmission. An alternative retrofit kit is available from Creusot-Loire, which includes a GIAT 105mm main gun mounted in an FL-1 5 turret.

Below: *Virtually all tank chassis and the associated automotive systems are used as a basis for a family of specialised support vehicles, such as bridge-layers, repair and recovery vehicles, and so on. This AMX-13 conversion was developed as a field ambulance, Its tracks giving excellent cross-country capability and enabled it to reach casualties in the forward areas, while the armor protected the crew and the patients.*

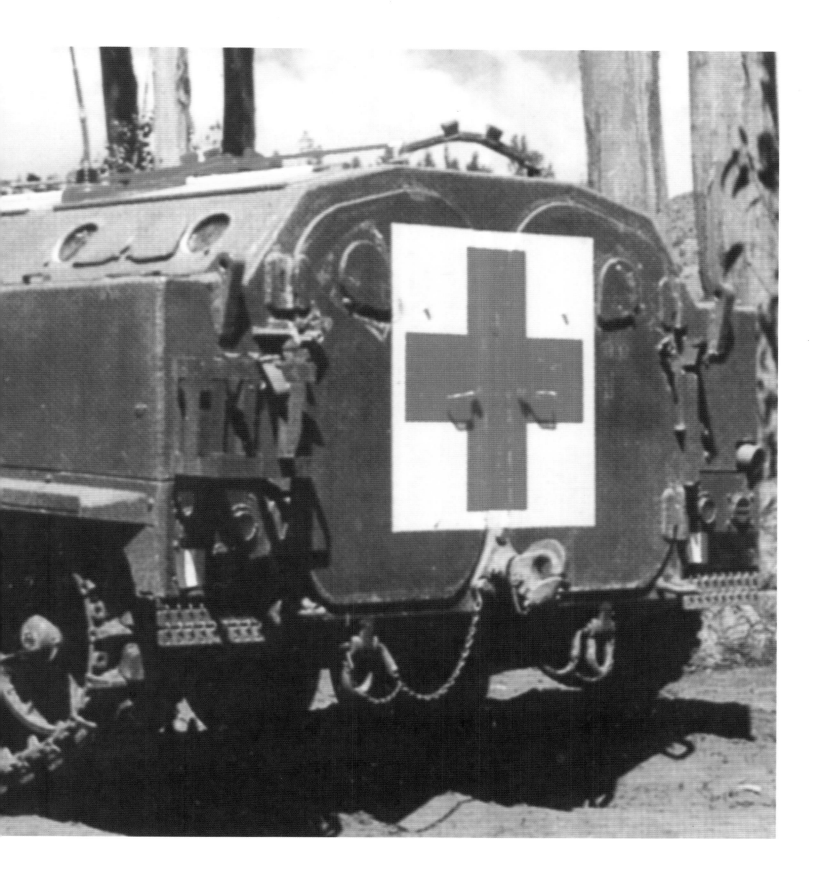

FV214 Conqueror Heavy Tank

❖

IN THE LATE 1940s NATO became apprehensive about the threat from Soviet Josef Stalin 3 heavy tanks. The British response was the Conqueror, armed with a 120mm gun and with a chassis based on that developed for the abortive FV 200 Universal Tank. The hull was of all-welded construction, while the large turret was a single-piece casting. The driver was seated at the right front of the hull, with ammunition stowed to his left and the commander had his own, entirely independent cupola. The engine was a more powerful version of the Rolls-Royce Meteor used in the Centurion, while the Horstmann suspension consisted of four units, each with two road wheels on each side.

Main armament was a 120mm gun with separate-loading ammunition, with 35 rounds of HESH and APDS. There were two 0.3in machine-guns: one coaxial with the main gun, the second on the commander's cupola, where it could be laid and fired from within the turret.

After lengthy development, Conqueror was issued to armored regiments in Germany on a scale of nine per regiment, usually organized into three three-tank troops, one to each tank

squadron, where their task was to provide long-range anti-tank support for the Centurion. The Conqueror proved difficult to maintain and its electrical system gave trouble, but one of its most serious shortcomings was its range of a mere 95 miles(153km). Its weight made it difficult to move along roads or across bridges, but it was surprisingly agile cross-country. Once Centurions armed with the L7 105mm were in service, Conqueror was quietly faded out.

A total of 180 Conquerors was built, plus some armored recovery vehicles (ARV) designated FV219.

SPECIFICATIONS

Country of origin: United Kingdom.
Crew: 4.
Armament: One 120mm gun; one .3in machine-gun co-axial with main armament; one .3in ranging machine-gun on commander's cupola, six smoke dischargers on each side of the turret.
Armor: 178mm (7.12in) maximum.
Dimensions: Length (overall) 38ft (11.58m); length (hull) 25ft 4in (7.721m); width 13ft 1in (3.987m); height (overall) 11ft (3.353m).

Weight: Combat 145,600lb (66,044kg).
Engine: M.120 No.2 Mk.1A 12-cylinder petrol engine with fuel injection system developing 810bhp at 2,800rpm.
Performance: Road speed 21.3mph (34km/h), range 95 miles (153km); vertical obstacle 3ft (0.914m); trench 11ft (3.352m); gradient 60 per cent.

Left: *The British Conqueror, built solely to defeat Soviet JS-series and T-10 heavy tanks, was armed with the then very large caliber 120mm gun with separate ammunition.*

T-10 Heavy Tank

THE STANDARD RUSSIAN heavy tanks during the closing years of World War II were the JS (Josef Stalin) series, which led to the post-war JS-10, but, following the denunciation of the Soviet dictator by Khruschev, the name was hastily changed to T-10. This was a large tank with a combat weight of 114,600lb (52,000kg) and armed with the powerful 122mm gun, for which 30 separately loaded rounds were carried. The tank also mounted two 12.7mm DShK machine-guns. There was a crew of four, - commander, gunner, loader and driver - with the latter seated in the front center, the other three in the turret.

The T-1OM was a development of the T-10, with a number of major improvements. The main gun was essentially the same, but had a multi-baffle muzzle-brake and a fume extractor, and was stabilized in both elevation and traverse. Most important of all, the T-10M had a HEAT round with a muzzle velocity of 2,953ft/s (900m/s), which would penetrate 18in (460mm) of armor. Also, the two 12.7mm machine-guns were replaced

by the later, heavier 14.5mm types.

In the Soviet Army T-10s were formed into special battalions and attached to divisions as required. The T-10 was also used by Egypt and Syria in the 1973 Middle East campaign, where it was normally used to provide long-range anti-tank support to the T-55/T-62 tanks.

Below: Soviet T-10 tank on maneuvers in the 1950s. Note the 122mm gun, the most powerful tank gun in the world at that time.

Inset right: Soviet T-10M in the streets of Prague, maintaining Soviet power over eastern Europe following the Czech uprising.

SPECIFICATIONS

Country of origin: Russia.
Crew: 4.
Armament: One 122mm gun; one 14.5mm machine-gun co-axial with main armament; one 14.5mm anti-aircraft machine-gun.
Armor: 20-250mm (0.79-10.8in).
Dimensions: Length (gun forward) 34ft 9in (10.6m); length (hull) 23ft 1in (7.04m); width 11ft 8in (3.566m); height 8ft (2.43m) without anti-aircraft machine-gun.

Weight: Combat 114,640lb (52,000kg).
Engine: V-2-IS (VK2), 12-cylinder water-cooled diesel developing 700hp at 2,000rpm
Performance: Road speed 26mph (42km/h); range 155 miles (250km); vertical obstacle 2ft 11in (0.9m); trench 9ft 10in (3m); gradient 60 per cent.

M 103 Heavy Tank

❖❖

DEVELOPMENT OF THIS TANK started in 1947 and two prototypes, designated T43, were completed in 1948, followed by four modified T43E1. This model was placed in production and 400 were built between 1952 and 1954 by Chrysler, although official standardization as M103 was not given until 1953. Once in service many faults were found, and, as as every tank needed some 150 modifications, all were placed in storage, not returning to service until 1958.

An unsolved problem was M103's poor mobility, not surprising as it had the same power train as the M47 medium tank, which was some 10 tons (10,161kg) lighter. M103 also broke down repeatedly and had a very short operational range. As soon as the M60 was in production the Army very quickly discarded the unpopular M103.

The US Marine Corps acquired 219 M103s from the Army and upgraded them to M103A1 standard, which included an improved fire-control system and a basket suspended beneath the turret. The Marines

subsequently upgraded 153 of these to M103A2 standard, which involved many improvements, including a new diesel engine (the same as that in M48A5 and M60), which resulted in much greater reliability and range. It was phased out in 1972-74.

Main armament consisted of the M58 120mm gun, with a .3in coaxial machine-gun and Browning 0.5in antiaircraft machine-gun. The crew comprised commander, gunner, driver, and two loaders, who were necessary because of the separate ammunition.

SPECIFICATIONS

Country of origin: USA.
Crew: 5.
Armament: One M58 120mm gun; one .3in M57 or M1919A4E1 machine-gun co-axial with main armament; one .5in M2 anti-aircraft machine-gun.
Armor: 12mm-178mm (0.47in-7.12in).
Dimensions: Length (gun forward) 37ft 1½in (11.315m); length (hull) 22ft 11in (6.984mm); width 12ft 4in (3.758m); height 9ft 5½in (2.88m).

Weight: Combat 125.000lb (56,700kg).
Engine: Continental AV-1790-5B or 7C 12-cylinder air-cooled diesel engine developing 810hp at 2,800rpm.
Performance: Road speed 21mph (34km/h), range 80 miles (129km); vertical obstacle 3ft (0.914m); trench 7ft 6in (2.286m); gradient 60 per cent.

Left: *An M103A2 of 1st Marine Division at Camp Pendleton, California, in March 1965. The M103 was a failure in the Army, but the Marine Corps sorted out most of its problems, resulting in the M103A1 and then M103A2, the latter being at least adequate, if not outstanding. The Marines phased it out in 1973, when it was replaced by the M60.*

M60/M60A1/M60A3 Main Battle Tank

❖

BY THE MID-1950s the M48 was established as the standard tank of the US Army. In 1957 one of these M48s was fitted with a new engine for trials purposes and in late 1958 it was decided to arm the new tank with the British 105mm L7 series gun, which was then being built in the United States under the designation M68. This was deemed to be such a different tank that it was designated the M60 and in 1959 the first production order for the new tank was placed with Chrysler. The type entered production at the Detroit Tank Arsenal in late 1959, with the first production tanks being completed the following year. From late 1962, the M60 was replaced in production by the M60A1, which had a number of improvements, the most important being the redesigned hull and turret, which were now of all-cast construction.

The driver is seated at the front of the hull with the other three crew members in the turret, commander and gunner on the right and the loader on the left. The Continental diesel and the transmission

are at the rear, the latter having one reverse and two forward ranges. The M60 has torsion-bar suspension and six road wheels, with the idler at the front and the drive sprocket at the rear; there are four track-return rollers.

The M68 105mm gun has powered elevation and traverse; a 7.62mm machine-gun is mounted coaxially with

Below: M60A3, with the crew undergoing anti-gas training. It is armed with the M68 105mm gun and has a well-shaped turret, but note the overall height, which is just under 12ft (9.5m) to the roof of the turret.

SPECIFICATIONS

Country of origin: USA.
Crew: 4.
Armament: One M68 105mm rifled gun; one M73 7.62mm co-axial machine-gun; one M85 12.7mm anti-aircraft machine-gun.
Armor: Classified.
Dimensions: Length (including main armament) 30ft 11in (9.4m); length (hull) 22ft 9in (6.95m); width 11ft 11in (3.63m); height 10ft 9in (3.27m).

Weight: Combat 107,900lb (48,987kg).
Engine: Continental AVDS-1790-2c, 12-cylinder, air-cooled, diesel engine developing 750hp at 2,400rpm.
Performance: Road speed 30mph (48km/h); range 300 miles (480km); vertical obstacle 3ft 0in (0.92m); trench 8ft 6in (2.6m); gradient 60 per cent.

(Data for M60A3)

the main armament and there is a 12.7mm M85 machine-gun in the commander's cupola which can be aimed and fired from within the turret. Infra-red driving lights are fitted as standard and infra-red/white light is mounted over the main armament. All M60s have an NBC system. The tank can also be fitted with a dozer blade on the front of the hull. It can ford to a depth of 4ft (1.2m) without preparation, 8ft (2.4m) with the aid of a kit, or 13.5ft (4.1m) with the aid of a snorkel.

A radical departure was made with the M60A2, developed in the mid-1960s, in which a standard M60 hull was mated to a new turret mounting the (then) new 152mm gun/launcher, which fired either a Shillelagh missile or various types of 152mm round.

Meanwhile, plans were being made to improve the 105mm gun-armed version, leading to the M60A3. A new fire control system, laser rangefinder and computer substantially enhanced the probability of a

first-round hit, later helped even more by the addition of a Tank Thermal Sight. Many of these M60A3s came from new production, but others were upgraded M60A1s. The M60 series was phased out of US front-line service in 1997, although a number remain in the inventory with Reserve and Army National Guard units.

Many M60s will remain in service with foreign armies for years to come, the largest single current user being the Israeli Army, which has som 1,350 M60s,

M60A1s and M60A3s, which are being constantly upgraded. All have been given more powerful engines, while the locally produced M68 105mm rifled gun has been fitted with an Israeli-developed thermal sleeve. Israeli M60s have also been fitted with Blazer explosive reactive armor, and a newer appliqué armor, MAGACH-7, has also been fitted, which gives increased protection against both chemical and kinetic energy projectiles. A new fire control system called MATADOR is also being installed. Other known users are: Austria; Bahrain; Bosnia; Brazil; Egypt; Greece; Iran; Jordan; Morocco; Oman; Portugal; Saudi Arabia; Singapore; Spain; Sudan; Taiwan; Thailand; Tunisia; Turkey; and Yemen.

The M60 served as the primary main battle tank of the US Army and Marine Corps for two decades until replaced by the M1. It was criticized for its considerable height of 10.8ft (3.3m) and a perceived limitation in its cross-country

Opposite: *An M60A1; the device atop the fume extractor launches small flash grenades as visual signals of a hit during exercises.*

Below: *A joint exercise in South Korea aboard an M60A3 of the US Army's 2nd.72nd Armor, 2nd Infantry Division.*

capabilities, but over 15,000 were built by Chrysler and it has performed satisfactorily in all the combats in which it has participated. Its last operational service under the US flag was in Operation Desert Shield/Desert Storm when 1st Marine Expeditionary Force fielded 210 M60A1s which played a very active role in the advance into Kuwait City.

Left below: *The crew of a US Army M60A1 at daily maintenance, scrubbing through the barrel, guided by a very watchful NCO.*

Inset below: *M60A1 of the Israeli Armored Corps, which bought many hundreds and has regularly updated them over the years.*

Left: *US Marine Corps M60A1 rolls down the main street of Tok Sok Ri, near Pohan in the Republic of Korea; September 1986.*

Inset above. *The original M60, which was, in essence, an M48 hull and turret, but armed with the license-built M68 105mm gun..*

Left: *The M60A1 was an upgraded version of the M60, the main improvement being a totally new turret of better ballistic shape.*

Inset above: *An original M-60 (note turret shape) being used as part of an aggressor force in Exercise Sentry Castle 81.*

Left: *The M60A3 had many improvements including a new fire control system, laser rangefinder and ballistic computer.*

Inset below: *The business end of the M68 105mm gun; designed in the UK it has been built in many countries including the USA.*

T-62 Main Battle Tank

❖

THE T-62 WAS DEVELOPED in the late 1950s as the successor to the earlier T-54/T-55 series (q.v.), and was first seen by Western observers in May 1965. In appearance it was very similar to the earlier T-54/T-55, but with a longer and wider hull, a new turret and main armament, and could easily be distinguished as the T-54/-55s had a distinct gap between their first and second road wheels, whereas the T-62's road wheels are more evenly spaced. Further, the T-54/-55 had a bore evacuator at the muzzle, while in the T-62 it was situated virtually mid-way.

The hull of the T-62 was of all-welded construction with the well-sloped glacis plate being 4in (10cm) thick. The turret, which was hemispheric in shape, as on T-54/-55 but somewhat larger, was of cast armor, which varied in thickness from 6.7in (17cm) at the front to 2.4in (6cm) at the rear. The driver was seated at the front of the hull on the left side, with the other three crew members in the turret, the commander and gunner on the left and

the loader on the right. The 12-cylinder, water-cooled diesel engine and transmission were at the rear of the hull. The suspension was of the well-tried torsion bar type, and consisted of five road wheels with the idler at the front, and the drive sprocket at the rear.

The U-5TS 115mm gun was the first modern smoothbore tank gun to be fielded, causing some surprise in the West. It had an elevation of +17° and the usual Soviet depression of -4°. Two main types of ammunition were carried: High Explosive Fin-Stabilized Armor-Piercing Discarding

SPECIFICATIONS

Country of origin: Russia.
Crew: 4.
Armament: One U-5TS 115mm gun; one PKT 7.62mm PKT machine-gun co-axial with main armament; one DShK 12.7mm anti-aircraft machine-gun (optional).
Armor: 20mm-242mm (0.79in-9.52in).
Dimensions: Length (overall) 30ft 7in (9.33m); length (hull) 21ft 9in (6.63m); width 11ft (3.35m); height (without anti-aircraft machine-gun) 7ft 10in (2.4m).

Weight: Combat 88,200lb (40,000kg).
Engine: Model V-55-5 12-cylinder water-cooled diesel engine developing 580hp at 2,000rpm.
Performance: Road speed 31mph (50km/h); range (without additional fuel tanks) 280 miles (450km); vertical obstacle 2ft 8in (0.8m); trench 9ft 2in (2.8m); gradient 60 per cent.

Sabot (FSAPDS) and High Explosive Anti-Tank (HEAT). The FSAPDS round had a muzzle velocity of 5,512ft/s (1,689m/s) and an effective range of 1,750 yards (1,600m). When this type of sub-caliber round is fired, the sabot (the disposable "slipper" round the projectile) drops off after the round has left the barrel and the fixed fins of the projectile stabilize it in flight. Being fin-stabilized, such a round does not need to be "spun-up" by rifling in the barrel, which was the reason for the smoothbore. This FSAPDS round was capable of penetrating 11 .8in (30cm) of armor at a range of 1,094 yards (1,000m). The round was manually loaded, but once it had fired the gun automatically returned to a set angle, at which the empty cartridge case was extracted from the breech, moved on to a chute and then ejected through a small hatch in the turret rear.

A PKT 7.62mm machine-gun was mounted coaxially with the main armament. When the T-62 first entered service it did not have an anti-aircraft machine-gun, but most were subsequently fitted with the standard DShK 12.7mm weapon, mounted on the loader's cupola; tanks thus fitted were designated T-62A.

There were three main variants of the T-62. The T-62M (also known as T-62A) was an improved MBT, the T-62K was a command tank and the M 1977 was an armored recovery vehicle. Some versions for the Soviet Army mounted the 122mm D-49S gun, but were phased out fairly rapidly.

Approximately 20,000 were built, most in the Soviet Union, but some in Czechoslovakia, and at its peak approximately 14,000 were in service with the Soviet Army. The type was exported to many countries (but not to the Warsaw Pact, apart from Czechoslovakia), including: Afghanistan (100); Angola (72); Algeria (325); Cuba (160); Egypt (600); Ethiopia (172); Iran (150-200); Iraq (1,600); Libya (900), Syria (1,020), Vietnam (220) and Yemen (100). Israel captured at least 100 and pressed them into service for some years, and others were also exported to Mongolia and North Korea, but numbers are not known. Many of these remain in service around the world, although numbers decrease annually, and some of the survivors are being upgraded by the addition of new armor, tracks, sideskirts, and guns.

Left: *The T-62 was well-designed, particularly with its small, virtually hemispherical turret, and well armed, introducing a 115mm gun at a time when virtually all Western tanks mounted 105mm guns. It was also agile, its powerful engine and low ground pressure resulting in excellent cross-country performance. Above all, however, like most Soviet Cold War tanks, it was built in vast numbers, posing a very menacing threat to NATO planners.*

Leopard 1 Main Battle Tank

THE LEOPARD 1 started as a collaborative project with France, but when this split the West Germans ordered the tank for its own army, the first production vehicle being delivered in September 1965. There were two German production lines, the last of which closed in 1979, but reopened in 1981 to meet orders from Greece and Turkey. A third production line was established in Italy to meet the Italian order. Leopard 1 has a crew of four, with the driver in the right front, the other three in the turret. All versions of Leopard 1 are armed with the British 105mm gun, for which 55 rounds are carried. Secondary armament consists of two 7.62mm machine-guns, one coaxial, the other in a flexible mounting on the turret roof. Leopard 1 had a high power:weight ratio, which gave it exceptional battlefield agility. The design was modified throughout its life. Leopard 1A1 had appliqué armor and a thermal sleeve on the gun, while Leopard 1A2 was built with thicker armor from the start. Leopard 1A3 had a new turret and

Leopard 1A4, a new, fully integrated fire control system. In the 1980s/90s most existing Leopards were upgraded by the addition of a new fire control system; these were known as Leopard 1A5, although there were differences in the make of system actually installed. Once the Cold War was over most users "cascaded" their Leopard 1s to other armies.

Below: *Leopard 1A3, one of several models of this very successful German tank, which sold in large numbers. It was agile, reliable, well-armored by the standards of the time, and armed with the British L7 105mm gun.*

SPECIFICATIONS

Country of origin: Germany.
Crew: 4.
Armament: One 105mm gun; one 7.62mm machine-gun co-axial with main gun; one 7.62mm machine-gun on turret roof; four smoke grenade dischargers on each side of the turret.
Armor: 10mm-70mm (0.4in-2.8in).
Dimensions: Length (including main armament) 31ft 4in (9.54m); length (hull) 23ft 3in (7.1m); width 10ft 8in (3.25m); height 8ft 8in (2.64m).

Weight: Combat 93,394lb (42,400kg).
Engine: MTU MB 838Ca M-500 10-cylinder multi-fuel engine; 830hp at 2,200rpm.
Performance: Road speed 40mph (65km/h); range 373 miles (600km); vertical obstacle 3ft 9in (1.15m); trench 9ft 10in (3.0m); gradient 60 per cent.

Vickers Main Battle Tank

❖

A VERY SUCCESSFUL PRIVATE VENTURE, the Vickers MBT originated in the 1950s when India decided to undertake tank production. The design competition was won by Vickers in 1961 and after they had built two prototypes and a few production vehicles, kits of parts were sent to the newly-completed factory in India until the Indians were able to assume total responsibility. Designated Vijayanta (= victorious), 2,200 were built and gave a good account of themselves in the Indian-Pakistani conflict.

Vickers sought a balance between armor, mobility and firepower in a conventional design and within a weight limit of 38 tons (38,610kg). The engine and transmission were the same as those in the British Army's Chieftain MBT, while the suspension was based on that of the Centurion. The main armament was the L7 105mm rifled gun, which was aimed using the ranging machine-gun technique. Some 44 rounds of 105mm ammunition were carried, together with 3,000 rounds for the two 7.62mm machine-guns and 600 rounds for the ranging machine-gun. Apart from Indian production, Vickers also produced 70 MBT

Mark 1 for Kuwait.

Vickers produced an improved version, the Mark 3, which had better armor, improved suspension, and a new powertrain; there were two sales: Kenya - 76 and Nigeria - 108. The Mark 3(M), produced in anticipation of a Malaysian order, was fitted with ERA and air-conditioning, while the weight was kept down to 39 tons (39,900kg), but no order was placed.

Below: The Vickers MBT was based on the company's experience with the Centurion, but simplified and lightened to make it suitable for countries outside the NATO area. It was very successful and some 2,200 were built.

SPECIFICATIONS

Country of origin: United Kingdom.
Crew: 4.
Armament: One Royal Ordnance L7A1 105mm rifled gun; one 12.7mm co-axial ranging machine-gun; one co-axial L37A2 7.62mm general-purpose machine-gun; one L37A2 anti-aircraft machine-gun; two six-barrel smoke grenade dischargers.
Armor: Maximum 80mm (3.15in).
Dimensions: Length (including main armament) 32ft 1in (9.79m); length (hull) 24ft 10in (7.56m); width overall 10ft 5in (3.17m); height 10ft 1in (3.1m).
Weight: Combat 88,107lb (40,000kg).
Engine: Detroit Diesel 12V-71T turbocharged 12-cylinder engine developing 720bhp at 2,500rpm. Perkins 4,10 4-stroke diesel auxiliary power unit.
Performance: Road speed 31mph (50km/h), range 330 miles (530km); vertical obstacle 2ft 9in (0.83m); trench 9ft 10in (3m); gradient 60 per cent.

M60A2 Main Battle Tank

❖

IN THE EARLY 1960s the US Army found itself with the (apparently) very promising Shillelagh tank missile system, which is described in detail in the M551 Sheridan entry, nearing the end of its development. The Shillelagh had always been intended for both MBTs and the Sheridan reconnaissance tank, but with the repeated delays to the MBT70 program there was no heavy vehicle to field the missile in, particularly in the region of major threat, Western Europe.

As a result, it was decided to develop what appeared to be a low-risk interim solution, by taking the existing hull, suspension and power-train of the M60A1 (q.v.) and mating them with an entirely new turret mounting the revolutionary gun/missile system. This new project was initially designated M60A1E2 and was authorized in 1964, with the first pilot vehicle being completed in September 1965.

The M60A1 E2 had a turret of cast steel, but of a completely novel shape, being very long and narrow, which was intended, at least in part, to present the

minimum cross-section to the enemy when hull-down. The commander was at the rear in a sophisticated but rather high cupola, with the 152mm gun/launcher at the front. The tank carried 13 Shillelagh missiles and 33 conventional 152mm rounds, both with HEAT warheads.

Left below: An M60A1E2, one of the experimental tanks which led to the M60A2. This allied the M60 hull and automotive system to a totally new, long, narrow turret.

Right below: Another M60A1E2. The 152mm gun/missile launcher was at the heart of the concept and proved a dismal failure.

SPECIFICATIONS

Country of origin: USA.
Crew: 4.
Armament: One M162 152mm gun/launcher; one 7.62mm M73 machine-gun co-axial with main armament; one 12.7mm M85 anti-aircraft machine-gun in commander's cupola.
Armor: Not known.
Dimensions: Length (gun forward) 24ft 0in (7.33m); length (hull) 22ft 11in (7.0m); width 11ft 11in (3.63m); height 10ft 10in (3.31m).

Weight: Combat 128,120lb (58,115kg).
Engine: One Continental AV1-1790-2A, V-12, four-stroke diesel, 750bhp at 2,400rpm.
Performance: Road speed 31mph (50km/h); range 370 miles (595km); vertical obstacle 3ft 0in (0.91m); trench 8ft 8in (2.66m); gradient 60 per cent.

The fire-control system was particularly complicated for its day, with the commander sitting in a fully rotating, independently stabilized cupola, in order to provide an accurate, fire-on-the-move capability. There was a full-solution, ballistic computer coupled to a laser rangefinder, and both commander and gunner had passive night vision devices. Only the gunner was able to launch and guide the missile, but the commander was able to aim and fire the main weapon in a gun engagement, by day or night, with the same accuracy as the gunner. In addition, the commander, having acquired a target using his cupola, could then press a button to align the turret with the target in order to designate the target to the gunner for a missile engagement.

The hull was that of the M60A1, but despite the original intentions some modifications were necessary, including the installation of air compressors and compressed-air storage bottles. These were required to provide a closed-breech scavenging system to clear the gun tube after firing, so that noxious fumes from the propellants were not allowed back into the turret.

The program was beset by difficulties

from the start; these involved the missile system, the combustible cartridge for the conventional round, turret stabilization, and the integration of the new turret into the M60A1 hull. Because of all these problems, overall system reliability was very poor. There were tactical problems as well, since the weight had crept up from a planned 52 tons to 57 tons, while the overall height of 11 ft 11 in (3.63m) was very considerable, particularly for European-type warfare.

The controversy came to a head in 1966 with a dispute between those who wanted to put the new tank into production as soon as possible and others who wanted to find answers to the great number of unresolved problems before the system was put into the hands of troops. Unfortunately, the former won and an

Opposite: *Two production M60A2s on exercise. One of the many criticisms of this design was the height of the tank.*

Below: *An M60A2 fires a 152mm shell. These shells had a combustible case, another technological innovation, and another source of constant problems in practice.*

order for 300 was placed in 1967 and some tanks were actually deployed to the 7th (US) Army in Europe. So severe were the problems, however, that production was suspended in 1969 and it was not until late 1971 that the tank was accepted into service as the M60A2. A total of 526 M60A2s were eventually built, which were deployed to US units in Western Europe and the Continental USA. The M60A2s in Europe were quietly withdrawn to the USA in 1979 and then all were withdrawn from service in the early 1980s.

With the M551 and MBT-70, the M60A2 was yet another sad chapter in history of tank development in the US Army in the 1960s and 1970s.

However, matters would eventually come right with the outstanding M1 Abrams, as will be described in a later entry.

Below: M60A2s in West Germany. The large sleeve around the barrel was a bore evacuator, which cut-down the fumes inside the turret.

Right inset: A gunner of the first unit to field the M60A2 S B Company, 1st Battalion, 32nd Armor of the 3rd Armored Division.

Left: *A remarkable shot as a Shillelagh missile leaves its launcher tube. A total of 13 missiles were carried and only the gunner was able to launch and guide the missile, which had a large HEAT warhead.*

M551 Sheridan Light Tank

❖❖

THE M551 SHERIDAN and its revolutionary weapons system were among the greatest disappointments in tank history and remain a prime example of what can go wrong when too much new technology is assembled into one system.

Sheridan was designed around the 152mm M81 gun/missile launcher, which was to be capable of firing either conventional ammunition or the MGM-51 Shillelagh antitank missile and was very similar to the systems used in M60A2 and MBT-70

(see separate entries). Sheridan was a reconnaissance vehicle, but the Shillelagh system was supposed to give it a long range anti-tank capability, as well. The vehicle was also required to be fully amphibious and to be capable of being dropped by parachute from aircraft such as the C-130.

The August 1959 operational requirement was for a "new armored vehicle with increased capabilities over any other weapon in its own inventory and that of any adversary" and in 1960 General Motors (Allison Division) was

awarded a design contract for the Armored Reconnaissance Airborne Assault Vehicle (ARAAV). The first prototype XM551 was completed in 1962, and followed by another 11 prototypes. The production contract was awarded to Allison in 1965, with the first production vehicles completed in 1966 and fielded in 1968 under the designation M551

Below: M551 Sheridans at a depot in Europe awaiting their crews from the USA in a REFORGER (REinFORce GERmany) exercise. Note the large caliber barrel for the 152mm gun/missile launcher system.

SPECIFICATIONS

Country of origin: USA.
Crew: 4.
Armament: One 152mm gun/missile launcher; one 7.62mm machine-gun co-axial with the main armament; one 12.7mm anti-aircraft machine-gun; four smoke dischargers on each side of turret.
Armor: Classified.
Dimensions: Length 20ft 8in (6.30m); width 9ft 3in (2.82m); height (overall) 9ft 8in (2.95m).

Weight: Combat 34.898lb (25,830kg).
Engine: Detroit 6V53T six-cylinder diesel developing 300bhp at 2,800rpm.
Performance: Road speed 45mph (70km/h), water speed 36mpg (59km/h); range 373 miles (600km); vertical obstacle 2ft 9in (0.83m); trench 8ft 4in (2.54m); gradient 60 per cent.

Sheridan. Production ended in 1970 after some 1,700 vehicles had been built.

The MGM-51 Shillelagh missile was developed by the Army Missile Command and the Philco-Ford Corporation, and was 45in (1,143mm) long and weighed 50lb (26.7kg). It was powered by a single-stage, solid-propellant Amoco Chemicals motor with a burn time of 1.2 seconds, which accelerated the missile to a speed of some 2,630mph (4,233km/h); steering was by four spring-loaded fins which popped out as the missile left the tube. The flight was then controlled using a SACLOS (= semi-active command-to-line-of-sight) guidance system in which the gunner simply had to keep the cross-hairs of his sight on the target from launch to impact. On leaving the tube, the missile was programmed to fly slightly under the line-of-sight until moving back into it at a point some 1,250yd (1,143m) down range, whereupon it responded to correction signals over the infra-red link from the tracker. The warhead was a 15lb (6.8kg) shaped-charge and with a 6in (153mm) diameter it was extremely effective against the armor of the day. Range of the MGM-1A missile was 2,200yd (2,000m), increasing to 3,280yd (3,000m) with

MGM-1B. Some 228 vehicles left the production line without the missile guidance hardware and all vehicles sent to Vietnam had it removed prior to leaving the USA.

As a gun, the weapon fired three types of round, HEAT-MP, WP and canister, all of which used a combustible cartridge case. The 152mm tube was relatively short and was initially fitted with both a bore evacuator and a scavenging (ie, cleaning) system which used jets of carbon dioxide to blow any remnants of the combustible casing out of the open breech. Unfortunately, combustion was seldom complete and when the breech was opened burning fragments were ejected into the turret, which was alarming for the crew and potentially lethal with other live rounds present. To overcome this, a

Left below: M551 Sheridan had a built-in screen which could be erected and collapsed quickly, making it fully amphibious.

Right below: A Sheridan in April 1975. The bore evacuator seen here was later removed and a new scavenging system installed.

closed-breech scavenging system (CBSS) was installed during production from hull #700 onwards and retrofitted to survivors of hulls #1-699. The result of firing a very powerful gun in such a light vehicle was a tremendous recoil, causing discomfort for the crew, interfering with the missile electronics and damaging anything not fitted with proper shock absorbers, particularly the radio system. The normal load-out of a Sheridan was eight missiles and 20 rounds of ammunition. Secondary armament comprised a 7.62mm coaxial machine-gun and a 12.7mm machine-gun on the commander's cupola. The latter could not be fired from within the turret, so that the commander had to expose his head and shoulders to fire it, which was not ideal in Vietnam.

The hull was all-aluminum and the turret welded steel; the vehicle was, therefore, light enough to be dropped by parachute, but the aluminum armor was so thin that it could be penetrated by RPG-7 rockets and 12.7mm heavy machine-gun rounds. The suspension and the underside of the hull were also particularly vulnerable to mines. The driver sat in the front center, the other three in the turret, loader on the left, gunner and commander on the right. The power unit was at the rear and comprised a diesel, driving the tracks through an Allison powershift transmission. The torsion-bar suspension consisted of five road wheels, with the drive sprocket at the rear, idler at the front. There were no track-return rollers. Sheridan had a permanently-fitted flotation screen and, when erected, could

cross rivers using its tracks for propulsion.

Some 500 Sheridans went to Vietnam, where many deficiencies were revealed and major losses incurred, making it unpopular with the troops. In addition to the problems mentioned above, it was found that the high tropical humidity could damage both the all-electric fire control system and the combustible shell casing, while mines sometimes caused live rounds to detonate, with catastrophic consequences.

The Sheridan began to be phased out of the US inventory from 1978. However, Sheridan-equipped units took part in both Operations Just Cause (Panama, 1989), and Desert Shield. (Saudi Arabia, 1991), while over 300 "visually-modified" Sheridans represented threat tanks and armored vehicles at the National Training Center in Fort Irwin, California well into the 1990s.

All in all, it was a sorry story and as a final irony there is no record of the Shillelagh missile ever being used in anger.

Opposite: *M551 Sheridan driver takes a drink on exercise in Saudi Arabia. Note the large caliber of the gun/missile launcher.*

Below: *Armament of the M55 Sheridan included the roof-mounted 0.5in (12.7mm) M2HB machine-gun seen here.*

Left below: *M551 Sheridan light tank is landed from an airborne C-130 transport aircraft using the Low Altitude Parachute Extraction System (LAPES).*

Right below: *The commander of a three-man Sheridan crew in his cupola aims the 0.5in (12.7mm) Browning M2HB heavy machine-gun, intended mainly for air defence.*

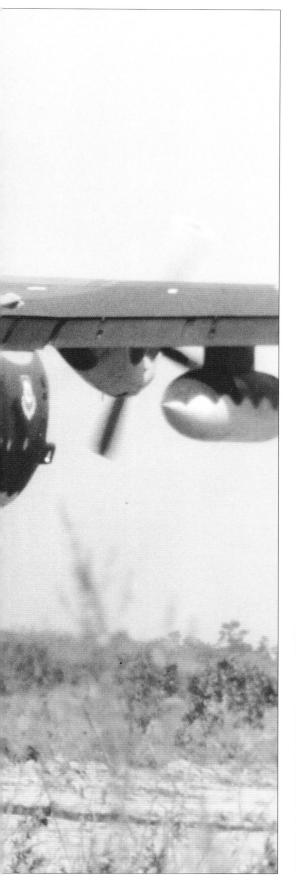

Below: *Sheridans on patrol during an exercise in Saudi Arabia. The two soldiers by the left-hand tank demonstrate how small this tank was, but the whole project soaked up an enormous slice of the defense budget.*

Inset: *One of many criticisms was that the commander had to expose his upper body to fire the machine-gun. This was a major hazard in Vietnam and shields were fitted to offer some protection from snipers.*

Left: *A crewman takes the first step in erecting the flotation screen, which took a matter of minutes, but could not be done under enemy fire. Once water-borne, propulsion was by means of the tracks.*

Inset: *When firing the 152mm shell, there was a tremendous recoil, as it was a very large gun for such a relatively small vehicle. In addition, the turret was filled with noxious gas and burning remnants of the case and a scavenging system was developed to get rid of them. The recoil, however, remained a major problem.*

Stridsvagn Strv-103C Main Battle Tank

WHEN IT APPEARED IN 1961 the Swedish "S-tank" aroused great interest as it seemed to revolutionize tank design, promising lighter, smaller, more mobile MBTs. The three-man crew was located in a central fighting compartment, the driver/gunner on the left, facing forwards and behind him the radio operator, who faced the rear and drove the tank backwards, when required. The commander was on the right and could control the vehicle, if desired.

Main armament was a lengthened version of the British L7 105mm gun, with the barrel mounted rigidly in the glacis plate, thus removing the need for a turret. This reduced both height and weight, and enabled the first automatic loader to be installed, holding 50 rounds. Power was provided by a diesel engine for normal operations, with a gas-turbine boosting power for combat. The gun was aimed using the hydropneumatic suspension to either adjust the elevation or to slew the tank for traverse, which could only be done at the halt. The suspension was locked as the gun was fired.

The S-tank bristled with innovations and

300 were produced in 1966-71. It was widely tested, the British Army even leasing a complete armored squadron for a protracted field trial. But it proved less successful than first thought and no further similar designs were produced, even the Swedes choosing the Leopard 2 as its successor.

Below: The Swedish Strv-103 (front, left) was an attempt to rethink the design of the tank, the major feature being a fixed 105mm gun aimed by moving the tank on its tracks.

Inset: Frontal view of the Strv-103 shows just how much of the hull had to be exposed for a "hull-down" firing position.

SPECIFICATIONS

Country of origin: Sweden.
Crew: 3.
Armament: One L74 105mm rifled gun; two 7.62mm co-axial machine-guns, one 7.62mm anti-aircraft machine-gun (commander); eight smoke dischargers (four on each side of turret).
Armor: All-welded steel.
Dimensions: Length (including main armament) 29ft 6in (8.99m); length (hull) 23ft 1in (7.04m); width 11ft 11in (3.63m); height 7ft 11in (2.43m).

Weight: Combat 93,712lb (42,500kg).
Engine: Detroit Diesel 6V-53T 6-cylinder, water-cooled, diesel engine developing 290hp at 2,800rpm; Boeing 553 gas turbine, 490shp at 38,000rpm.
Performance: Road speed 31mph (50km/h); range 242 miles (390km); vertical obstacle 2ft 11in (0.9m); trench 7ft 6in (2.3m); gradient 60 per cent.

AMX-30B2 Main Battle Tank

❖

IN 1956 FRANCE AND GERMANY drew up a common requirement for a new MBT, the plan being that each would design a tank to the same general specifications. Then, after testing prototypes, the best would enter production for use in both armies, as well as that of Italy. Like many subsequent international tank programs, it all which came to nothing; France built the AMX-30, Germany the Leopard 1 and Italy bought the US M60.

The AMX-30 entered service in 1967.

The hull was of cast and welded construction, while the turret was cast in one piece, with the driver seated at the front left of the hull and the other three in the turret, commander and gunner on the right and loader on the left. The engine and transmission were at the rear and could be removed as a complete unit in under an hour. The torsion-bar suspension had five road wheels and five track-return rollers, with the drive sprocket at the rear and the idler at the front.

Main armament was a French-designed 105mm rifled gun, with a 20mm cannon

mounted to its left, which could be elevated independently, enabling it to be used against slow-flying aircraft and helicopters. There was a 7.62mm machine-gun on the commander's cupola, and four smoke-grenade launchers. Ammunition comprised: 105mm - 47 rounds; 20mm - 500 rounds; 7.62mm - 2,050 rounds.

Initially the gun fired a unique HEAT round in which the shaped charge was mounted inside a sleeve, linked by ball races so that the outer body spun rapidly to maintain stability and accuracy, while

SPECIFICATIONS

Country of origin: France.
Crew: 4.
Armament: One 105mm gun; one 20mm cannon or one 12.7mm machine-gun co-axial with the main armament (see text); on 7.62mm machine-gun on commander's cupola; two smoke discharges.
Armor: 3.1in (79mm) maximum.
Dimensions: Length (including main armament) 31ft 1in (9.48m); length (hull) 21ft 8in (6.59m); width 10ft 2in (3.1m); height (including searchlight) 9ft 4in (2.85m).

Weight: Combat 79,366lb (36,000kg).
Engine: Hispano-Suiza HS-110 12-cylinder water-cooled multi-fuel engine developing 720hp at 2,600rpm.
Performance: Speed 40mph (65km/h); range 373 miles (600km); vertical obstacle 3ft 1in (0.93m); trench 9ft 6in (2.9in); gradient 60 per cent.

the charge itself rotated at a much slower rate. The object was to reduce the dispersion of the hot metal jet, but the idea was never repeated by the French, and in 1980 a more conventional APFSDS projectile entered service.

The AMX-30 could ford 6ft 7in (2m) without preparation and a snorkel fitted over the loader's hatch to increase this to 13ft 2in (4m). The AMX-30S was developed for use in desert conditions; modifications included modified engine and adjusted gearbox ratios to improve desert performance, as well as sandshields over the air intakes.

In 1979 it was decided to upgrade the French Army's version with a much improved and fully integrated fire-control system, a new gearbox and other more minor improvements. Designated AMX-30B2, the French Army received 166 new-builds in the early 1980s and a further 493 AMX-30s were brought up to the -B2 standard. An ERA package was developed for the AMX-30B2, but was only fitted to the tanks in two battalions of the Rapid Reaction Force. The AMX-30 sold reasonably well abroad, but two more designs, developed specially for export - AMX-32 and AMX-40 - did not win any orders.

Left: The AMX-30 was the French competitor for the first European tank program, but when it was clear that the German Leopard I would win, the French withdrew. The gun was a French 105mm in which the non-spinning projectile traveled inside a rotating sleeve.

FV4201 Chieftain Main Battle Tank

Following its frequently traumatic experiences against German tanks in World War II the British Army has always given top priority to protection and firepower, while accepting some limitations on mobility. Thus, when a staff requirement was issued in the 1950s for an MBT to replace Centurion, the result was the best armored tank of its generation, with the most powerful main gun. Seven prototypes of the new FV4201 Chieftain were completed between 1959 and 1962, and following protracted development problems with the engine, transmission and suspension, the first of some 900 Chieftains entered service with the British Army in 1967.

The Chieftain had a hull front of cast construction, while the rest of the hull was welded; the turret was a single-piece casting. The driver was positioned centrally in the front of the hull in a semi-reclined position, which enabled the overall height of the tank to be kept to a minimum. In the turret, the commander and gunner were on the right and the

loader on the left.

One of the major innovations of the Chieftain was the L11 120mm rifled gun. At the time, the British had recently achieved a great success with their L7 105mm gun which had become the virtual NATO standard, so it caused some surprise when Britain then became the first to move to another, and larger caliber.

Below: *Most MBT designs generate recovery vehicles based on the same chassis; here a Chieftain battle tank (right) is towed by a Chieftain armored recovery vehicle (ARV). Note the spade at the front of the ARV.*

SPECIFICATIONS

Country of origin: United Kingdom.
Crew: 4.
Armament: One L11 series 120mm gun; one 7.62mm machine-gun co-axial with main armament; one 7.62mm machine-gun in commander's cupola, one .5in ranging machine-gun; six smoke dischargers on each side of the turret.
Armor: Classified.
Dimensions: Length (gun forward) 35ft 5in (10.79m); length (hull) 24ft 8in (7.52m); width overall (including searchlight) 12ft (3.66m); height overall 9ft 6in (2.89m).

Weight: Combat 121,250lb (55,000kg).
Engine: Leyland L.60 No 4 Mk 8A 12-cylinder multi-fuel engine developing 750bhp at 2,100rpm.
Performance: Road speed 30mph (48km/h), road range 280 miles (450km); vertical obstacle 3ft (0.91m); trench 10ft 4in (3.15m); gradient 60 per cent.

When originally introduced, the gunner was provided with a 0.5in (12.7mm) ranging machine-gun, whose ammunition was ballistically matched to the 120mm rounds, and he was thus able to obtain precise ranging information for the main gun. This was a very simple and effective system compared to the contemporary cross-turret optical rangefinders, but it was replaced by an even more effective method of range-taking in the 1970s,

using the Barr & Stroud laser rangefinder. The 120mm gun was also fitted with a muzzle reference system, fume extractor and a thermal sleeve, and fired Armor-Piercing Discarding Sabot (APDS), Armor-Piercing Fin-Stabilized Discarding Sabot (APFSDS) and High Explosive Squash Head (HESH) rounds. Later the Marconi Integrated Fire Control System was installed, while over 300 British Army Chieftains were fitted with the Thermal

Observation and Gunnery Sight (TOGS), which had been developed for the Challenger MBT.

Various "add-on" devices were developed for the tank, to be fitted when the tactical situation required it, including a dozer blade and a deep fording kit. In 1986, the British Army fitted appliqué armor, codenamed Stillbrew, which enhanced armor protection at comparatively small cost and with only a

small effect on mobility. Other versions of the Chieftain included armored repair and recovery vehicles, armored recovery vehicles and the armored vehicle-launched bridge (AVLB). Part of the British Army's Chieftain fleet was replaced in the 1980s by the Challenger 1 and the remainder in the 1990s by the Challenger 2 (q.v.).

The Chieftain was very popular with the British Army, but did not obtain any export successes with other NATO armies.

The Imperial Iranian Army placed an order for 700 Chieftains in 1971, followed by another order for 125 of an improved version called the Shir 1 and 1,225 of an even more advanced version called the Shir 2. The original Chieftains all arrived in Iran, but none of either version of the Shir were actually delivered, due to the collapse of the Shah's regime. These were used in the war against Iraq during which the latter captured a number and pressed

Left below: *All British MBTs have a "tank telephone" at the rear to enable an infantryman to talk to the tank commander, without climbing onto the hull.*

Right below: *Essential members of a British armored regiment are the mechanics from the Royal Electrical and Mechanical Engineers (REME); this one is working on a Chieftain.*

them into service. The Israeli Army trialled a number of Chieftains, but a potential order was blocked for political reasons. Small quantities of Chieftain were bought by Kuwait (20) and Oman (15), while Jordan subsequently purchased 90 Shir 1s, which were designated the Khalid (qv). The Shir 2 design became the basis of the British Army's Challenger 1 MBT (q.v.).

Below: *The Chieftain's main gun was the first of a new generation of 120mm weapons, but unlike the later German smoothbores, British 120mm tank guns have always been rifled.*

Inset: *Chieftain on the cross-country circuit at the test center at Chobham, England. Note how the turret was configured with a large "nose" thus avoiding the need for a mantlet.*

Left: *Rapid changes of engines in the field are essential for all tanks. Here a REME crew changes the engine on a Chieftain at the British Army's training unit at Suffield in Canada, using a crane mounted on their FV 434 fitters' repair vehicle.*

Left: *In a tank-versus-tank engagement the accuracy of the first round is essential and a factor that became important in the 1980s was that the longer gun tubes then being introduced could suffer from "muzzle droop" (ie, a bend due to its own weight). This was an infinitesimal amount but could be just enough to cause a "miss" rather than a "hit." This was overcome by the "muzzle reference system" (MRS), seen here at the end of the Chieftain's 120mm barrel. A laser on the turret shone a beam onto a mirror in the MRS and any offset in the reflected beam indicated the "droop," which was then fed into the fire-control computer and the solution amended accordingly.*

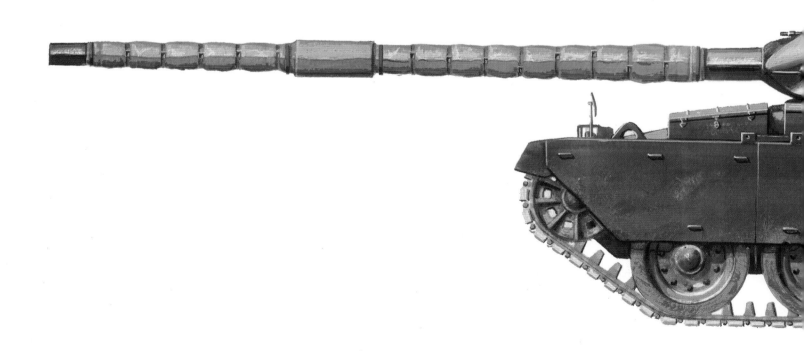

Opposite: *A troop of Chieftain MBTs on exercise. It was a popular tank in the British Army and it equipped the armored regiments of the British Army of the Rhine (BAOR) for some 20 years. It also sold well in the Middle East, where it saw combat in the hands of the Iranian Army during the ten-years long Iran/Iraq war.*

Below: *The Chieftain was a remarkably compact design, its height being kept down by the driver's semi-reclining position when the tank was "closed -down." After the great success of the British L7 105mm gun, this was the first NATO tank to move to the new generation of 120mm guns and the very long tube is clear from this artwork.*

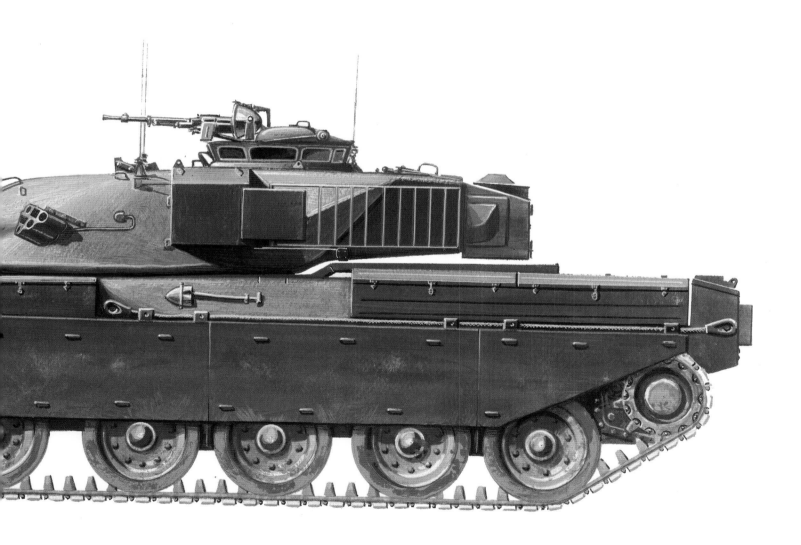

Engesa Osório Main Battle Tank

IN THE EARLY 1980s Brazilian company Engesa was one of the world's largest manufacturers of wheeled AFVs, and designed and produced a light tank, the X1A2, for the national army. Then, in the 1980s, it designed a totally new MBT,

Osório, mainly for the Brazilian Army, but also for export. The turret was designed, built and equipped by British company, Vickers, with two versions: EE-T1, armed with the British L7A1 rifled 105mm gun, and EE-T2 armed with the GIAT 120mm

smoothbore. Automotive power was provided by a Deutz 765bhp diesel, giving a very respectable power/weight ratio of 18.6hp per tonne, while the hydropneumatic suspension was designed and manufactured by Dunlop.

Several countries showed strong interest in Osório, the most important being Saudi Arabia, where it did particularly well in desert trials. Serious consideration was given to building it in Saudi Arabia. Unfortunately, circumstances combined to bring the project to naught, the most important being that the end of the Cold

War resulted in many second-hand tanks becoming available, and the Brazilian Army acquired ex-US M60s and ex-Belgian Leopard Is at give-away prices. Then various other deals in which Engesa was involved went wrong, including possible sales to Iraq and Libya, and the company went bankrupt and ceased trading. It was a sad end to a very promising design.

SPECIFICATIONS

Country of origin: Brazil.
Crew: 4.
Armament: GIAT 120mm smoothbore main gun (see text); one 7.62mm machine-gun coaxial with main gun; one 7.62mm/12.7mm machine-gun on turret roof; three single-barrelled smoke grenade dischargers on each side of turret.
Armor: Not known.
Dimensions: Length 33ft 1in (10.1m); width 10ft 8in (3.26m); height 9ft 6in (2.89m)

Weight: Combat 90,388lb (41,000kg).
Engine: Deutz MWM TBD-234-V12 12-cylinder turbocharged diesel; 765bhp at 2,300rpm.
Performance: Road speed 43mph (70km/h); range 342 miles (550km); vertical obstacle 3ft 8in (1.15m); trench 9ft 10in (3.0m); gradient 65 per cent. (*Specifications are for EE-T2 armed with 120mm gun.*)

Left: *Despite being its country's first attempt at MBT design, the Brazilian Osorio MBT was well-designed and very capable. EE-T1, seen here on desert trials, was armed with the British L7 105mm rifled gun, which was fitted with a muzzle reference system (MRS), thermal jacket and bore evacuator. Note the anti-aircraft machine-gun on a very basic pintle mounting.*

Inset: *Osorio EE-T1 on winter trials, showing the clean shape of the turret, very well sloped glacis plate and six-wheeled suspension. The thick and heavy skirts provided good protection, down almost to the axle level. The Osorio attracted considerable interest but was thwarted by the sudden end of the Cold War and the financial difficulties of its maker, Engesa.*

MBT-70/KPz-70

❖

THE MBT70 (Main Battle Tank 1970) remains a salutary example of what can go wrong in a military development project. In the United States the 1960s were a time of technological revolution, while within NATO the fashion was for collaboration and standardization, all of which came together in the MBT70 US/German project, with disastrous results. Development began in 1965 and everything about the MBT 70 was innovative, none more so than the 152mm gun/missile launcher which fired either a HEAT round with a combustible cartridge case, or a guided missile, the tactical concept being that the missile would be used at longer and the gun at shorter ranges. An autoloader reduced the crew to three - a novel idea at the time - but all three were concentrated in the turret, in order to reduce the height of the hull. The driver sat in a counter-rotating cupola, which was supposed to face forward whatever movements the turret made. This again proved to be a major problem and all drivers complained of disorientation

and motion sickness. Other innovations included the variable-height hydropneumatic suspension and the gas-turbine engine.

The result was an extremely expensive fiasco, which suffered from seemingly endless technical problems and ever-escalating costs. An austere version was produced but that, too was a failure and Congress banned all future funding in 1972.

Below: The MBT-70 introduced many innovations, including a 152mm gun/launcher, placing the driver in the turret, hydropneumatic suspension and a gas-turbine engine. It was a very expensive fiasco.

SPECIFICATIONS

Country of origin: USA/ Federal Republic of Germany.
Crew: 3.
Armament: One 152mm smoothbore gun/missile launcher; one 20mm cannon on turret roof; eight single barrelled smoke grenade launchers on each side of turret.
Armor: Cast steel.
Dimensions: Length not known; width 11ft 6in (3.51m); height 7ft 6in/6ft 6in (2.29m/1.98m) (see text).

Weight: Combat 105,273lb (47,750kg).
Engine: US version, Continental multi-fuel, air-cooled engine, 1,475hp; German version, Daimler-Benz multi-fuel, water-cooled engine, 1,500hp.
Performance: Not known.

Leopard 2 Main Battle Tank

❖

THE LEOPARD 2 MBT originated as a national fall-back against the possible failure of the US/FRG MBT-70 (q.v.) program and when this happened the Germans pushed ahead, with 17 prototypes completed by 1974. The layout of the Leopard 2 is conventional, with the driver at the front, turret with commander, gunner and loader in the center, and the engine and transmission at the rear. The complete powerpack, which was originally developed for the MBT-70, can be removed in about 15 minutes. It was originally believed that Leopard 2's armor was of the spaced type, but it was revealed in 1976 that it uses the British-developed Chobham armor, which consists of layers of steel and ceramics. The suspension system is of the torsion-bar type with seven roadwheels, the drive sprocket at the rear and the idler at the front, and there are four track return rollers.

Early prototypes were armed with a Rheinmetall 105mm smoothbore gun, but later prototypes and all production tanks have the 120mm smoothbore gun.

This fires Fin Stabilized Armor-Piercing Discarding Sabot anti-tank rounds and a fin-stabilized multi-purpose round, intended for use against field fortifications and other battlefield targets. The cartridge case is semi-combustible and only the cartridge stub, made of conventional steel, remains after the round has been fired. The job of the loader is eased by the use of the hydraulically-assisted loading mechanism. A standard 7.62mm MG3 machine-gun is mounted co-axially with the main armament and another MG3 is installed on the loader's hatch for use in

SPECIFICATIONS

Country of origin: Germany.
Crew: 4.
Armament: One Rheinmetall 120mm smoothbore gun; one MG3 7.62mm co-axial machine-gun; one MG3 7.62mm anti-aircraft machine-gun; 16 smoke dischargers (eight on each side of turret).
Armor: Spaced, multi-layer.
Dimensions: Length (including main armament) 31ft 9in (9.67m); length (hull) 25ft 4in (7.72m); width 12ft 2in (3.7m); height 8ft 2in (2.48m).

Weight: Combat 121,475lb (55,150kg).
Engine: MTU MB-873 Ka-501 12-cylinder liquid-cooled diesel engine developing 1,500bhp at 2,600rpm.
Performance: Road speed 45mph (72km/h); range 600 miles (550km); vertical obstacle 3ft 7in (1.1m); trench 9ft 10in (3m); gradient 60 per cent.

Left: *Leopard 2. Note the flatness of the upper deck, absence of shot traps at the turret/hull interface, flat faces of the turret and the Rheinmetall smoothbore 120mm gun.*

Inset above: *Two Leopard 2s in service with the German Army. The square planform of the turret is clearly visible, which was made possible by the use of "special" armor.*

the anti-aircraft role. A very advanced fire-control system is fitted, which includes a combined laser and stereoscopic rangefinder, and the gun is fully stabilized, enabling it to be laid and fired on the move with a high probability of the round hitting the target.

The Leopard 2 has established an enviable reputation and has been tested by a number of armies. The US Army evaluated a special tank designated "Leopard 2 Austere Version" (Leopard 2AV) against the US-designed XM1, from which the latter emerged victorious. In the late 1980s the British also examined a different version known as Leopard 2 (Improved), but again this failed to win an order against the national rival, in this case Challenger 2.

The German tank has won four major foreign orders and a fifth at secondhand. The first foreign customer was the Netherlands, who purchased 445, which were delivered between 1981 and 1986. Of these, 114 were sold to Austria in the mid-1990s and the rest are being upgraded to Leopard 2A5 standard; Sweden purchased 280 tanks from Germany, of which 160 were early model Leopard 2s from German Army stocks and are

designated Stridsvagn 121 in Sweden, while the remainder are new-build Leopard 2A5s (see below). Spain ordered 219 Leopard 2A5s (see separate entry), but obtained 108 Leopard 2A4s from the German Army on a five year lease; these were delivered in 1995-1996.

Switzerland took delivery of 350 Leopard 2s between 1987 and 1993, and there it is known as Pz67 Leo. It is

anticipated that most, if not all of them, will be upgraded to the Leopard 2A5 standard at some point.

Variants include a bridging vehicle, an armored recovery vehicle and a driver training vehicle, all of which have been ordered by both the Dutch and German Armies. Known trials versions include one with a 55-caliber 120mm gun and another with a 140mm gun.

The Leopard 2 entered service in 1978 and various improvements have been either incorporated into the design or retrofitted into service vehicles since that time. In the late 1980s, however, a major improvement program was set in train, consisting of two elements. The first, designated KWS-1, involved installing a new 120mm 52-caliber weapon, while the other - KWS-II - is typified by the

Opposite top: *Leopard 2 in hull-down firing position. Note the smoke-grenade launchers on the side of the turret, seven-wheel torsion bar suspension and skirting plates.*

Opposite bottom: *The Leopard 2 has proved a major success, selling well within other NATO countries, as well as neutral Sweden and Switzerland.*

Below: *The tactical signs on this Leopard 2 indicate a "Class 60" bridge classification and that it belongs to 3 Company, 184th Armored Battalion.*

reshaping of the front of the turret to give it a unique (arrowhead) profile. This is the result of fitting new, removable panels to increase protection against both kinetic energy (ie, APFSDS/APDS) and chemical (ie, HEAT) rounds. Additional armored panels are also fitted to the skirts to improve protection of the suspension and the side of the hull. The interior of the turret has been lined with a spall inhibitor.

The tank's electronic and electrical systems are considerably improved. This includes a new all-electric gun-control system, new navigation system, a modified laser ranging system, a thermal sight for the commander, and a television camera at the rear feeding a monitor on the driver's console, enabling him to see where he is going when reversing.

In 1994 the KWS-II package was

approved for installation in 225 of the current German fleet of 1,857 Leopard 2s, which was completed by the end of 1998. The Royal Netherlands Army also modified all 330 of its Leopard 2s to Leopard 2A5 standard, which was completed in late 2000.

Sweden has ordered 120 new-build Leopard 2A5s under the national designation Strv-1 22 (Stridsvagn = battle

tank), also known as Leopard 2(S). These not only have all the improvements of the German/Dutch program, but also have further, Swedish-developed, armor protection on the front, sides and turret roof, a modular command system, and a new, eye-safe laser ranging device. These Strv-122s are in addition to the 160 ex-German Army Leopard 2A4s delivered in 1995; Sweden has an option on a further 90 Strv-1 22s.

Spain has ordered 219 Leopard 2A5s which are being built under licence, under the designation Leopard 2A5E (E = Espana). To fill the gap before these become available, the Spanish Army obtained 108 Leopard 2A4s from the German Army on a five year lease. Other orders are from Denmark, Finland, Greece, Norway and Poland.

Below: *The 120mm gun of this Leopard 2 fires non-spinning projectiles, which means that the barrel is not rifled. This has found wide acceptance and has been adopted by the US Army for its Abrams M1A2.*

FV101 Scorpion Light Tank/Reconnaissance Vehicle

❖

This very successful family of light fighting vehicles were designed as reconnaissance vehicles, but the gun-armed versions have been (and still are) frequently used as light tanks. The design originated in the early 1960s with a British Army requirement for a new reconnaissance vehicle, which was eventually met by two separate designs, Combat Vehicle Reconnaissance (Tracked) and Combat Vehicle Reconnaissance (Wheeled), of which only the former concerns us here. The first prototype Scorpion CVR(T) was completed by Alvis in 1969 and production started in 1971, with the first examples entering service in 1972.

The Scorpion was the first all-welded aluminum vehicle to be accepted by the British Army, and is a very light and compact vehicle, with a front-mounted engine, driving the tracks through the forward sprocket. The driver sits at the left front with the engine to his right and the transmission beneath his feet. The engine is the same as used in the Fox 4x4 vehicle.

The turret is towards the rear with the commander on the left and gunner on the right. The suspension uses five cast aluminum road wheels and torsion bars. A flotation screen is permanently carried, collapsed around the top of the hull and when this is erected the Scorpion is propelled in the water by its tracks at speeds (depending on the current) of up to

Below: *The Scorpion was the finest light tank of its generation; light, very fast and agile, and with an effective 76mm gun. Red signs on tank and men indicate "enemy" on an exercise in West Germany.*

SPECIFICATIONS

Country of origin: United Kingdom.
Crew: 3.
Armament: One L23A1 76mm main gun; one L37A2 7.62mm machine-gun co-axial with main gun; three single-barrelled smoke dischargers on each side of turret.
Armor: Aluminum.
Dimensions: Length (hull) 15ft 8in (4.8m); width 7ft 0in (2.13m); height (to turret roof) 6ft 9in (2.1m).

Weight: Combat 17,800lb (8,073kg).
Engine: Jaguar J60 No1 Mk100B, 4.2 litre 6-cylinder petrol engine, 190bhp at 4,750rpm.
Performance: Road speed 50mph (80.5km/h); range 400 miles (644km); vertical obstacle 1ft 7in (0.5m); trench 6ft 10in (2.1m); gradient 60 per cent.

5mph (8km/h). The vehicle has spectacular performance and the ground pressure is so low that it can frequently cross ground that is so soft that a man is not able to walk on it.

The 76mm gun which arms the standard Scorpion was a lightweight development of a gun which had previously armed the British Saladin armored car. It fires High-Explosive Squash Head (HESH) and High Explosive (HE) rounds with a range of 5,500yd (5,000m), and smoke, which has range of 4,000yd (3,700m). Elevation limits are +35° degrees to -10° with a 360°

traverse, which was originally manually controlled but latterly was electrical. This was a very effective gun but some users wanted a heavier weapon, and a new version of the vehicle was developed armed with the Belgian Cockerill 90mm, whose main ammunition is a fin-stabilized HEAT round, but it also fires fin-stabilized HESH and HE, as well as smoke and canister rounds. The Scorpion 90 also has a laser rangefinder, an integrated fire-control system and electrical traversing. Many Scorpion 90 users have specified diesel engines and the Perkins T6-3544 is

about the only one which can be squeezed into the small space available. The Scorpion 90 is somewhat heavier: 19,230lb (8,723kg) compared to the standard model's 17,800lb (8,073kg).

A 7.62mm machine-gun is mounted coaxially with the main armament. Although not normally fitted, some users have also specified an anti-aircraft machine-gun in a flexible mounting on the turret roof. Three smoke-grenade dischargers are mounted on each side of the turret. Standard equipment includes an NBC pack and night-vision equipment for

both the driver and gunner.

The original requirement was to use a commercially off-the-shelf (COTS) engine and the Jaguar J60 was selected, a six-cylinder petrol engine, moderated from 260hp to 190hp for this application. This engine had powered a number of most successful sports cars in the 1960s and 1970s, and offered a high power output for a small space requirement, which was considered more important than both the danger of using petrol in a fighting vehicle and its relatively high fuel consumption. Most operators purchased the vehicle with the Jaguar engine but Malaysia, Indonesia and Venezuela specified diesel engines.

The basic vehicle was adapted for a large number of roles and the family included: the FV101 (Scorpion) reconnaissance vehicle with 76mmn gun; FV 102 (Striker) anti-tank vehicle with five Swingfire missile launchers; FV 103 (Spartan) personnel carrier; FV 104 (Samaritan) ambulance; FV 105 (Sultan) command vehicle; FV 106 (Samson) recovery vehicle; FV 107 (Scimitar) reconnaissance vehicle with 30mm Rarden cannon; Streaker, a high-mobility load carrier, and numerous others.

The CVR(T) family was produced in both the UK and Belgium and approximately 4,000 had been produced by the time production ceased in the mid-1990s.

Below: *British Army Scorpion crosses a temporary bridge, laid by Royal Engineers. Scorpion was powered by the same engine as the famous Jaguar XK-120 and the tank also performed like a sports car.*

Type 74 Main Battle Tank

❖

The first tanks for the post-war Japanese Ground Self-Defense Force (JGSDF) (ie, army) were 470 M24 Chaffees and 360 M4 Shermans, but it was quickly appreciated that these were designed for men somewhat taller than the average Japanese soldier. As a result, the Type 61 was designed and built, which was generally similar to the M47 Patton, but slightly smaller. The Type 61 entered service in 1962, but the project had already started for a successor, to enter service in the 1970s.

The first two prototypes, known as STB-1s, were completed by Mitsubishi in late 1969. Further prototypes were then built and, following trials and finalization of the design, the new vehicle, designated Type 74, entered production at Mitsubishi's new tank plant in 1973. A large number were produced for the JGSDF, but there were no exports as it is Japanese government policy not to export arms or weapons of any type. Layout of the Type 74 is conventional, with the driver at the front of the hull on the left and the other three crew members in the turret, with the commander and gunner on

the right and the loader on the left. The engine and transmission are at the rear of the hull. The suspension is of the hydropneumatic type and consists of five road wheels, with the drive sprocket at the rear and the idler at the front, but with no track-return rollers. The suspension can be adjusted by the driver to suit the type of ground being crossed, so that when crossing a rocky, broken area, for example, the

Below: *Japan's Type 74 had hydropneumatic suspension and was armed with the British L7 105mm gun. It was low compared to contemporary tanks of other nations.*

SPECIFICATIONS

Country of origin: Japan.
Crew: 4.
Armament: One L7 series 105mm gun; one 7.62mm machine-gun co-axial with main armament; one .5in anti-aircraft machine-gun, six smoke dischargers.
Armor: Classified.
Dimensions: Length (gun forward) 30ft 10in (9.41m); length (hull) 22ft 6in (6.85m); width 10ft 5in (3.18m); height (with anti-aircraft machine-gun) 8ft 10in (2.67m) at a ground clearance of 2ft 2in (0.65m).

Weight: Combat 83,776lb (38,000kg).
Engine: Mitsubishi 10ZF Model 21 WT 10-cylinder air-cooled diesel developing 750bhp at 2,200rpm.
Performance: Maximum road speed 33mph (53km/h); range 186 miles (300km); vertical obstacle 3ft 3in (1m); trench 8ft 10in (2.7m); gradient 60 per cent.

suspension would be adjusted to give maximum ground clearance, but when taking up a firing position the suspension would be adjusted to give minimum ground clearance. The limits to such clearance are from a minimum of 8in (20cm) to a maximum of 2ft 2in (65cm). It can also be used to give the tank a tactical advantage, so that when the tank is on a reverse slope, the suspension can be lowered at the front and increased at the rear to enable the main

armament to be depressed further than normal. Thus, while the main gun has a normal elevation of +9° to -6°, the hydropneumatic suspension can be used to increase it to +15° orlower it to -12.5°. The only other production tank with this type of suspension was the Swedish S-tank, which needed it as the gun was fixed to the hull; it was also tried on the German/American MBT-70, but the project was cancelled.

The Type 74 is armed with the British L7

series 105mm rifled tank gun, built under licence in Japan. A 7.62mm machine-gun is mounted co-axial with the main armament. The fire control system includes a laser rangefinder and a ballistic computer, both of which are produced in Japan. Prototypes had an automatic loader, but this would have cost too much to install in production tanks. A .5in M2 anti-aircraft machine-gun is mounted on the roof. On the prototypes this could be aimed and fired from within

the turret, but this was also found to be too expensive for production vehicles.

In designing the Type 74 MBT the Japanese sought, and managed, to combine the best features of contemporary tank design within a weight limit of 83,702lb (38,000kg). A total of 873 were built. There was only one variant of the Type 74, the Type 78 Armored Recovery Vehicle, which is provided with a hydraulically-operated crane, winch and a dozer blade at the front of the hull. It has been produced in small numbers. The Type 74 chassis, was also used for the Type 87 35mm SP anti-aircraft gun, of which 12 were produced.

The latest Japanese tank is the MBT 90 which weighs 110,000lb (50,000kg). It is fitted with a unique hybrid torsion-bar/hydropneumatic suspension, which, as with the Type 61, enables the driver to change the attitude of the tank to achieve the optimum position. The main armament is a Mitsubishi-produced version of the Rheinmetall 120mm smooth bore and, again, the electronics are of a very high order.

Left: *A total of 873 Type 74s were built, all for the Japanese Ground Self-Defense Force, since the post-war Japanese Constitution forbids the export of warlike equipment. The chassis was also used for an armored recovery vehicle and a self-propelled anti-aircraft gun; both were built in very small numbers.*

T-72 Main Battle Tank

◆◆

THE T-72 BEARS A certain resemblance to the T-64, but was, in fact, developed at a quite different design bureau. It entered production in 1971 and was in service by 1973, although not reported publicly by Western experts until 1977. As in all recent Russian MBTs, the driver is seated centrally under a well-sloped glacis plate, which has transverse ribs and a splashboard. The other two crew members are seated in the turret, the commander on the right and the gunner on the left. All T-72s built for use by armies of the former Warsaw Pact had an interior lining of a special synthetic, lead-based material, which was intended to provide some degree of protection against two of the products of a nuclear explosion: for the crew against neutron radiation and for the electronic equipment against electro-magnetic pulses.

Except in the earliest version, the main gun is the 2A46 125mm smoothbore, fitted with a light alloy thermal sleeve and a fume extractor, and firing three types of ammunition, using an automatic loader,

which, unlike that in T-64, has a horizontal feed system. Ammunition comprises APFSDS-T, HEAT-IFS and HEAT-IFS, all three of which come in two parts: the projectile and a combustible cartridge case with a metal stub. Theoretical rate of fire is 8 rounds per minute, although whether this could be achieved, let alone sustained, on the battlefield is a different matter.

Below: The T-72 mounts a 125mm gun, with a thermal jacket and bore evacuator, which fires three types of ammunition. It uses an automatic loader, thus reducing the crew to three.

SPECIFICATIONS

Country of origin: Russia.
Crew: 3.
Armament: One 2A46 125mm gun; one PKT 7.62mm co-axial machine-gun; one NSVT 12.7mm anti-aircraft machine-gun.
Armor: "Special" type.
Dimensions: Length (including main armament) 30ft 4in (9.24m); length (hull) 22ft 10in (6.95m); width 15ft 7in (4.75m); height 7ft 10in (2.37m).

Weight: Combat 90,310lb (41,000kg).
Engine: V-12 diesel engine developing 780hp at 2,000rpm.
Performance: Road speed 50mph (80km/h); road range 300 miles (483km); vertical obstacle 2ft 8in (0.85m); trench 8ft 10in (2.7m); gradient 60 per cent.

There is a single, narrow snorkel tube for deep-fording rivers, which fits over the gunner's periscope mounting. Such a tube provides no means of escape for the crew in the event of something going wrong whilst underwater and the whole tactic of fording is very unpopular with the soldiers serving in Russian armored units.

The second version, T-72A, entered service in June 1979 and incorporated a considerable number of improvements, the most important of which were the definitive 2A46 125mm gun, laser rangefinder and night sights. It also had a new type of diesel engine, improved suspension, a new smoke-grenade launcher system, and greatly increased armored protection, especially on the forward part of the turret. There was a parallel command version (T-72AK). A number of T-72As were later given additional ERA and were re-designated T-72AV. All this additional armor on the tank's frontal and upper surfaces was a clear response to the increased threat posed by NATO's ever improving anti-tank weapons, especially the "top attack" munitions, which were starting to enter service at this time.

The T-72B, first seen by Western observers in 1985, incorporated yet further improvements, including the 2A46M 125mm gun which could launch the AT-1 1 missile, a beam-rider with a maximum range of 5,500yd (5,000m). The 2A46M was fitted with a thermal

jacket and fume extractor, but was also the first Russian tank gun to use a muzzle reference system. Introduced in 1992, the T-72BM was an improved production version for the Russian Army, with a large number of ERA tiles fitted in manufacture, giving greatly enhanced protection against HEAT and APFSDS rounds. The T-72s produced for the Soviet/Russian Army had parallel export versions, although these usually appeared later and frequently did not have all the sophisticated

equipment of their Soviet originals. All T-72s, with the exception of command tanks, have the mountings necessary for mine-clearing ploughs at the front of the hull.

With such a large number of the various models of T-72 in service around the world, it is not surprising that there should be a large number of upgrade packages on the market, being supplied by French, Russian, Ukrainian and Yugoslav companies.

Production of the T-72 and its variants has now ended, some 20,000 having been produced in four State armaments factories in Russia, as well as in Czechoslovakia, and Poland. The Type 72M1 was produced in India as the Ajeya and in Iraq as the Assad Babyle (Lion of Babylon). It was also produced in the former Yugoslavia as the M-84, which differed from the T-72 in a number of respects.

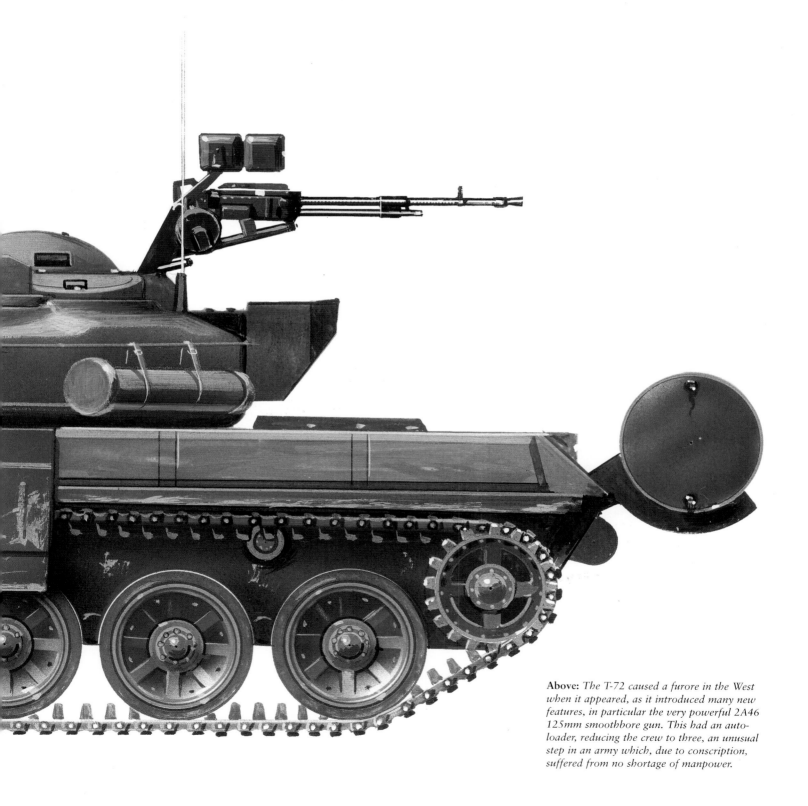

Above: *The T-72 caused a furore in the West when it appeared, as it introduced many new features, in particular the very powerful 2A46 125mm smoothbore gun. This had an auto-loader, reducing the crew to three, an unusual step in an army which, due to conscription, suffered from no shortage of manpower.*

Right: *This top view of the T-72 shows its neat design. The glacis plate is well-sloped with the driver's position in the center. Note the hatches for the driver and gunner in the turret and the snorkel tube stowed at the turret rear.*

Opposite top: *Very smart T-72s and proud crews on parade in Moscow during the Cold War. All such parades were watched with great interest by Western observers as they revealed the latest trends in Soviet military equipment.*

Opposite bottom: *The Red Army was so proud of the T-72 that, in the very unusual gesture, seen here, they showed it to French observers and cameramen at a Guards tank regiment barracks just outside Moscow. Note the very low turret, spring-loaded skirting plates, dozer blade for digging into a new position, and the cut-away ammunition on the glacis plate.*

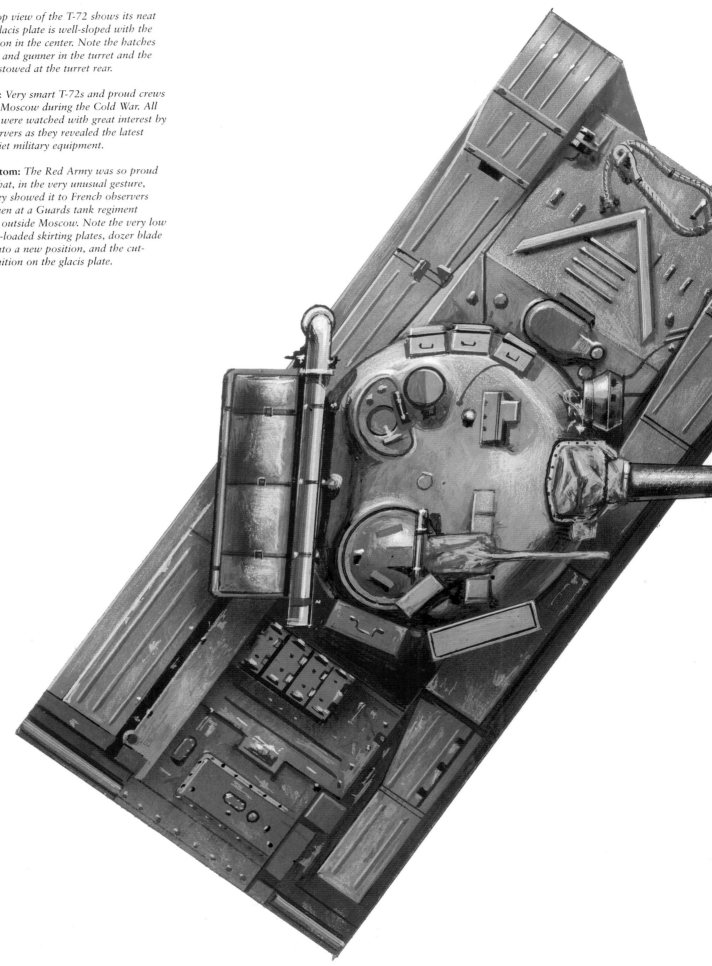

T-64 Main Battle Tank

◆◆

THE DRIVER OF THE T-64 sits in the front center, with the other two crewmen in the turret, commander on the right, gunner on the left. The gun is a 125mm smoothbore, one of the largest-caliber tank guns to attain service, with a vertical ammunition stowage system for its automatic loader. This reportedly gave trouble in its early years, injuring a number of crewmen.

The suspension has six small, dual roadwheels mounted on hydropneumatic arms, an unusual arrangement in the Russian army, which has used large roadwheels and torsion bars since the Christie tanks of the 1930s. The T-64K is a minor variant designed for use as a command post tank, for which it carries extra radios, reducing the number of rounds of 125mm ammunition carried. A telescopic mast, carried on the outside of the hull, is erected whenever the tank is stationary. Three major versions of the T-64 have been identified. The first was the initial production version described above. Next came the T-64A, which had a

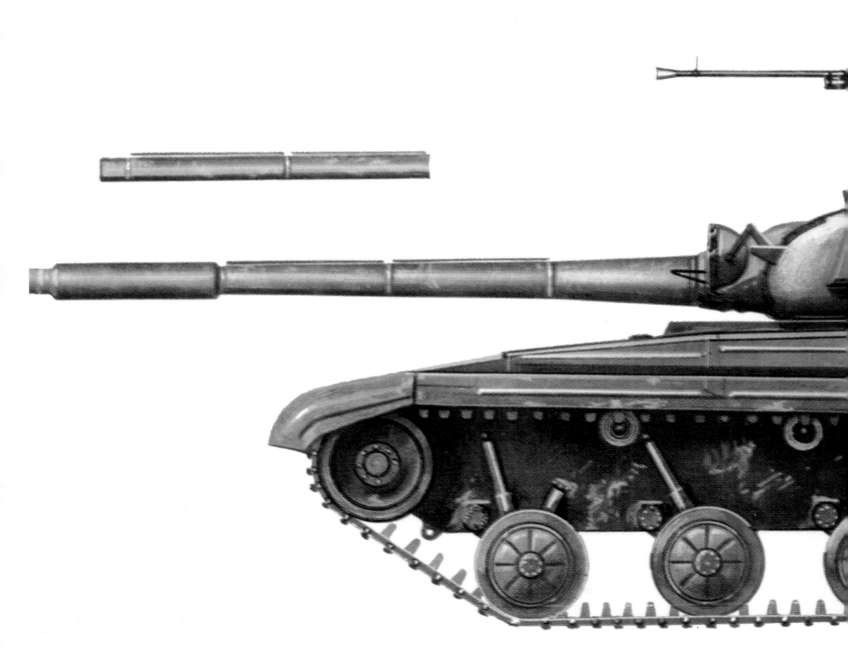

number of minor modifications, then T-64B with a new version of the 125mm smoothbore gun, which can also launch an anti-tank guided weapon, designated AT-8. No T-64s were exported and the type served only with the Soviet Army and remains in service with various armies of the former Soviet Union.

Below: *The T-64 was one of many impressive new tank designs produced by the Soviet Army during the Cold War. The T-64 was never exported, but it remains in service with a number of armies of the states which once were integrated into the Soviet Union.*

SPECIFICATIONS

Country of origin: Russia.
Crew: 3.
Armament: One 2A26 125mm gun; one PKT 7.62mm co-axial machine-gun; one 12.7mm anti-aircraft machine-gun.
Armor: Classified.
Dimensions: Length (including main armament) 32ft 6in (9.90m); length (hull) 24ft 5in (7.45m); width 15ft 3in (4.64m); height 7ft 3in (2.20m).

Weight: Combat 92,512lb (42,000kg).
Engine: 5DTF, 5-cyclinder opposed piston liquid-cooled diesel engine developing 750hp at 2,000rpm.
Performance: Road speed 47mph (75km/h); road range 250 miles (400km); vertical obstacle 2ft 8in (0.8m); trench 8ft 10in (2.7m); gradient 60 per cent. (*Data apply to T-64B*).

Merkava Main Battle Tank

❖

FOR MANY YEARS the Israeli Armored Corps used a wide collection of foreign tanks, including British Centurions, US M48s and M60s, and various Soviet types captured in the Arab-Israeli wars. The aim, however, was to develop a tank based on their own experiences and tailored to meet their particular requirements. As explained elsewhere in this book, all tanks are the result of a compromise between firepower, protection and mobility, and in the Israeli case the top priority is protection, since, being a small country with much less of a manpower base than their larger neighbours, Israel cannot afford large losses. This became particularly clear in the 1967 campaign and a design and development team was then established under the leadership of Major-General Israel Tal. The outcome was the Merkava (Chariot), the first prototype of which was completed in 1974, although it was not revealed publicly until 1977. The first production vehicles were issued to the Army in 1979 and the type saw initial combat in

Lebanon in 1982.

There are five known models. The original Merkava Mark 1 was armed with the widely-used M68 105mm gun. This was succeeded by the Mark 2a, which had better armor protection and improved fire control, and then the Mark 2b, with yet more improvements to the armor, plus new fire control software; this version also introduced an internally-mounted 60mm mortar. All Mark 1s and 2as have been brought up to Mark 2b standard. The Mark 3, which entered service in 1989 was virtually a new tank, but the major

SPECIFICATIONS

Country of origin: Israel.
Armament: One M68 105mm rifled gun; one co-axial 7.62mm machine-gun; two 7.62mm anti-aircraft machine-guns; one 60mm mortar.
Armor: See text.
Dimensions: Length (gun forward) 28ft 5in (8.65m); length (hull) 24ft 5in (7.54m); width 12ft 2in (3.70m); height (to turret roof) 8ft 9in (2.66m).

Weight: Combat 132,160lb (60,000kg).
Engine: Teledyne Continental AVDS-1790-6A V-12 diesel developing 900hp.
Performance: Road speed 29mph (46km/h); range 250 miles (400km); vertical obstacle 3ft 1in (0.95m); trench 9ft 10in (3.0m); gradient 70 per cent.

(Data for Mark 1.)

Left: The Merkava was designed to meet the specific needs of the Israeli Army. Among these were placing the engine forward, thus giving extra protection for the crew and releasing space in the rear for a compartment for extra ammunition or six infantry soldiers.

visible change was replacement of the 105mm gun by a new 120mm smoothbore, developed in Israel. A much revised suspension was also used, together with a new engine and transmission. Another major innovation was a system of modular armored protection in which plates are attached by bolts, enabling them to be changed to meet different threats or when better ballistic technology becomes available.

All Mark 3s have since been upgraded to Mark 3 Baz (= falcon), which has a totally new fire control system, whose capabilities include locking on to a target and then automatically tracking it. The latest version, which entered service in 2001, is the Mark 4, which retains the 120mm gun but has yet further enhancements in the field of fire control, armor and defensive systems. It is estimated that about 1,400 Merkava Marks, 2, 3 and 4 tanks are in service with the IDF.

The layout of the Merkava is unusual, with the engine and transmission at the front of the tank, which is intended to increase crew protection, since the Israeli Army would much rather save the crew and lose the tank. The driver is seated forward and on the left, with the engine to his right. The turret has an exceptionally small frontal cross-section and a well-sloped front, presenting an extremely small target when the tank is in a hull-down position. There is a layer of "special" armor on the turret front and sides. Inside, the commander and gunner are seated on the right, with the loader on the left. Like many other modern tanks, the turret has a large bustle, which normally acts as a "shot-trap" but in the Merkava a skirt of heavy chains is suspended from the outer edge of the bustle, kept in position by dense weights. As a result, incoming HEAT projectiles detonate on hitting the chains rather than on the turret ring, which would usually have disastrous consequences.

The suspension comprises six road wheels per side with the drive sprockets at the front and idlers at the rear. There are return rollers and there are armored skirts to protect the top half of the tracks, the suspension and the sides of the hull from damage by HEAT weapons.

Placing the engine at the front has created considerable space at the rear of the tank. This is normally used to house ammunition, but can also be used to accommodate a maximum of six fully equipped infantrymen or commandos. However, the space and the door also allow the crew to enter or leave from the rear out of sight of the enemy, and for ammunition to be resupplied from the rear rather than over the sides of the tank. Additional communications facilities can also be installed in place of some of the ammunition to enable the tank to be used as a command post.

The main gun on the Marks 3 and 4 is the Israeli Military Industries (IMI) 120mm smoothbore. This is totally enveloped in a new type of thermal sleeve, which is intended to improve accuracy by eliminating distortion of the barrel due to the effects of weather, heat and shock. The ammunition store contains 50 rounds of 120mm ammunition. The tank is also equipped with three 7.62mm machine-guns, of which one is coaxial and the other two mounted on the roof of the turret; some 10,000 rounds of ammunition are carried. There is also a 60mm mortar, which is installed in the turret and which can be loaded, aimed and fired by the crew from inside the turret. It is used to fire high explosive and illuminating bombs, and thus conserve main gun ammunition.

Merkava Mark 3 is powered by a Teledyne diesel which delivers 1,200bhp, compared to the 900bhp engine installed in Merkava Marks 1 and 2. Merkava Mark 3 carries 1,400 litres of fuel. The Merkava Mark 4 is powered by the MTU 1200hp V-12 diesel engine, which is assembled under license by General Dynamics Land Systems in the United States.

Right: *Gunner's position inside the Merkava tank. Sophisticated weapons require sophisticated controls, but all must survive the rigors of cross-country driving, the shocks from non-penetrating hits on the outside of the tank, and the recoil of firing the tank's own very powerful gun.*

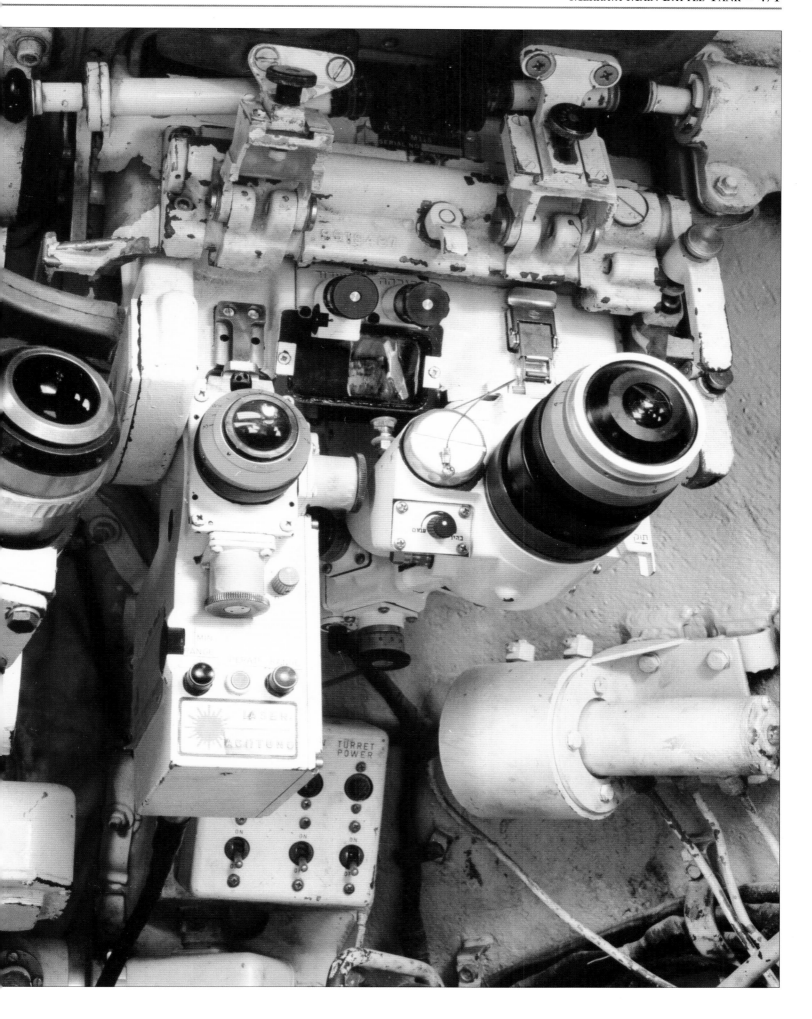

M1 Abrams

❖

Having fielded the M60, the US Army started an international project with the Federal Republic of Germany designated the MBT-70 (see separate entry), but this turned into a controversial and expensive fiasco, which was eventually cancelled. A new competition was then run for a replacement, which was won by Chrysler; this entered production as the M1 in 1979, with first deliveries in February 1980.

Four major versions were produced - M1, M1 (Improved), M1A1 and M1A2. The M1, of which 2,674 were built, was armed with the M68 rifled 105mm gun, with the last 300 - M1 (Improved) - having better armored protection. The M1A1, produced from 1985 through 1993, has the Rheinmetall 120mm smoothbore gun and numerous other enhancements, including improved suspension, new turret, increased armor protection, and a nuclear-chemical-biological (NBC) protection system; 403 M1A1s were also built for the US Marine Corps. The latest M1A2 includes all M1A1 features, plus a

new commander's station. A total of 77 new M1A2s were built, but approximately 1,000 of the original M1s are being rebuilt to this standard.

The hull and turret are constructed of "special" armor and the main gun is fully stabilized, enabling it to be aimed and fired while on the move. Secondary armament comprises a coaxial 7.62mm

Below: *After the fiasco of the MBT-70 the US Army needed a successful tank and received it in the shape of the M1 Abrams, which has set the international standard in the 1990s and the first decade of the 21st century.*

SPECIFICATIONS

Country of origin: United States of America.
Crew: 4.
Armament: One M256 Rheinmetall 120mm smoothbore gun; one M240 7.62mm co-axial machine-gun; one M2 12.7mm and one M240 7.62mm anti-aircraft machine-gun.
Armor: Classified.
Dimensions: Length (including main armament) 32ft 3in (9.83m); length (hull) 25ft 11in (7.92m); width 11ft 11in (3.66m); height 9ft 6in (2.89m).

Weight: Combat 125,890lb (57,154kg).
Engine: Textron Lycoming AGT-1500 gas-turbine developing 1,500hp at 30,000rpm.
Performance: Road speed 41mph (67km/h), range 300 miles (480km); vertical obstacle 3ft 6in (1.07m); trench 9ft 0in (2.74m); gradient 60 per cent.

machine-gun and two machine-guns on the turret roof, a 12.7mm at the commander's station and a 7.62mm at the loader's station. M1 carries 55 rounds of 105mm and M1A1/M1A2 40 rounds of 120mm, and all also carry 1,000 rounds of 12.7mm and 11,400 rounds of 7.62mm machine-gun ammunition. The design incorporates extensive measures for the protection of the crew, particularly against fire and NBC.

The M1 is powered by the Textron Lycoming AGM-1500 gas-turbine, which prolonged service use has demonstrated to be very reliable, mechanically simple and particularly easy to service. However, it is also noisy, emits a very hot exhaust, and is thirsty on fuel, although the logistic support during Desert Storm was so effective that this was not a problem.

Over the past 20 years, some foreign armies have reduced their tank crews from four to three, but not the US Army which has retained the traditional crew of four. The driver sits at the center front in a semi-reclined seat, where he is protected by the very well-sloped glacis plate. The other three are in the turret, the commander and gunner on the right, the loader on the left. The commander can cue the gunner's sight without any verbal communication and can also fire the main gun without reference to the gunner.

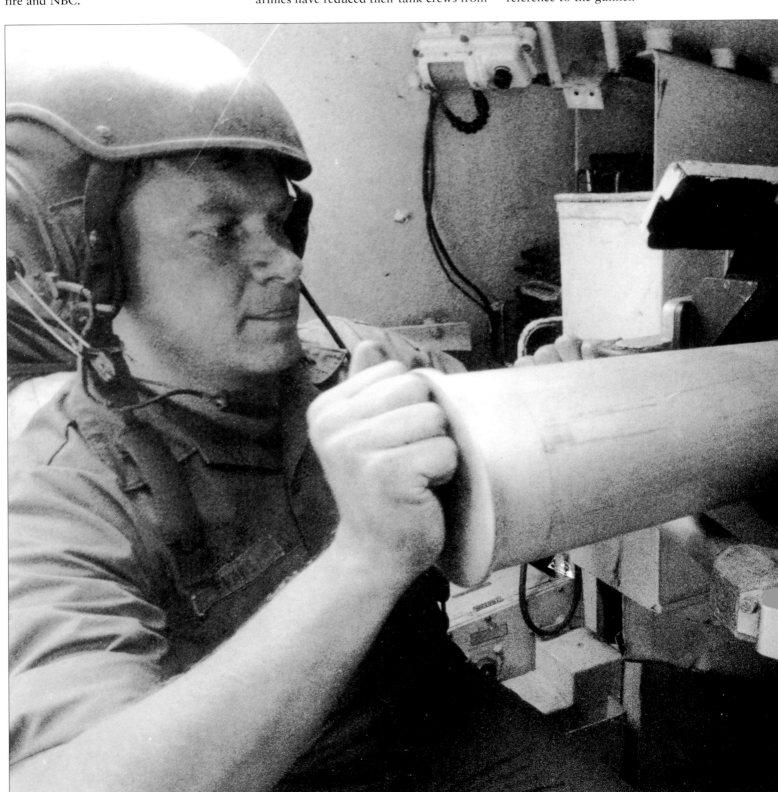

M1A1(HAP) (= heavy armor package) was produced for tanks destined to fight in Europe, in which parts of the hull, particularly at the front, were fabricated from a new type of armor, essentially depleted uranium (DU) encased in steel. M1A1D is a program to digitize the M1A1 under the System Enhancement Program (SEP), which involves installing the digital command and control package, as well as replacing some of the remaining analog units, with new digital units.

In Operations Desert Shield/Desert Storm 1,848 US MBTs (mostly M1A1s, but also a number of M1s and M1A1(HAP)) faced some 500 modern T-72s, about 1,600 older T-62s and about 700 1950s vintage T-54s. Prior to the land advance Allied air power destroyed some 50 percent of the Iraqi tanks, but as soon as the Abrams were unleashed they quickly dealt with the remainder in their sector, destroying large numbers while incurring only 18 battle losses, of which nine were permanent and nine were repaired. Not one crewman was lost.

In summary, approximately 10,000 are in service world-wide, with the only new-build vehicles being produced in Egypt. The US Army's fleet comprises: M1 - 2,674, all to be converted to M1A2; M1 Improved - 894; M1A1 - 4,796; M1A2 new-build - 77.

Left: *The loader on an M1 Abrams loads the shell into the M68 105mm gun. This British-designed gun was the same weapon as used in the M60-series (except for M60A2), but was replaced in the M1A1 by the US-made version of the German Rheinmetall 120mm smoothbore cannon.*

Opposite: *AZ platoon of M1A1s on a training exercise in Germany. The highly sloped faces are designed to prevent an incoming high-velocity round from penetrating.*

Below: *The driver has a direct view when opened up, but for the closed-down condition the hatch (to his left in this picture) is pulled across and he looks out through a periscope.*

Below: *An early model M1 Abrams, armed with a 105mm rifled gun; note the bore extractor and thermal sleeve. Secondary armament comprises a coaxial 7.62mm machine-gun, a second M60 7.62mm machine-gun on a pintle above the loader's hatch, and an M2HB 0.5in (7.62mm) machine-gun above the commander's hatch.*

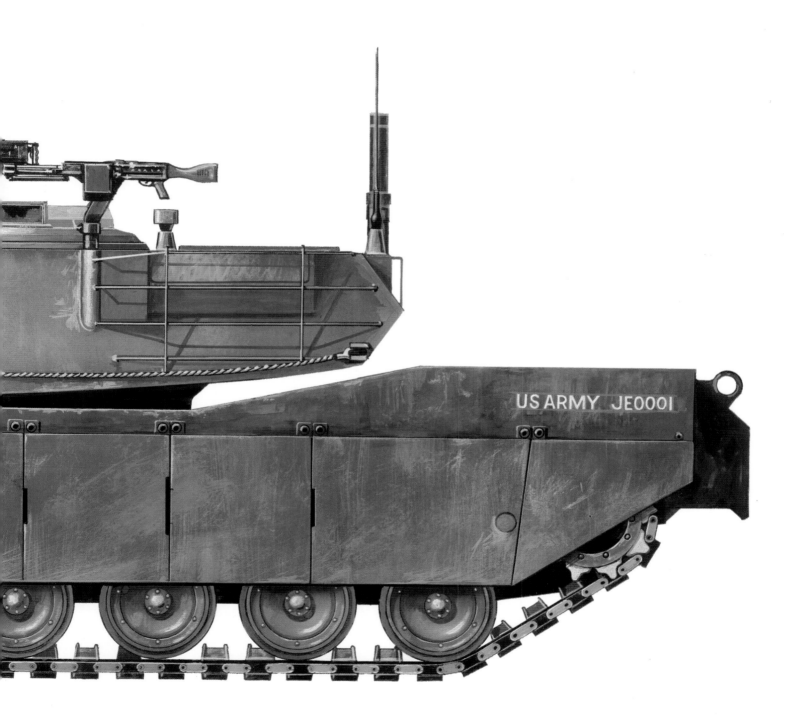

Opposite top: *The tubes on the left fire smoke grenades to show an exercise hit; the orange device is a flashing light for peacetime road travel.*

Opposite bottom: *Its turret reversed, an M1 travels along a road during an exercise; note unusual camouflage paint scheme.*

Below: *The streak of light shows the very flat trajectory followed by the 120mm APFSDS high velocity round of this M1A1.*

Left: *After all the tribulations of the MBT-70 and the long development period of the M1, the Abrams has turned out to be a splendid tank. It did very well in the Gulf War and has been bought by a number of foreign armies. Further development has slowed down as US national attention turns to a different type of warfare, but the M1 will remain in service for many years to come.*

Type 69 Main Battle Tank

Having started out by producing virtual carbon copies of Soviet tanks in the 1950s, China now produces far more tanks today than any other country. A typical product was the Type 69, which was a development of the Chinese Type 59, a license-built version of the Soviet T-54. As in the Type 59, the driver sat in the front left, with the remaining three crewmen in the turret.

In the first production batch two different types of gun were installed: some had a new 100mm smoothbore (Type 69-I), others the same 100mm rifled tube as the Type 59 (Type 69-II). After extensive testing, it was concluded that the rifled gun was superior and production of the Type 69-I terminated with the 150th tank.

The Type 69-II fired a range of Chinese-designed and produced ammunition, including three types of APF'SDS, plus HEAT, HE and APHE. The gun was fully stabilized, there was a Tank Laser Rangefinder-I mounted above the mantlet and the Tank Simplified Fire

Control System (TSFCS) was fitted. Most Type 69-IIs had an externally- mounted laser rangefinder, but the TSKS-L system incorporates a laser integrated with the gun sight and mounted inside the turret. A later version was armed with a 105mm rifles gun, presumably a licence-build copy of the Royal Ordnance L7.

The Type 69 has been exported in respectable quantities, mainly to the Middle East. The Royal Thai Army ordered some 500 Type 69-IIs under the local designation Type 30, but it is believed only about 50 were delivered.

SPECIFICATIONS

Country of origin: China.
Crew: 4.
Armament: (Type 69-I) One 100mm smoothbore gun; one Type 54 12.7mm co-axial machine-gun; one Type 59T 7.62mm anti-aircraft machine-gun. (Type 69II). One 100mm rifled gun; one Type 54 12.7mm co-axial machine-gun; one Type 59T 7.62mm anti-aircraft machine-gun.
Armor: 1.5in-8in (39mm-203mm).
Dimensions: Length (including main armament) 28ft 5in (8.66m); length (hull) 20ft 6in (6.24m); width 10ft 10in (3.29m); height 9ft 3in (2.81m).
Weight: Combat 81,500lb (37,000kg)
Engine: Model 12150L-7BW V-12 liquid-cooled diesel developing 580hp at 2,000rpm.
Performance: Road speed 31mph (50km/h); range 273 miles (440km); vertical obstacle 2ft 7in (0.79m); trench 8ft 10in (2.7m), gradient 60 per cent.

Left: *Main armament of all versions of the Chinese Type 69 was a 100mm gun, but this was smoothbore in some versions and rifled in others. Although not sophisticated by Western or Soviet standards, it was a major step forward in Chinese armored fighting vehicle design, and was manufactured in large numbers.*

Challenger 1 Main Battle Tank

With the Chieftain (q.v.) accepted for service in 1963, the staffs of the British Army turned their sights towards the next generation tank. The first attempt was an international project with West Germany, which started in 1970, but, as with every other collaborative project of that era, this fell apart in 1977. Meanwhile, a low-key national project had been in progress, albeit at a slow tempo, as an insurance policy, which was just as well, and in 1977 it moved into full gear.

Meanwhile, the Chieftain had attracted large orders from the Shah of Iran and a developed version had been produced for the Iranian Army, designated the Shir 1. This led in turn to the Shir 2, a much more advance MBT, whose development was mainly funded from the Iranian order. Unfortunately for the British, the Shah was then deposed by Ayatollah Khomeini and the new Iranian government promptly cancelled any further work or deliveries. Vickers then produced a new version of the Shir 2, altered to suit British Army requirements, and this was ordered into

production in 1978, entering service with the British Army as the Challenger 1 in 1984. A total of 420 had been delivered by the time production ended in mid-1990. Challenger 1 hull was fabricated from Chobham armor, with a steeply sloping glacis plate, which combined to give a high degree of ballistic protection. The large angular turret housed an L11A5 120mm rifled gun (the same as later versions of

Below: The British Challenger 1 was armed with the L30 120mm rifled gun. Note the driver's position, inset into the glacis plate, seen here with the hatch cover in the open position.

SPECIFICATIONS

Country of origin: United Kingdom.
Crew: 4.
Armament: One Royal Ordnance L30 120mm rifled gun; one McDonnell Douglas 7.62mm co-axial Chain-Gun; one L37A2 7.62mm anti-aircraft general-purpose machine-gun; two five-barrel smoke grenade dischargers.
Armor: Chobham.
Dimensions: Length (including armament) 37ft 11in (11.55m); length (gun to rear) 32ft 4in (9.86m); width 11ft 7in (3.52m); height 8ft 2in (2.49m).

Weight: Combat 127,775lb (60,000kg).
Engine: Perkins CV12 TCA 12-cylinder 60° V direct injection 4-stroke liquid-cooled diesel engine developing 1,200bhp at 2,300rpm. Perkins 4,108 4-stroke diesel auxiliary power unit.
Performance: Road speed 35mph (56km/h), range 340 miles (550km); vertical obstacle 2ft 11in (0.9m); trench 7ft 8in (2.34m); gradient 60 per cent.

Chieftain), which was fitted with a bore evacuator and a muzzle reference system. When other armies moved from 105mm to 120mm they chose a smooth-bore barrel since they no longer saw a need to use HESH ammunition, but the British were convinced of its value as a complement to APFSDS and so carried on using a rifled barrel. Challenger 1 experienced considerable trouble with its original engine and transmission, which took some time to put right.

Challenger 1 managed to earn considerable bad publicity, which reached its peak when the British Army decided to withdraw from the Canadian Army Trophy, an international tank gunnery contest among NATO teams in the Germany-based Northern and Central Army Groups. However, a Challenger Improvement Program (CHIP) was established and the tank and its systems were progressively improved, which was just as well, because when the Gulf War broke out in 1990-91, the British Army sent a complete armored division to Saudi Arabia, which included 176 Challenger 1s. In the event, these performed exceptionally well and showed a high degree of mechanical reliability, with the tanks in the forward armored regiments each covering an average of 217 miles (350km) in the 100-hour ground war, in the course of which there were just two breakdowns in the entire force. The 120mm gun proved very accurate and more than half the engagements involved the use of High-Explosive Squash Head (HESH) rounds, which, as mentioned

above, the British continued to use with their 120mm gun, even though most other armies had ceased to do so. The record spoke for itself, as during the Gulf War the Challenger 1s destroyed some 300 Iraqi tanks and not one British tank was destroyed in return.

Intense speculation about a future MBT for the British Army culminated in the late 1980s with an announcement that there would be an international competition for a Challenger replacement. The four competitors were the Leopard 2 (Improved) from Germany, the M1A1 Abrams from the USA, the Leclerc from France and the Challenger 2 from the UK. After an intensive evaluation of the competing designs the Challenger 2 was selected, subject to passing a series of "milestones" which would demonstrate that it fully met the British Army's requirement.

It was originally intended to replace about half the Challenger 1 fleet with Challenger 2s, but it was subsequently decided to replace them all. As a result, Challenger 1s were progressively replaced by Challenger 2s, the process being completed in late 2001. Some Challenger 1 hulls are now used for specialist vehicles, such as AVLBs or ARVs, while the remainder will be either sold or scrapped.

Below: *A Challenger 1 pauses during an exercise in Germany, with an Armoured Recovery Vehicle to its right. The turret is facing to the rear and below the gun is the engine compartment, housing a Perkins 12-cylinder, 4-stroke, liquid-cooled, 1,200bhp diesel, which gives the tank a high degree of agility.*

Hyundai K1
Main Battle Tank

❖

THE REPUBLIC OF KOREA (RoK) Army has traditionally used American equipment and its tank corps was equipped with a succession of such tanks, including the M47 and M48A5. It came, therefore, as something of a surprise when the RoK Army issued invitations in the mid-1970s for proposals for a new MBT, which was to be designed to South Korean specifications, with a view to production in South Korea. Several manufacturers submitted proposals and the Chrysler Defense (later General Dynamics Land Systems Division) design was selected in 1980. Two prototypes, designated XK-1, were built in considerable secrecy and sent to the Aberdeen Proving Grounds in Maryland, USA, for testing in 1983. Production started in 1984 at the Hyundai factory at Changwon under the designation K1 MBT and several tank battalions had been equipped with the new MBT by the time it was revealed to the public in late 1987. The total RoK Army requirement is believed to be well over 1,000.

The tank is of conventional design with

the vulnerable parts of the hull constructed of British-designed and American-manufactured Chobham armor. There is a four-man crew, with the driver sitting in the front compartment on the left. The commander is seated in the turret on the right of the gun with the gunner in front of and below him, and the loader on the left of the gun.

Two prototypes of a new version, K1A1, started testing in 1996. These are armed with a Rheinmetal 120mm smoothbore gun and it is probable that many K1s will be modified in due course.

SPECIFICATIONS

Country of origin: Republic of Korea (South Korea).
Crew: 4.
Armament: One M68A1 105mm rifled gun; one 7.62mm co-axial machine-gun, one 12.7 anti-aircraft machine-gun (gunner) and one 7.62mm machine-gun (loader); 12 smoke dischargers (six on each side of turret).
Armor: Composite.
Dimensions: Length (including main armament) 31ft 9in (9.67m); length (hull) 24ft 6in (7.48m); width 11ft 10in (3.60m); height (to turret top) 7ft 5in (2.25m).
Weight: Combat 112,335lb (51,000kg).
Engine: MTU MB 871 Ka-501 12-cylinder water-cooled diesel engine developing 1,200hp at 2,600 rpm.
Performance: Road speed 40mph (65km/h); range 310 miles (500km); vertical obstacle 3ft 4in (1.0m); trench 9ft 0in (2.74m), gradient 60 per cent.
(Data for K1 armed with 105mm gun)

Left: *Specialist versions of the K1-M include this Armoured Vehicle Launched Bridge (AVLB), which carries a 72ft (22m) British No 8 bridge that can span a 67ft (20.5m) gap.*

Above top: *The original K1 is armed with an M68A1 105mm rifled gun firing NATO standard ammunition, with a coaxial M60E2 machine-gun and a second M60 atop the turret.*

Above: *The K1A1 differs from the K1-M in being armed with the M268 120mm smoothbore gun, although the M60E2 co-axial MG is retained.*

Leclerc Main Battle Tank

◆◆

I N THE LATE 1970s the French and German armies undertook a collaborative project to replace the AMX-30 and Leopard 1 MBTs, but this collapsed in December 1982 and the French undertook the design of a new tank designated Engin Principal de Combat (EPC).

The first prototype was running in late 1989 and the vehicle was named the Leclerc after a successful World War II commander. The Leclerc is generally similar to contemporary Western MBTs, but has an automatic loader, reducing the crew to three

men. The hull and turret are constructed of welded steel to which is added modular segments of composite armor, which is claimed to have high resistance to kinetic energy and chemical rounds. The prototype turret was very angular, but the production tanks sport a long, low turret of excellent ballistic shape.

The GIAT 120mm smoothbore has a chamber the same size as that on the German Rheinmetall gun to ensure commonality of ammunition, but the tube is longer, imparting a higher muzzle velocity to the projectiles. The gun also uses a compressed-air system to

expel fumes automatically after firing. The automatic loader contains 22 rounds of ready-use ammunition and is mounted in the long turret bustle, separated from the fighting compartment by a bulkhead. The co-axial weapon is a 12.7mm machine-gun, with a 7.62mm machine-gun on the turret roof, which is fully controlled from within the tank. Power is provided by a diesel, with gas-turbine for auxiliary power.

Below: French Army armor/infantry combat team, with a wide range of vehicles, including, at the front, thirteen Leclerc MBTs, one of the most powerful current battle tanks.

SPECIFICATIONS

Country of origin: France.
Crew: 3.
Armament: One GIAT 120-26 120mm smoothbore gun; one 12.7mm co-axial machine-gun; one 7.62mm anti-aircraft machine-gun; two nine-barreled smoke grenade discharges.
Armor: Spaced, multi-layer.
Dimensions: Length (including main armament) 32ft 5in (9.87m); length (hull) 22ft 7in (6.88m); width 12ft 2in (3.71m); height 8ft 4in (2.53m).

Weight: Combat 1120,172lb (54,500kg).
Engine: Uni-Diesel V8X-1500 Hyperbar 8-cylinder liquid-cooled diesel engine developing 1,500hp at 2,500rpm; SACM Turbomeca gas turbine auxiliary power unit.
Performance: Road speed 44mph (71km/h); range 341 miles (550km); vertical obstacle 4ft 1in (1.25m); trench 9ft 10in (3m), gradient 60 per cent.

T-90 Main Battle Tank

❖❖

THE PROTOTYPE T-90 first ran in 1990 and the first production models were delivered to the Russian Army in 1994. Production has continued since, but at a very slow rate compared with previous Soviet/Russian tank programs, with only about 200 in service by the year 2000.

Main armament is a 125mm smoothbore gun, fitted with a fume extractor and surrounded by a thermal jacket. The autoloader holds 22 projectiles and charges, and there are a further 21 stored elsewhere in the tank. The gun, which is the same as that mounted in the T-72 and T-80, fires the same APFSDS, HEAT and HE-FRAG rounds. In addition, however, it has a new and unique type of fragmentation round which can be detonated from the tank as it passes over the target, thus giving it a top-attack capability. The 125mm gun can also launch the laser-guided Refleks missile, which has a tandem warhead, enabling it to attack tanks fitted with ERA. Although some recent Russian tanks have been powered by a gas turbine, T-90 has a four-

stroke diesel engine, with a multi-fuel capability, enabling it to run on diesel fuel, gasoline, kerosene or benzine. The T-90 has been ordered by India (310 vehicles), but no other orders have so far been announced.

Below: *The Russian T-90 has a crew of three and is armed with a 125mm smoothbore gun, which is fed by an autoloader. This weapon fires a variety of projectiles, including the laser-guided Refleks missile. Some T-90s have been built for the Russian Army, but the largest current order is some 310 for India.*

SPECIFICATIONS

Country of origin: Russian Federation.
Crew: 3.
Armament: 2A46M 125mm smoothbore gun; one PKT 7.62mm machine-gun co-axial with main gun; one remote-controlled NSVT 12.7mm machine-gun on turret roof; six single-barrelled smoke grenade dischargers on each side of turret.
Armor: Composite, with added ERA.
Dimensions: Length (including main gun) 31ft 3in (9.53m); length (hull) 22ft 6in (6.86m); width 12ft 5in (3.78m); height (to turret roof) 7ft 4in (2.23m).
Weight: Combat 102,513lb (46,500kg).
Engine: V-84MS 4-stroke, 12-cylinder diesel, 840bhp at 2,000rpm.
Performance: Road speed 37mph (60km/h); range 342 miles (550km); vertical obstacle 2ft 10in (0.85m); trench 9ft 2in (2.8m); gradient 60 per cent.

C1 Ariete Main Battle Tank

❖

THE ITALIAN ARMY used American MBTs for many years after World War II, but in 1970 it ordered Leopard ls from Germany, with 200 built in Germany and 720 in Italy. The first post-war Italian MBT was the OF-40, with 36 built, all for the UAE. Then, in 1982 the Italian Army issued a requirement for a new MBT, one criterion being that it must be built in Italy. Design work started in 1984, the first prototype ran in 1986 and the first production vehicle was delivered in 1995.

The Ariete is a conventional design, armed with a 120mm smoothbore, designed and manufactured by OTO Breda. The chamber is identical with that of the Rheinmetall 120mm smoothbore, thus ensuring commonality of ammunition. The gun fires APFSDS and HEAT-MP rounds, together with smoke and illuminating rounds. The gun is mounted in a fixed mantlet and has a two-axis stabilization system. There are also eight smoke dischargers, four on each side of the turret.

The hull is of all-welded steel construction with a layer of "advanced armor" on the

nose and glacis plate. The turret is well shaped with an angled face, unlike some modern tanks which have a vertical face. The torsion-bar suspension system has seven roadwheels with four return rollers and is protected by skirts. Production for the Italian Army ended in mid-2002; there have been no export orders.

Below: *Production of the C1 Ariete (= ram) took place from 1995 to mid-2002. The tank, gun, engine and most components were of all-Italian design and manufacture, but no export orders were won and the type is almost certain to be the last MBT to be designed in Italy.*

SPECIFICATIONS

Country of origin: Italy.
Armament: One OTO Melara 120mm smoothbore gun; one 7.62mm co-axial machine-gun; one 7.62mm anti-aircraft machine-gun.
Armor: See text.
Dimensions: Length (gun forward) 31ft 3in (9.52m); length (hull) 24ft 11in (7.60m); width 11ft 10in (3.6m); height (commander's cupola) 8ft 0in (2.45m).

Weight: Combat 119,000lb (54,000kg).
Engine: One IVECO V-12 MTCA turbo-charged inter-cooler 12-cylinder diesel developing 1,300hp at 2,300rpm.
Performance: Road speed +40mph (+65km/h); range +342 miles (+550km); vertical obstacle 6ft 10in (2.1m); trench 9ft 10in (3.0m); gradient 60 per cent.

Above: *The C1 Ariete's gun is a 120mm smoothbore, which was designed and developed by OTO Melara. This Italian company has produced some of the most successful post-war naval guns, which now equip many warships in dozens of navies around the world.*

Below: *The external lines of the C1 Ariete are remarkably neat and uncluttered for an MBT. There are reports that a more advanced C2 version is under development, but whether a new, heavy MBT will ever be required, let alone built, is a matter for conjecture.*

Vickers Defence Challenger 2 Main Battle Tank

◆◆

THE PRIVATE COMPANY, Vickers Defence, started company-funded design work on a successor to the Challenger main battle tank in the mid-1980s, which led in 1988 to a contract to proceed to a demonstration phase, which involved the construction of nine prototypes. All of these were completed by late 1990 and in June 1991 the company received a production contract for 140 new tanks, now named Challenger 2 (with the original Challenger becoming Challenger 1), which comprised 127 main battle tanks and 13 of a specialized driver-training version. Formal type acceptance was given in mid-1994, completing a process in which the Challenger 2 was the first tank for the British Army to be designed and developed entirely by an independent industrial company (rather than at a government research and development [R&D] establishment) since World War II. It was also the first major project to have set reliability goals laid down in a fixed-price contract.

The initial intention of the British

Ministry of Defense (Army) had been to replace only half the Challenger 1 fleet with Challenger 2s, but in July 1994 this decision was rescinded and an additional 268 (259 MBTs, plus nine more driver training tanks) were ordered, so that the entire Royal Armoured Corps would be equipped with Challenger 2s. Despite entering many competitions, the only overseas order for Challenger 2 has been

Below: *Initially intended to replace only half the Challenger 1 fleet, Challenger 2 is now re-equipping all armored regiments in the British Army.*

SPECIFICATIONS

Country of origin: United Kingdom.
Crew: 4.
Armament: One Royal Ordnance L30A1 rifled gun; one Hughes L94A1 7.62mm Chain Gun co-axial with the main gun; one L37A2 7.62mm remote-controlled machine-gun on turret roof; five single-barrelled smoke grenade launchers on each side of the turret.
Armor: Second generation, Chobham type.
Dimensions: Length 37ft 8in (11.5m); width 11ft 6in (3.52m); height (to turret roof) 8ft 2in (2.5mm).

Weight: Combat 137,500lb (62,500kg).
Engine: Perkins CV-12 TA Condor V-12 12-cylinder diesel, 1,200bhp at 2,300rpm.
Performance: Road speed 35mph (56km/h); range 280 miles (450km); vertical obstacle 2ft 10in (0.9m); trench 7ft 8in (2.34m); gradient 60 per cent.

from the Oman, which ordered 18 in 1993 and a further 20 in 1997.

The Challenger 2 incorporates well over 150 improvements compared to Challenger 1, together with a totally new turret, and, despite its name, is in reality a completely new tank. The hull is generally similar to that of the Challenger 1, with the driver sitting centrally, with an unusual shallow trough in the glacis plate to enable him to see. The other three crewmen are in the turret, which is fabricated from new, second-generation Chobham armor, with the commander and gunner on the right of the gun, and the loader on the left. The hull and turret are constructed of welded steel and Chobham armor, and are of exceptionally good ballistic shape. The gun control and stabilization systems are all-electric, thus overcoming the vulnerability problems associated with hydraulic or mixed hydraulic/electric systems.

Main armament is the new Royal Ordnance L30 rifled gun, which was the crucial element in the CHARM (CHallenger ARMament) package, which included the gun, a new charge system, and a new and more effective anti-tank round with a depleted uranium (DU) penetrator. The barrel is fitted, as is now normal practice, with a thermal sleeve and muzzle reference system, which are part of the measures designed to optimize the possibility of a first-round hit. There is also a fume extractor, to reduce the amount of noxious fumes passing into the turret. The barrel is the first in any British tank to be chrome-plated and is 55 calibers (i.e., 21.7ft [6.6m]) long. Sixty-four projectiles are carried, together with 42 charges, the latter being stowed in armored boxes below the turret ring for maximum safety. It was planned at one stage that the L30 gun would be retrofitted to the Challenger 1 tanks not being replaced by Challenger 2, but as no Challenger 1s are being retained, that plan is no longer necessary.

The Challenger 2 was the only new MBT introduced in the 1990s to mount a rifled (as opposed to smoothbore) 120mm main gun. This is due to the British Army's continuing belief in the value of the HESH/HEP round. When such a round hits a tank the high-explosive forms, for the briefest moment of time, a circular "cake" on the outside of the armor plate, which is then detonated by a charge in the base of the projectile. The shock from this explosion dislodges a large scab from the inside wall of the tank, and this then ricochets at high velocity around the crew compartment, killing or wounding the crew and destroying or damaging the equipment. The British Army firmly believes that this type of round is necessary as a complement to the high-velocity, kinetic energy round (APDS and APFSDS) and has therefore insisted on retaining a rifled barrel, since the HESH round depends on spin stabilization for in-flight stability and cannot be fired from a smoothbore barrel. A McDonnell Douglas 7.62mm Chain Gun is mounted co-axially with the main gun and a second 7.62mm anti-aircraft machine-gun is mounted on the turret roof.

Right: *On and around the turret are a number of sensors; they include a stabilized sight; wind, humidity and temperature gauges; laser detectors; and other classified devices.*

The power unit is a Perkins diesel with a rated output of 1,200bhp. The TN37 transmission of the Challenger 1 was long considered to be insufficiently flexible and has been replaced in the Challenger 2 by theTN54 model, which has six forward and two reverse gears. This power train was, in fact, installed initially in the Challenger Armored Repair and Recovery Vehicle (ARRV) and 12 of these were deployed to Saudi Arabia for Operation Desert Storm where they achieved 100 per cent availability, a truly remarkable figure.

The Challenger 2 project was required to meet a gruelling and very demanding In-Service Reliability Demonstration (ISRD) milestone, which involved 12 army-crewed vehicles from September to December 1998. This was successfully achieved and the targets were not only met, but actually exceeded by a considerable margin.

The first regiment to be equipped, the Royal Scots Dragoon Guards, stationed in Germany, started to take delivery of Challenger 2 tanks in January 1998 and received the 38th and last in time to meet the stipulated June 1998 in-service deadline. Deliveries of Challenger 2 then continued and all six of the British Army armored regiments were fully equipped with their tanks and associated logistic support package by the end of 2000.

The Omani version has some modifications to cope with the high temperatures of the Gulf region. These include improved airflow in the engine compartment and air-conditioning. A newer version, now being offered for export, is the Challenger 2E, which has an MTU power pack, increased fuel tankage, steering wheel (as opposed to tillers) and a 12.7mm machine-gun on the turret roof replacing the 7.62mm MG.

The British and Omani armies have also purchased Challenger 2 driver training tanks, which weigh the same as the MBT, but have a fixed turret which accommodates the instructor (who has full dual controls) and four students.

Like most other major armies, the British Army is now trying to decide what to do next. The old threat of massive tank battles in central Europe has receded, to be replaced by far smaller campaigns in distant countries, which requires a smaller, lighter, more easily deployable fighting vehicle. On the other hand, so long as some armies, particularly those in the Middle East, retain large, sophisticated MBTs, there will be a need to match and defeat them. So, army staffs have to decide whether to develop a new main battle tank in the 50-60 ton range and armed with a 120mm (or larger) gun, or to move to something radical. It is a difficult and challenging dilemma to solve.

Left above: *The box above the muzzle houses the Muzzle Reference System, which measures even the tiniest variation in the barrel.*

Left: *Challenger 2 is powered by the very successful Perkins 12-cylinder diesel engine (1,200hp at 2,300rpm), driving a David Brown TN-54 epicyclic transmission with six forward and two reverse gears.*

TIMELINE

1906   **1908**   **1910**   **1912**   **1914**   **1916**

• **1914**

(Oct) In Britain, Lt Col E Swinton proposes that armored caterpillar tractors should be built to break through the Western Front trenchlines.

(Nov) J L Breton makes the first French proposal for vehicles as track assault weapons. His idea of a mechanical wire cutter was expanded by E Brillié of the Schneider Company who proposed fitting a cutting device to an armored 'Baby Holt' tractor.

• **1906**

First commercial tracked vehicle—a converted steam agricultural tractor—is built by the American Holt Manufacturing Co.

• **1916**

(Jan) The first fighting tank ran on its own tracks in Britain. Successive trials convinced skeptics that here was a practical device deserving full-scale production.

(March) In Britain, Swinton begins recruiting a special tank force.

(Sep) At the Battle of Flers Courcellette, France, the British send a tank into action for the first time.

(Oct) Britain forms the first Tank Corps

• **1911**

The first of several 'paper' projects for a tracked fighting vehicle is produced by Austrian engineer G. Burstyn.

• **1915**

Britain and Russia test the trench-crossing capabilities of tracked and wheeled suspensions. Designs for gigantic machines are abandoned as too vulnerable. Britain chooses to develop tracked vehicles after experimenting with various cross-country machines.

(June) In Britain, Swinton produces the first definitive paper specifying the technical and tactical requirements for a tank. This enabled the first tank designers, William Tritton and Walter Wilson, to work towards a recognizable objective.

• **1912**

Australian engineer L. de Mole proposes the second main 'paper' project for a tracked machine but does not specify any armament.

(Dec) The first actual use of the word 'tank' was brought about by the need to disguise the existence of the special assault weapon in Britain.

1918 1920 1922 1924 1926 1928 1930 1932 1934   1936

- **1917**

(April) The first French tank goes into action. In Palestine the British also use a tank for the first time in a desert campaign.

(Nov) The first tank offensive is made by 476 British tanks near Cambrai, France.

- **1918**

(Jan) The US forms a tank corps.

(Feb) The A7V, Germany's first tank, enters service.

(Aug) The largest tank offensive of World War I is made by 604 Allied tanks to the east of Amiens, France.

(Sep) The US tank corps make their first battlefield appearance during the Battle of St. Mihiel Salient, France.

- **1927**

Japan's first tank, an experimental machine, is completed.

- **1934**

France forms the first genuine mechanized division—the Division Légère Mécanique—which includes a brigade of 220 tanks.

The first German tank to be produced in quantity appears. It is called an agricultural tractor for reasons of secrecy but it is later named the Pz Kpfw I.

- **1935**

The first German armored (Panzer) division is formed.

- **1936**

The Soviet T-27 and T-38 become the first tanks to be carried by aircraft.

- **1931**

France introduces the first cast turrets in the D1.

1938	1940	1942	1944	1946	1948	1950	1952	1954	1956	1958

• 1938

The first British armored (or 'mobile') division is formed.

• 1945

(Jan–Feb) The final German tank offensive of World War II, launched to counter the Soviet invasion of Hungary, is defeated by overwhelming opposition.

(March) Allied armored forces lead the greatest amphibious river crossing over the Rhine river into Germany.

• 1952

Soviet PT76 amphibious tanks become the first tanks to use hydro-jets as a means of water propulsion.

• 1939

Germany launches the first tank invasion across the Polish frontier.

• 1942

The M4 Medium Tank enters service in U.S. Tank Corps, the most prolific media tank of World War II.

• 1950

(Jan–Aug) 1000 US and North Korean tanks are sent into action in Korea.

• 1956

The first major tank victory since World War II is won by Israel against Egypt during the Suez Crisis.

(Oct) First uninhibited use of tanks to control rioting occurs in Budapest, Hungary.

• 1941

The first major jungle war with tanks commences in Asia across scattered localities from Bataan to the Dutch East Indies.

• 1951

10 M24s are broken down and airlifted to French forces at Dien Bien Phu in Indochina during the infamous siege.

The Swiss decide to build their first production tank, the Pz 58. The prototype appears in 1958.

• 1943

Germany develops the most powerful tank engine of World War II, a 1,200hp Daimler-Benz for the Maus.

(July) World War II's greatest tank battle takes place between 6000 German and Soviet tanks at Kursk.

1960 1962 1964 1966 1968 1970 1972 1976 1980 1984 1986 1988 1990 1992 1994 1996

1960's

NBC warfare protection begins to be incorporated into most tanks and armored vehicles.

1960

Aluminum armor is used for the first time on the US M113 APC and the hull of the Sheridan.

During the Vietnam War (lasting until 1975) approximately 3,000 North Vietnamese tanks are deployed to meet approximately 1,000 South Vietnamese, US, and Australian tanks.

1980

Iran and Iraq deploy thousands of tanks during a protracted war that lasts until 1988.

1990

Iraqi tanks spearhead the invasion of Kuwait. A UN coalition force, including some 4,200 tanks, liberates Kuwait in January 1991 and destroys approximately 3,800 enemy tanks.

1967

(June) During the Six Day War some 1,000 Israeli tanks are deployed to meet an Arab coalition armored force.

1973

(Oct) During the Arab-Israeli War some 2,000 Israeli tanks are deployed to meet an Arab coalition armored force.

GLOSSARY

AMMUNITION AND ARMOR.

AP. Armor piercing.

APDS. Armor Piercing, Discarding Sabot. Sub-caliber (q.v.) round held in place by a sabot which falls away as it leaves the muzzle. Made of dense material, e.g. tungsten carbide or depleted uranium. Spin stabilized in flight.

APFSDS. Armor Piercing, Fin-Stabilized, Discarding Sabot. As for APDS but a longer, non-spinning round, fitted with fins.

Appliqué armor. Add-on armor.

Armor. Steel plate to protect the vehicle against incoming rounds. It should be noted that, in order to restrict the weight, the thickness varies, with the thickest on the front, thinnest on the rear.

Chobham armor. Special form of armor developed at the British R&D center at Chobham in the 1970s.

DU. Depleted Uranium. Very dense, non-radioactive material, used in some APDS and APFSDS rounds, and also some modern armors.

ERA. Explosive Reactive Armor. Small segments of material which explodes when hit, thus deflecting incoming APDS and APFSDS rounds.

HE. High Explosive.

HEAT. High Explosive Anti-Tank. Also known as "Hollow-Charge." Pierces armor by concentrated jet of molten high explosive.

HESH. High Explosive Squash Head. Also known as High Explosive Plastic (HEP). Designed so that on impact with tank the HE forms a "cake" which is then detonated and the shock wave dislodges a large metal scab from the interior.
MP. Multi-Purpose. Modern round for

Rheinmetall 120mm round, which can be used against tanks or bunkers, or soft target, such as infantry and artillery positions.

Spaced armor. Two layers of armor with gap in between, in which the outer layer causes HEAT or HESH warhead to detonate and dissipate their energy in the gap.

Sub-caliber. A round whose diameter is less than that of the barrel and which is held in place by a sabot; see APDS, APFSDS.

TANK TERMINOLOGY

Basket. Framework suspended below a turret which rotates with the turret.

Bustle. Overhang at the rear of a turret.

Return roller. Small diameter roller which supports track clear of the top of the roadwheels.

Coaxial. Machine-gun located next to the main gun which is elevated and trained simultaneously with the main gun.

Cupola. A special position for the tank commander, usually with its own controls and sighting devices.

Drive sprocket. The wheel which transfers power from the transmission to the tracks.

Glacis plate. The frontal armored plate of the tank.

Idler. The unpowered wheel at the opposite end to the drive sprocket.

Mantlet. Large armored plate designed to prevent incoming rounds from penetrating the small gaps surrounding inner end of the barrel.

Road wheel. Wheel running along that section of the track in contact with the ground.

Skirt/skirting plate. Vertical plate hanging from the track guard to protect the running gear, suspension and side of the hull from HEAT rounds.

Sponson. Found only in early tanks, this was a gun position sticking out from the side of the tank.

Volute. A suspension springing system used in many US tanks in the 1930s and 1940s. See M4 Sherman entry.

TANK TYPES

Cruiser. British term used in 1930s and 1940s for a fast battle tank, intended for independent operations; ie, as opposed to "infantry" tank (see below).

Heavy, medium, light tanks. These are relative terms, which can only defined in terms of the period in which they are used.

Infantry tank. British term used in 1930s and 1940s for a heavily armored, slow-moving tank designed to give direct support to infantry.

MBT. Main Battle Tank. Came into use from 1960s onwards to denote a fighting tank of approximately 30 tons or more.

Tankette. A small, fast, two-man vehicle, usually armed with one machine-gun, Popular in the 1920s.

GUN TERMINOLOGY

Bore evacuator. Circular sleeve around barrel, which extracts noxious fumes after a round has been fired to prevent them escaping into the fighting compartment.

Caliber. The internal diameter of the barrel. Up to about 1960s UK and US used inches, but since then have adopted the metric system, which has always been used by most other countries. Caliber is also used as a measure of barrel length. Thus, a 105mm 50-caliber barrel is 105 x 50 = 5.25m (17.2ft) long.

Pounder. Until about 1950 British tank and anti-tank guns were categorized by the weight of shell, expressed in Imperial pounds. In modern terms their calibers were: 2-pounder S 40mm; 6-pounder S 57mm; 17-pounder S 76.2mm; 20-pounder S 83.4mm.

Muzzle brake. A device on the end of a barrel which deflects some of the gasses which follow a round forwards, thus reducing the recoil which has to be absorbed within the turret.

NATIONAL TANK DESCRIPTORS

United States
Vehicles for test and trials are given the prefix "T"; thus, T26.

Vehicles officially accepted for production are given the prefix "M"; thus, M4, M48, etc. This started with the M1 Combat Car in 1937 and continued to the M60, but restarted at M1 with the modern Abrams tank.

Major modifications of in-service vehicles are given a letter suffix (but not "E") and minor modifications a further numerical suffix. Thus, M60, M60A1, M60A2, etc.

Experimental vehicles are given the suffix "E"; thus, T48E2.

From the late 1930s most major tanks have been given a name in addition to a number, which applies to the class as a whole. Thus, M4 Sherman, M1 Abrams. Normally these are the names of distinguished former generals. During World War II light tanks were given various names, including Locust and Hellcat.

British Tanks
British tanks were originally given mark numbers; eg, Mark I, Mark VIII, etc. From the 1920s they were designated with the letter A followed by a number, culminating with the A41 Centurion. Thereafter, they were given FV (fighting vehicle) numbers (eg, FV 200 Conqueror), but are more generally referred to by their names.
Tanks were given names from the 1930s onwards. In general, cruiser tanks were

given names starting with "C" (but Churchill was an infantry tank) and from the late 1940s onwards, all British main battle tank names have started with C.

Infantry tanks were given a miscellany of names; eg. Matilda, Valentine, Churchill, Black Prince.

German Tanks
German tanks received a variety of designations until the early 1930s when the title Panzer Kampfwagen (PzKpfw = armored fighting vehicle) was adopted. Thereafter, major service models were given a number, the series running from PzKpfw I of 1934 to PzKpfw VIII of 1945. Despite this apparently logical system there was an anomaly, possibly deliberately caused to mislead Allied intelligence, in that there were two totally unrelated PzKpfw Vs. A major modifications to a type was indicated by the word Ausfall (Ausf. = variant/model) followed by a letter: e.g., PzKpfw II Ausf B. Three World War II tanks were given names. Two of these were named after wild animals, Panther, Tiger I and II, while the third, the largest tank ever built in Germany was given the ironic name of Maus (mouse).

During World War II foreign tanks impressed into the German Army were given a "PzKpfw" designation followed by a national identifier in brackets; (f) = French; (t) = Czech. Thus, the French Char SOMUA S-35 became PzKpfw 35C 739 (f), and the Czech LT-35 became PzKpfw 35 (t).

There have only been two post-war German tanks, which continued the wild animal theme with the name Leopard, although it should be noted that Leopard 2 bears no design relationships to Leopard 1. Modified versions are indicated in the same way as US tanks, e.g. Leopard 1A1, Leopard 1A2, etc.

Japanese tanks
Up to 1945, Japanese tanks were given a "type" designation in which the figure denoted the year of the dynasty in which it was accepted for service. Thus, the Type 95 appeared in the 95th year of the Showa dynasty, etc, etc.

Since 1945 Japanese tanks have been given a type number which approximates to the date of acceptance into service; thus, Type 61, Type 74, etc.

MISCELLANEOUS

Armored Personnel Carrier (APC). Wheeled or tracked vehicle designed to carry infantry troops at similar speed and with a similar cross-country capability to tanks. They have sufficient armor to protect against small arms fire only.

Armored Vehicle Launched Bridge (AVLB). US term for a tank chassis carrying a bridge which can be laid to cross major gaps, rivers, etc. Also known as "bridge-layer."

Power-to-Weight Ratio. This provides a rough measure of the tank's agility by expressing the ratio of weight divided by engine power in horsepower. Thus, a tank with a power-to-weight ration of 22hp/ton would be appreciably more agile than one with a ratio of 18hp/ton. These figures can, however, be misleading since it depends on how the power output is measured.

Self-propelled (SP) artillery. This comprises a howitzer (ie with elevation over 45°) mounted on a tracked chassis. During World War II the guns were usually in open mounts, but today they are mounted in a rotating turret similar to but much larger than those used on tanks.

Standardization. US term for the process of officially accepting a new weapon for service; for example, "the T43E1 was standardized as the M103."

Tank destroyer. A fighting vehicle, usually tracked, whose sole mission is to destroy tanks. It is usually tracked and armed with an anti-tank weapon which is typically mounted in the glacis plate with limited (sometimes, no) traverse. (German term is jagdpanzer).

INDEX